The Holocaust

The Holocaust
The Third Reich and the Jews
Second edition

David Engel

LONDON AND NEW YORK

First published 2000 by Pearson Education Limited
Second edition published 2013

Published 2013 by Routledge
2 Park Square, Milton Park, Abingdon, Oxon OX14 4RN
711 Third Avenue, New York, NY 10017, USA

Routledge is an imprint of the Taylor & Francis Group, an informa business

ISBN: 978-1-4082-4994-9 (pbk)

British Library Cataloguing in Publication Data
A CIP catalogue record for this book can be obtained from the British Library

Library of Congress Cataloging in Publication Data
A CIP catalog record for this book can be obtained from the Library of Congress

Set by 35 in 10/13.5pt ITC Berkeley

Introduction to the series

History is narrative constructed by historians from traces left by the past. Historical enquiry is often driven by contemporary issues and, in consequence, historical narratives are constantly reconsidered, reconstructed and reshaped. The fact that different historians have different perspectives on issues means that there is also often controversy and no universally agreed version of past events. *Seminar Studies* was designed to bridge the gap between current research and debate, and the broad, popular general surveys that often date rapidly.

The volumes in the series are written by historians who are not only familiar with the latest research and current debates concerning their topic, but who have themselves contributed to our understanding of the subject. The books are intended to provide the reader with a clear introduction to a major topic in history. They provide both a narrative of events and a critical analysis of contemporary interpretations. They include the kinds of tools generally omitted from specialist monographs: a chronology of events, a glossary of terms and brief biographies of 'who's who'. They also include bibliographic essays in order to guide students to the literature on various aspects of the subject. Students and teachers alike will find that the selection of documents will stimulate discussion and offer insight into the raw materials used by historians in their attempt to understand the past.

Clive Emsley and Gordon Martel
Series Editors

Contents

Publisher's acknowledgements		x
Note on place names		xi
List of maps		xii
Chronology		xiii
Who's who		xvii
Glossary		xx
Maps		xxix

PART ONE   ANALYSIS   1

1	STUDYING THE HOLOCAUST	3
	Holocaust and genocide	4
	Who is right?	7
	Studying the Holocaust historically	9
2	THE JEWS	11
	Jewish origins	11
	The Jews in Christian Europe	12
	In modern times	14
3	HITLER, NAZIS, GERMANS, AND JEWS	19
	The Jews in Hitler's world view	20
	Jews in the ideology and programme of Nazism	22
	Jews in German public opinion	25
	True believers and the First World War	27
	Ordinary men or ordinary Germans?	29
4	1933–41: A TWISTED ROAD?	31
	A diabolical plot of the work of 'only men'?	32
	The state of documentation	34

A step-by-step process?   37
Jewish policy and global strategy   40

5   RESPONDING TO PERSECUTION   44
Perceiving the threat   44
To leave or not to leave?   47
Communal leadership: coping and resisting   49
Zionism, German Jewry, and world Jewry   51
External obstacles to emigration   53

6   THE TRANSITION TO KILLING   56
Why begin killing?   57
The means of murder   65
Organizing the transports   67

7   RESPONDING TO MURDER   71
Information and imagination   71
Communal responsibility and strategies for survival   75
The unofficial community and resistance   78
Local non-Jewish leaders and populations: opposition and complicity 81
Beyond the Nazi realm   87

8   HUMANITY, MODERNITY, AND THE HOLOCAUST   90

PART TWO   DOCUMENTS   99

1   The definition of 'genocide', by the word's inventor   100
2   From an early speech by Hitler about the Jews   101
3   An ex-Nazi evaluates the anti-Jewish aspect of National Socialism,
    1939   102
4   Hitler and Horthy discuss the fate of Hungarian Jewry, April 1943 103
5   Kristallnacht in German public opinion   104
6   Germans confront the deportation of their Jewish neighbours, 1941 105
7   The Lublin reservation   106
8   A German Jewish editor assesses the impact of the Nuremberg laws 107
9   A German Jewish woman describes her experience in the early
    Nazi years   108
10 A Jewish man commits suicide in protest over exclusion from
    the German nation   110
11 A German Jewish leader describes the 'return to Judaism'   110

12	A Zionist explains how his movement can help German Jews	111
13	A Polish report describes conditions for Jews after the German conquest	112
14	Goering instructs Heydrich to prepare a 'total solution' of the Jewish question	113
15	Notes by Goebbels on a meeting with Hitler concerning the implications of Germany's declaration of war against the United States	114
16	Invitation to the Wannsee conference	114
17	An eyewitness describes a mass shooting in the Soviet Union	116
18	A *Sonderkommando* member describes the Bełżec killing centre	117
19	The Polish underground reports the liquidation of the Warsaw ghetto	119
20	An early assessment of German policy towards Jews in occupied Poland	120
21	The story of a mass shooting is met with disbelief	121
22	The first Jewish intuition of a Nazi murder programme	122
23	A youth movement member becomes an underground courier	123
24	A Jewish underground party informs the Polish government-in-exile of a plan to murder all Polish Jews	125
25	The Warsaw *Judenrat* offers to regulate Jewish forced labour	126
26	The leader of the Białystok *Judenrat* preaches 'salvation through work'	127
27	The head of the Łódź ghetto announces the deportation of children	128
28	A Warsaw ghetto resident comments on Czerniaków's suicide	129
29	Self-help and alternative leadership in Warsaw	130
30	Hiding in a bunker	130
31	*Żegota* appeals for funds to rescue Polish Jews	131
32	A plea to combat blackmail of Jews in hiding	132
33	Himmler comments on mass murder	133
	GUIDE TO FURTHER READING	134
	REFERENCES	144
	INDEX	149

Publisher's acknowledgements

We are grateful to the following for permission to reproduce copyright material:

Text
Document 7 from 'Divu'ah miMakor yehudi al gerush yehudei Bielsko-Biała el "haShemurah haYehudit" beEzor Lublin, mars 1940' (A Report on the Jewish Reservation in Lublin, March 1940), *Gal-Ed* 17, pp. CXXXI–CXXXIX (Engel, David 2000), reproduced with permission; Document 19 from 'Pro memoria o sytuacji w Kraju w okresie 1–25 lipca 1942 r.' (Memorandum on the situation in Poland, 1–25 July 1942), Polish Underground Study Trust, London, MSW 56/113, with permission from The Polish Underground Movement (1939–1945) Study Trust in London; Document 20 from 'An early account of Polish Jewry under Nazi and Soviet occupation presented to the Polish government-in-exile', February 1940, *Jewish Social Studies*, 45, pp. 1–16 (Engel, David 1983), copyright 1983 reproduced with permission of Indiana University Press via Copyright Clearance Center; Document 29 translated from *Pamiętniki z Getta Warszawskiego*, Warsaw, PWN (Grynberg, Michał, ed. 1993) pp. 41–42, reproduced with permission; Document 31 adapted from Yad Vashem Archives, O6/83, reproduced with permission; Document 32 adapted from *Konspiracyjna Rada Pomocy Żydom w Warszawie 1942–1945*, Warsaw, Państwowy Instytut Wydawniczy (Prekerowa, Teresa 1982) pp. 370–371 © by Teresa Prekerowa and Panstwowy Instytut Wydawniczy, Warszawa, 1981.

Plates
United States Holocaust Memorial Museum for Plates 1, 2, 4, 6, 7, 8, 9, 10, 11, 12, 13 and 14; Yad Vashem Photo Archive for Plate 5 and Centrum Judaicum Archive Berlin for Plate 3.

In some instances we have been unable to trace the owners of copyright material, and we would appreciate any information that would enable us to do so.

Note on place names

The names of cities given in the text are their official names in the language of the country to which they belonged on 31 August 1939. Hence Wilno instead of Vilnius or Vilna, but Kaunas instead of Kovno. Exceptions have been made for some cities whose names have well-known English forms (Prague, Vienna, Warsaw). Standard English names have been used for all larger political units.

List of maps

1 Europe and its Jews, January 1938   xxix

2 German, Hungarian, and Soviet expansion and the
dismemberment of Czechoslovakia and Poland, 1938–39   xxx

3 The Nazi orbit, 1942   xxxi

4 The murder of European Jewry   xxxii

Chronology

1933

30 January	Adolf Hitler appointed Chancellor of Germany.
9 March	Nazi party militias begin wave of anti-Jewish street violence throughout Germany.
1 April	Nazi regime sponsors one-day boycott of Jewish businesses.
7 April	Law for the Restoration of the Professional Civil Service enacted.
16 June	German Jewish Cultural Association founded.
17 August	*Haavara* agreement concluded.
8 September	Jewish organizations meeting in Geneva call for worldwide boycott of German products.
17 September	*Reichsvertretung* founded.
17 October	Law bans Jews from working for German newspapers.

1934

2 August	Upon the death of German President Hindenburg, Hitler becomes sole leader (*Führer*) of Germany.

1935

15 September	Nuremberg Laws proclaimed.

1938

13 March	Germany annexes Austria.
26 April	German government issues instruction confiscating Jewish businesses and requiring registration of Jewish-owned property.
5–15 July	Evian Conference.
26 August	Central Office for Jewish Emigration established in Vienna.

27 September	Jewish barristers banned from appearing in court.
28 October	14,000–17,000 Jewish residents of Germany with Polish citizenship deported to Poland.
7 November	Herszel Grynszpan, a Jewish student in Paris whose parents were deported from Germany to Poland, shoots Ernst vom Rath, a Germany embassy official, in revenge.
9–10 November	German government organizes *Kristallnacht*, ostensibly as collective punishment of Germany's Jews for Herszel Grynszpan's action.

1939

13–15 March	Germany occupies Czechoslovakia, creating the Protectorate of Bohemia and Moravia and the satellite state of Slovakia.
17 May	British White Paper restricts Jewish immigration to Palestine to an average of 15,000 per year for five years.
22 June	Jewish Emigration Office opened in Prague.
4 July	*Reichsvereinigung* replaces *Reichsvertretung*.
1 September	Germany invades Poland, conquering the country within a month.
17 September	Soviet Army occupies eastern Poland.
21 September	Reinhard Heydrich orders relocation of small Polish Jewish communities and establishment of Jewish councils.
12 October	Authorities in Vienna and the Protectorate deport first transports of Jews to Nisko reservation.
26 October	Jews in Generalgouvernement made subject to forced labour.
28 November	First ghetto established in Piotrków Trybunalski.

1940

9 April	Germany occupies Denmark and southern Norway.
10 May	Germany invades the Netherlands, Belgium, and France; Łódź ghetto sealed.
10 June	Italy enters the war on Germany's side.
22 June	France signs armistice with Germany and leaves war.
3 October	Vichy French government enacts anti-Jewish legislation.
15 November	Warsaw ghetto sealed.
24 November	Hungary, Romania, and Slovakia join Axis.
December	Emmanuel Ringelblum establishes secret Warsaw ghetto documentation project.

1941

12 February	Germans force establishment of countrywide Jewish council (*Joodse Rad*) in the Netherlands.
March	Adolf Eichmann appointed head of RSHA Jewish Affairs Section.
22 June	Germany invades Soviet Union.
23 June	First mass killings of Soviet Jews.
28 June	Pogrom in Iaşi (Romania).
31 July	Goering orders Heydrich to arrange 'final solution of the Jewish question'.
13 September	First deportations to Transnistria.
28–29 September	Mass shootings kill 33,771 Kiev Jews.
8 December	Gas vans begin operation at Chełmno.
31 December	First Jewish armed resistance unit formed in Wilno ghetto.

1942

20 January	Wannsee Conference.
March	First killings of Jews by gas at Sobibór, Bełżec, and Birkenau.
17 March–21 April	Liquidation of Lublin ghetto.
26 March	First deportation of Slovakian Jews to Auschwitz-Birkenau.
28 March	First deportation of French Jews to Auschwitz-Birkenau.
May	Bund tells Polish government-in-exile that Germans are engaging in 'the physical extirpation of the Jewish population on Polish soil'.
17 July	First deportation of Dutch Jews to Auschwitz-Birkenau.
22 July–12 Sept.	265,000 Jews sent from Warsaw ghetto to Treblinka.
28 July	Jewish Fighting Organization formed in Warsaw ghetto.
5 August	First deportation of Belgian Jews to Auschwitz-Birkenau.
November	German military advances halted at El-Alamein and Stalingrad; war turns in Allies' favour.
10 December	First deportation of German Jews to Auschwitz-Birkenau.
17 December	Allies condemn German murders of Jews.

1943

15 March	First deportation of Greek Jews to killing centres.
20–29 March	Bulgaria deports Jews from Thrace and Macedonia.
19 April–8 May	Warsaw ghetto uprising.
23 September	Liquidation of Wilno ghetto.
2 October	Rescue of Danish Jewry.

1944

15 May	First deportation of Hungarian Jews to Auschwitz-Birkenau.
6 June	Allied invasion of Normandy.
13 July	Soviet army liberates Wilno; Kaunas ghetto liquidated.
23 July	Soviet army liberates Majdanek.
30 August	Łódź ghetto liquidated.
31 October	Deportation of Slovakian Jews to Auschwitz-Birkenau resumed.
8 November	Death march of Budapest Jews.

1945

17 January	Auschwitz evacuated; prisoners begin death march.
27 January	Soviet army liberates Auschwitz-Birkenau.
8 May	Germany surrenders.

Who's who

Antonescu, Ion (1882–1946): Romanian general and dictator of the pro-German 'national legionary state', 1940–44. He ordered the mass murder of Jews in Bukovina and Bessarabia and the deportation of survivors to Transnistria, but he also prevented the killing of the Jews of Old Romania (the Regat) and southern Transylvania.

Arlosoroff, Chaim (1899–1933): Zionist leader and head of the Political Department of the Jewish Agency for Palestine. In 1933 he began negotiations with the Nazi government to permit German Jews to emigrate *en masse* to Palestine and to retain their property. These negotiations resulted in the Haavara agreement.

Barash, Efraim (1892–1943?): Head of the *Judenrat* in the Białystok ghetto.

Czerniaków, Adam (1880–1942): Head of the Warsaw *Judenrat*. In July 1942 he committed suicide rather than post an order for deporting Jews from the ghetto, although he did not warn Jews of the danger that faced them.

Eichmann, Adolf (1906–1962): SS official, central architect of the German murder programme. In 1938–39 he headed the Central Offices for Jewish Emigration in Vienna and Prague. Later he was appointed head of Jewish affairs for the RSHA. He supervised the logistics of deporting Jews from throughout Europe to the killing centres.

Frank, Hans (1900–1946): Head of the Generalgouvernement in Poland, 1939–45.

Gens, Jakob (1905–1943): Head of the ghetto administration in Wilno.

Globocnik, Odilo (1904–1945): SS and Police Leader of the Lublin district from November 1939; principal architect of Operation Reinhard.

Goebbels, Josef (1897–1945): Nazi Minister of Public Enlightenment and Propaganda, 1933–45, and *Gauleiter* (regional party leader) of Berlin.

Although not a central force in the making of Nazi Jewish policy, he was a principal instigator of the *Kristallnacht* violence and of the initial deportation of Jews from Berlin to the Łódź ghetto in October 1941.

Goering, Hermann (1893–1946): Principal Nazi leader after Hitler and Hitler's designated successor. Holding the title Reich Marshal, he was interior minister of Prussia, head of the German air force, plenipotentiary of the Four-Year Plan for economic revival, and minister of the economy.

Heydrich, Reinhard (1904–1942): Head of RSHA, Protector of Bohemia and Moravia, and organizer of the Einsatzgruppen. Heydrich was one of the primary planners and executors of the Nazi mass murder campaign.

Himmler, Heinrich (1900–1945): Head of the SS; along with Hitler and Goering the most powerful leader of the Third Reich. He oversaw the planning and execution of the murder campaign, supervising the work of Heydrich and Eichmann.

Horthy, Miklos (1868–1957): Regent of Hungary, 1920–1944. Although he resisted German demands to turn responsibility for Hungarian Jews over to the SS, his withdrawal from active political involvement between March and July 1944 opened the way for 430,000 Jews to be deported.

Karski, Jan (1914–2000): Polish underground courier. In 1940 and 1942 he transmitted eyewitness testimony about the fate of Polish Jews to the Polish government-in-exile. In 1942–43 he also informed British and US leaders about the systematic mass murder of Europe's Jews.

Kovner, Abba (1918–1987): Leader of the United Partisan Organization in the Wilno ghetto. Kovner was the first Jew known to have deduced the German murder plan and the first to call for Jewish armed resistance.

Lemkin, Raphael (1901–1959): Polish Jewish refugee legal scholar who coined the term 'genocide' in 1944.

Merin, Moshe (1906–1943): Head of the *Judenrat* in the Zagłębie region of Poland (eastern Upper Silesia), including the communities of Będzin and Sosnowiec.

Ringelblum, Emmanuel (1900–1944): Jewish historian and social worker from Warsaw. A leader of the Jewish self-help effort in the Warsaw ghetto, he established a clandestine information service and archive, which has become a principal source of information about how Jews in the ghetto lived under Nazi occupation. He was instrumental in gathering, collating, and transmitting information about mass murders of Jews.

Schindler, Oskar (1908–1974): German industrialist from Moravia (Czechoslovakia). He used his position as owner of an enamelware factory in Kraków as cover to save some 1,000 Jewish workers.

Tenenbaum, Mordechai (1916–1943): Leader of the resistance movement and rebellion in the Białystok ghetto.

Wallenberg, Raoul (1912–1947?): Special representative sent by the Swedish Foreign Ministry and US War Refugee Board to Budapest in 1944 to offer protection to Hungarian Jews threatened with death. By distributing special Swedish passports and establishing special Jewish hostels, Wallenberg managed to prevent the deportation or shooting of perhaps as many as 100,000 Jews.

Glossary

Aktion (*pl. Aktionen*): An operation leading to the killing of Jews, most commonly involving a mass roundup and removal to a killing site.

Arrow Cross: Radical right-wing Hungarian party founded by Ferenc Szálasi in 1939. It opposed the conservative Hungarian governments appointed by Miklos Horthy and was suppressed by them, even though those governments, like the Arrow Cross, favoured alliance with Nazi Germany. When Horthy sought to abandon the German alliance, the Arrow Cross militia, supported by German troops, staged a *coup d'état*. Once in control, the Arrow Cross began shooting, incarcerating, and deporting what remained of Hungarian Jewry. It is estimated that over 80,000 Jews fell victim to Arrow Cross violence.

Asocials: Nazi term referring to habitual criminals, vagrants, and beggars. Believing that criminality and vagrancy were hereditary, the Nazi regime incarcerated and sterilised many whom they branded 'asocial' without reference to any specific crime.

Auschwitz: German camp complex near the town of Oświęcim, in occupied Poland, 50 km west of Kraków. The main camp (Auschwitz I) was opened in June 1940 to house Polish political prisoners. A larger satellite camp, Birkenau (Auschwitz II), was built in late 1941, and a labour camp in the nearby village of Monowice (Monowitz or Auschwitz III) was operated by the IG-Farben chemical concern from May 1942. The Auschwitz complex became the largest and most notorious of all Nazi camps. Because almost 1.5 million Jews were put to death in the killing centre at Birkenau, Auschwitz has become a primary symbol of the Holocaust.

Bełżec: German killing centre on the Lublin–Lwów rail line. Some 450,000–500,000 Jews, mostly from ghettos in Poland, were killed there between March and December 1942.

Bermuda Conference: Anglo-American conference on refugees held on the Caribbean island of Bermuda, 19–30 April 1943. It was marked mostly by disagreements between the parties and the fear that concerted action to rescue Jews from Nazi-controlled Europe would interfere with the Allied war effort. The only substantive decision taken was to extend the mandate of the Intergovernmental Committee on Refugees that had been established at the Evian Conference of 1938.

Bessarabia: Romanian–Soviet border region between the Prut and Dniester Rivers. Mostly under Russian rule during the nineteenth century, it was awarded to Romania by the Paris Peace Conference in 1919. Soviet forces annexed the area in June 1940, but Romania reclaimed it in the wake of the German invasion of the USSR a year later. In anticipation of the reconquest, Romanian dictator Antonescu secretly ordered mass killings of the province's more than 200,000 Jews, who were charged with disloyalty. Well over half were killed in combined Romanian–German operations during July–August 1941. The remaining Jews were deported to Transnistria, beginning in September 1941; many thousands died en route.

Birkenau: Satellite camp of Auschwitz, known also as Auschwitz II, about 3 km from the main Auschwitz camp. It also functioned as the largest of the Nazi killing centres: almost 1.5 million Jews, 16,000 Soviet prisoners of war, and 20,000 Sinti and Roma were killed there between January 1942 and November 1944. It was the primary killing centre to which non-Polish, non-Soviet Jews were deported.

Bukovina: Former duchy of the Habsburg Empire, extending from the northeast end of the Carpathian Mountains to the Dniester River, awarded to Romania by the Treaty of St Germain (1919). The USSR annexed the northern half of the province in June 1940; Romania recovered it in June 1941. Like the Jews of Bessarabia, Bukovinian Jews were charged by the Romanians with supporting the Soviet enemy and subjected to revenge attacks by the Romanian army (together with German forces). Local Ukrainians also instigated pogroms against Jews. Over 20,000 Jews were killed in this fashion; another 57,000 were deported to Transnistria.

Bund: Jewish socialist party founded in 1897. In interwar Poland it was one of the largest Jewish political movements, and it played an important role in underground activities in the Polish ghettos. Its report of May 1942 included the first statement that the Germans had a programme to kill all Polish Jews.

Central Office for Jewish Emigration: Nazi-sponsored bureau established in Vienna in August 1938 to increase the pace of Jewish emigration from

Austria. A similar bureau was established in Germany in January 1939 and in the Protectorate of Bohemia and Moravia in July 1939.

Chełmno: The first Nazi killing centre. Located about 50 km west of Łódź, it employed sealed lorries for killing Jews by asphyxiation from exhaust fumes. Between December 1941 and March 1943, 320,000 people were murdered there, mainly Jews from western Poland.

Concentration camps: Camps employed for incarcerating political prisoners, 'asocials', and others deemed undesirable by the Third Reich because of their beliefs, behaviour, or presumed racial inferiority. They were not killing centres of the type used for mass murder of Jews (although concentration camps were located next to the killing centres at Auschwitz and Majdanek).

Death marches: Forced marches of prisoners over long distances, accompanied by brutal treatment. The term is most commonly applied to the march from Budapest to Vienna in November 1944 and to the westward march of prisoners from labour and concentration camps east of Berlin during the first four months of 1945, in flight from the advancing Soviet army.

Einsatzgruppe (pl. Einsatzgruppen): Special task forces under SS supervision, deployed first in Poland and later in the Soviet Union for eliminating potential resistance to German rule. During the invasion of the Soviet Union in 1941, they bore a major part of the responsibility for carrying out mass shootings of Jews.

Evian Conference: International conference on refugees, July 1938. Representatives of 32 countries came together in an effort to coordinate plans to absorb Jewish and other refugees from Germany. The conference established the Intergovernmental Committee on Refugees, but it generated virtually no practical results.

Four-Year Plan: Economic programme announced by Goering in September 1936, aimed at augmenting German industrial and armaments production and reducing its dependence on imports. It is widely viewed as a preparatory step towards an eventual invasion of the Soviet Union.

Führer: German for 'leader'. It was used as Hitler's title in the Nazi Party beginning in 1931. In 1934, when Hitler combined the offices of president and chancellor of Germany, *Führer* became his official designation as head of the German state and government.

Generalgouvernement: German-controlled territory carved out of Poland, incorporating the districts of Kraków, Lublin, Radom, and Warsaw (and Galicia after 1941), but excluding the western Polish provinces, which were annexed directly to Germany.

Genocide: Term coined by Raphael Lemkin in 1944 to refer to the destruction of a nation or ethnic group. The United Nations Genocide Convention of 1948 determined that genocide could occur through killing, torture, deprivation of adequate living conditions, or prevention of reproduction.

Ghetto: An urban area where Jews were compelled by law to reside. Between the sixteenth and eighteenth centuries ghettos were common in Italy and central Europe; the last such ghetto was dissolved in 1870. The Nazis revived the institution in occupied Poland and extended it to the Soviet territories conquered in 1941.

Haavara: (Hebrew: transfer) 1933 agreement between the Nazi government and agencies of the Zionist movement allowing German Jews migrating to Palestine to transfer a portion of their assets with them.

Hitler Youth: Nazi organization for boys aged 15–18; membership was compulsory from 1936. Along with the League of German Girls, it provided a principal avenue of indoctrination for the Nazi regime.

Intergovernmental Committee on Refugees: Body established by the Evian Conference in 1938. In 1939 it negotiated an arrangement allowing German Jews leaving the country to take their assets with them. The arrangement was not implemented due to the outbreak of war. During the war it was largely inactive.

Jewish Agency for Palestine: Body created in 1929 to represent the Jewish community of Palestine in political matters. Though including non-Zionists, it was closely associated with the Zionist movement.

Jewish Fighting Organization: Armed resistance group established in Warsaw in July 1942; principal force behind the Warsaw ghetto revolt. Branches were established in Białystok, Kraków, and other ghettos as well.

Jewish reservation: Idea floated within the Nazi regime in 1939–40, involving mass concentration of Jews in a single location. Proposed locations were Nisko (Poland) and Madagascar.

Judenrat (pl. Judenräte): Official Jewish administrations established at German behest in most east European ghettos and in several other occupied countries.

Killing centres: Term referring to six German-established locations (Chełmno, Bełżec, Sobibór, Treblinka, Majdanek, and Birkenau) to which Jews were transported from across Europe to be killed.

Kristallnacht: Nazi-organized anti-Jewish riot of 9–10 November 1938, in which synagogues were burned and Jewish property looted throughout Germany and Austria.

Labour camps: Camps where a minority of young, healthy Jews were exploited, along with non-Jews, as forced labourers instead of being killed immediately.

Law for the Restoration of the Professional Civil Service: The first major piece of Nazi anti-Jewish legislation. Adopted in April 1933, it removed Jewish government employees from their positions.

Madagascar Plan: Nazi plan to create a Jewish reservation on the east African island of Madagascar. Developed by the SS and the German foreign ministry, it received much attention within the Nazi regime in 1940, but it was abandoned late in the year, when the decision was taken to invade the Soviet Union.

Majdanek: Killing centre combined with concentration camp on the outskirts of Lublin. About 500,000 Jews, Poles, and Soviet prisoners were brought to the camp between October 1941 and July 1944; 150,000 Jews from many European countries were killed there in gas chambers.

Mein Kampf: Hitler's autobiography and main ideological tract, published 1925–28. Among other things, it is a principal source for the reconstruction of Hitler's ideas and plans concerning Jews.

Mischling (pl. Mischlinge): Category defined in the wake of the Nuremberg Laws, consisting of people with one or two Jewish grandparents who did not adhere to the Jewish religion and were not married to Jews. Because of their 'mixed blood', they were subject to certain restrictions in marriage and employment, which increased in severity in accordance with the percentage of Jewishness in an individual's pedigree.

Nazi Party: Common name of the National Socialist German Workers Party, founded in 1919 (known as the German Workers Party until 1920). Led by Hitler, it became the largest German political party in the July 1932 parliamentary elections. In January 1933 it took control of the government with Hitler as chancellor (premier); two months later it altered the German constitution and inaugurated the Third Reich.

Nisko Plan: Nazi scheme to create a Jewish reservation in the eastern Generalgouvernement, to which Jews from throughout the Nazi realm would be deported. Several tens of thousands of Jews were deported there from the Protectorate and western Poland in late 1939, but the operation was abandoned in early 1940 in favour of the Madagascar Plan.

Nuremberg Laws: Name for two German laws promulgated on 15 September 1935. The Reich Citizenship Law stated that only people with pure German blood could be German citizens; all others were classified as 'subjects'. The

Law for the Protection of German Blood and Honour outlawed marriages between citizens and subjects. In November 1935 a third category, *Mischlinge*, was added.

Operation Reinhard: Code name for the construction of the Bełżec, Sobibór, and Treblinka killing centres and their use in the murder of over 2 million Jews from the Generalgouvernement.

Protectorate of Bohemia and Moravia: German administrative unit established in the Czech lands following the conquest of Czechoslovakia in March 1939. Though officially run by Czechs, sole political authority actually rested with the German Protector and his officials.

Regat: Area of Romania comprising the two original Romanian provinces of Moldavia and Wallachia, excluding outlying regions (including Bukovina, Bessarabia, and Transylvania) annexed from 1913 on. Despite German pressure, Romanian dictator Antonescu refused to turn Regat Jews over to the Germans for deportation.

Reich Labour Service: German government labour battalion to which German men and women aged 19–25 could be conscripted for six months. It served as an important indoctrinatory vehicle for the Nazi regime.

Reichsvereinigung: Legally recognized official administration of the German Jewish community, established in 1939, replacing the *Reichsvertretung*. The *Reichsvereinigung der Juden in Deutschland* (Reich Association of the Jews in Germany) was a compulsory organization to which all Jews under German rule were compelled to belong. Its leaders were selected by the Nazi government, and its principal task was to effectuate mass Jewish emigration.

Reichsvertretung: Central organization of German Jewry under Nazi rule, established in 1933. The *Reichsvertretung der deutschen Juden* (Reich Representation of German Jews) was a voluntary social welfare organization; in 1935 it was ordered to change its name to the *Reichsvertretung der Juden in Deutschland* (Reich Representation of the Jews in Germany) – the Nuremberg Laws having made the term 'German Jews' untenable. In 1939 the *Reichsvertretung* was converted by government action into the *Reichsvereinigung der Juden in Deutschland* (Reich Association of the Jews in Germany).

'*Resettlement in the East*': German euphemism for deportation of Jews to killing centres.

RSHA: Acronym for *Reichsicherheitshauptamt* (Reich Main Security Office). Organized in September 1939 as a branch of the SS under Heydrich, the RSHA supervised the criminal police (Kripo), the secret political police (Gestapo), and the internal espionage service (SD).

SA: Acronym for *Sturmabteilung* (Storm division). Nazi party activist formation, often known as 'storm troops' or 'brownshirts'. More than 500,000 Germans had joined its ranks by the time the Nazis took power, and it became a major pressure group within the party, sometimes challenging Hitler's direction. It urged more radical, violent action against Jews than the Nazi government wished at first to undertake. It was purged of radical elements in 1934, after which it lost political significance.

SD: Acronym for *Sicherheitsdienst* (Security service). Domestic espionage arm of the Nazi Party, led by Heydrich. Its principal function was to gather intelligence concerning so-called internal enemies of the party and the German state. In 1939 it was subordinated to the RSHA.

SS: Acronym for *Schutzstaffel* (Protection squad). Nazi police force and Hitler's personal bodyguard corps, transformed under Himmler's leadership into the principal police agency in the Third Reich. Its primary task under Himmler was to survey and eliminate all activity that might threaten the Reich. In this capacity it supervised most of the German concentration camps and took on primary responsibility for controlling (and eventually killing) the Jewish population in German-occupied territories.

Salvation through work: Survival strategy employed by several Judenrat heads. It involved intensive Jewish-initiated exploitation of the industrial and labour resources of ghettos for German war production, in the hope that the Germans would regard Jews as too valuable to the German war effort to be killed.

Selection: Removal of young and healthy Jews from the ranks of those transported to killing centres, in order to exploit their labour or use them in medical experiments.

Sinti and Roma: The two largest European Gypsy groups, distinguished by language. Sinti were more numerous in Germany, Roma throughout Europe. The origins of both groups can be traced to India, and their presence was noted in Europe from the fifteenth century. There are many similarities between the treatment of Jews by the Third Reich and the treatment of Gypsies. Gypsies were victims of mass murder; estimates of the number killed range from 200,000 to 1,000,000.

Sobibór: German killing centre in eastern Poland. Some 200,000–250,000 Jews were killed in the Sobibór gas chambers between March 1942 and September 1943.

Sonderkommando: Name assigned to deportees selected upon arrival at killing centres to perform particularly gruesome duties associated with disposing of the bodies of the victims.

T4: Code name for a Nazi programme to kill mentally retarded and physically deformed individuals believed to present a danger of corrupting German racial stock. Operating in 1939–41, it was responsible for the development of techniques (including mass killing by asphyxiation) that were later employed in the murder of Jews. Some T4 workers were instrumental in the initial operation of the killing centres.

Transnistria: Ukrainian region between the Bug and Dniester Rivers, occupied by Romania from 1941 to 1944. The Romanian government deported some 150,000 Jews, mostly from Bukovina and Bessarabia, to Transnistria, where they were incarcerated in ghettos and camps and conscripted for forced labour. About 90,000 of the deportees died. In addition, some 185,000 Jews who had lived in the region before the Romanian occupation were murdered by German and Romanian forces.

Treblinka: German killing centre midway between Warsaw and Białystok. About 870,000 Jews were killed there between July 1942 and July 1943, almost all from the Generalgouvernement.

Ustaše: (Serbo-Croat: Insurgents) Units of a right-wing Croatian nationalist separatist paramilitary organization, led by Ante Pavelić. They came to power with Germany's creation of an independent Croatian satellite in 1941 and, without German assistance, initiated mass killings of non-Croatians, including 500,000 Serbs, 35,000 Jews, and 20,000 Gypsies.

Volk (pl. Völker): German word literally meaning 'people'. Hitler used it as a substitute for the term 'race', indicating a fundamental genetic division of humanity. *Völker*, in Hitler's view, were the repositories of all values.

Wannsee conference: Meeting held in Berlin in January 1942 to establish a timetable and coordinate the logistics of the transportation of European Jews to the killing centres.

War Refugee Board: US government agency established in January 1944 to explore possibilities for rescuing European Jews.

Weimar Republic: Name commonly used to designate the German republic established in February 1919. Fourteen years later it gave way to the Third Reich.

Yad Vashem: The official Israeli institution for studying and commemorating the Holocaust. Among other activities it maintains an extensive library and archive; it also honours and gathers information about non-Jews who risked their lives to assist Jews during the Holocaust.

Zionism: Modern Jewish political and ideological movement arguing that Jews constitute primarily a national group (comparable to Germans or Poles) instead of a religious one (comparable to Catholics or Muslims) and that as such they are entitled to political sovereignty over their historic homeland. During the early twentieth century the World Zionist Organization, established in 1897, encouraged Jewish migration to Palestine, where, it hoped, a large Jewish settlement would serve as the basis for a Jewish national home. Zionism was a controversial idea among Jews from its inception; nonetheless, from the end of the First World War it was one of the principal forces in European Jewish life.

Zyklon B: Trade name of prussic acid or hydrogen cyanide (HCN), a lethal substance used in the gas chambers at Birkenau.

Żegota: Code name for the Council for Aid to Jews, established under the aegis of the Polish underground in December 1942. It assisted some 4,000 Polish Jews to maintain themselves in hiding or under cover of false identity during the German occupation.

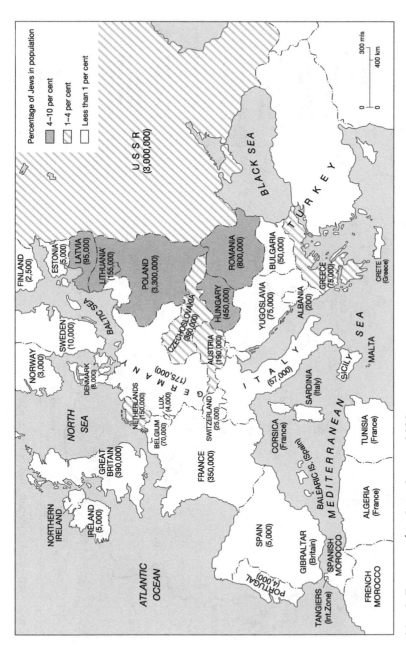

Map 1 Europe and its Jews, January 1938

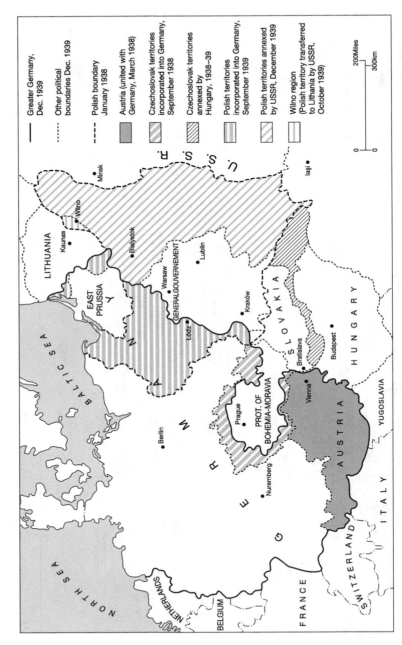

Map 2 German, Hungarian, and Soviet expansion and the dismemberment of Czechoslovakia and Poland, 1938–39

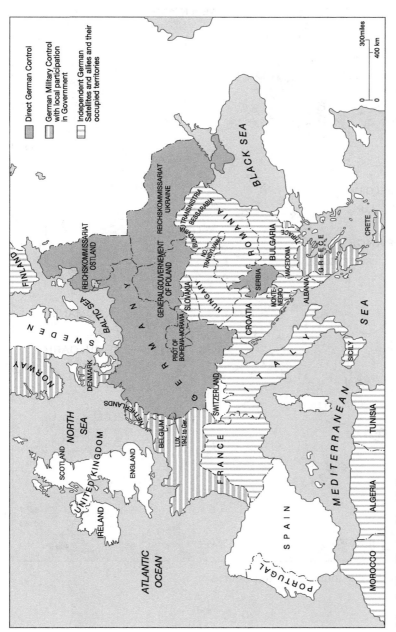

Map 3 The Nazi orbit, 1942

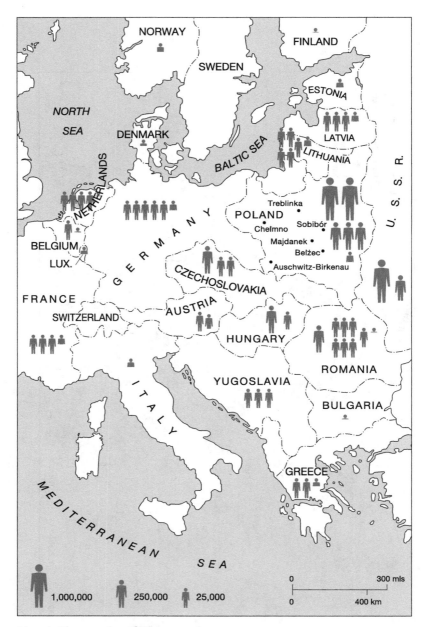

Map 4 The murder of European Jewry

Part 1

ANALYSIS

1

Studying the Holocaust

This book is about an encounter between two sets of human beings: on one hand the people who acted on behalf of the German state, its agencies, or its almost 66 million citizens between 30 January 1933 and 8 May 1945; on the other the almost 9 million Jews who lived in Germany, in twenty-one other European countries (Albania, Austria, Belgium, Bulgaria, Czechoslovakia, Denmark, Estonia, Finland, France, Greece, Hungary, Italy, Latvia, Lithuania, Luxembourg, the Netherlands, Norway, Poland, Romania, the USSR, and Yugoslavia), and in the French and Italian colonial territories (Algeria, Libya, Morocco, and Tunisia) that were either ruled directly or occupied by Germany or that made a formal alliance with it at any time during that interval. That encounter resulted in the death of about two-thirds of the latter group, in the large majority of cases as a direct result of actions taken by the former.

The 5.8 million Jews who died at German or German-allied hands, mostly during 1941–45, were almost all unarmed civilians who had committed no organized act of aggression against the German state or society and who posed no real threat to their well-being – at least in terms that made sense to reasonable people in the Western world. Yet the leaders of Germany actively sought their deaths. In fact, most of them came to regard the killing of Jews as one of their most important tasks, and from 1941 on they pursued that aim with ruthless vigour. In other words, the story of the encounter between the Third Reich (as the German state was known during almost all of the period in question) and the Jews ultimately became one of premeditated mass murder.

How the government of a modern state could come to such a conclusion – how it could undertake a program of systematic mass murder in the belief that doing so was one of the fundamental reasons for its existence – is exceedingly difficult for reasonable people to grasp. Yet thinking about the encounter between the Third Reich and the Jews as an act of murder actually suggests a way of working toward understanding. After all, there are certain questions that are routinely asked about any murder case that can be put to the case at hand as well. These are the questions of motive, means, and opportunity. What led the leaders of the Third Reich to believe that their Jewish victims needed to die? Once they reached that conclusion, how were those leaders able to act upon it with the precise degree of success they eventually achieved? How did they mobilize others to take part in the killing? How were people working on their behalf able to manoeuvre their victims into a position where it was possible to take their lives? Was there anything that some other agent could have done to stop the mass murder campaign or significantly to reduce the number of people who lost their lives because of it?

For many decades scholars have been working to find answers to those questions. They have learned much, but they are still far from knowing everything they would like to know. Moreover, not all of them agree about what the things they know really mean. After all, studying history isn't exclusively about discovering facts; it is also about figuring out how the facts connect with one another and how they help explain what historians (and, one hopes, others) want to understand. As it turns out, historians often disagree about these things, and their opinions about them sometimes change as new facts are brought to light.

This book will help readers learn the basic facts of the encounter between the Third Reich and the Jews – the who/what/when/where/how of the murder case. But it will also show them how different scholars have interpreted those facts and debated about how best to make sense of them. As readers will discover, many key questions about the encounter between the Third Reich and the Jews are far from settled. The book will highlight some of those problems, explain why they have yet to be resolved, and point readers towards ways of joining the conversation.

HOLOCAUST AND GENOCIDE

One of the most basic problems of interpretation stems from the fact that the encounter between the Third Reich and the Jews is often assigned a special name – the Holocaust.

That was not always the case. In fact, almost twenty years passed after the Third Reich fell and the Second World War ended before the encounter acquired its own particular label. Until that time the word 'holocaust' had been used as a catch-all term for almost any large-scale catastrophe. The great earthquake and fire that devastated San Francisco in 1906, the destruction caused by Japanese air raids in China in 1938, the anticipated outcome of global thermonuclear war – all of these were labelled 'holocausts' in the popular press throughout the world before the word (capitalized and preceded by the definite article) came widely to signify what befell Jews at the hands of the Third Reich and its allies.

Reserving the term 'the Holocaust' for the murder of two-thirds of European Jewry by the Third Reich suggests that that case of murder constituted a holocaust *par excellence*. Yet during the first two decades or so following the Second World War, most people did not understand it that way. The regime that ruled the Third Reich, governed by the National Socialist German Workers Party (the Nazis), was notorious for its brutality, and Jews were generally viewed as only one of many sets of victims. Those victims included political and religious dissidents (mostly socialists, communists, Jehovah's Witnesses, and political and religious leaders who spoke out against the Reich), vagrants, chronically unemployed persons, habitual criminals, male homosexuals from Germany and Austria, slave labourers, and members of groups targeted for wholesale killing, including the **Sinti** and **Roma** (commonly called Gypsies), Soviet prisoners of war, the mentally ill, and the physically disabled. Many members of these groups had been held in a highly-ramified network of concentration, labour, penal, and transit camps, where conditions were vicious and mortality dreadfully high. When British and American armed forces entered those camps in April–May 1945 and gained their first lasting impressions of Nazi atrocities, they found a population of perhaps 700,000 inmates, only about 100,000 of whom were Jews. As a result, it was difficult for them (as well as for the journalists who followed them and reported the horrors they saw) to see anything unusual in the experience of the Jews they met. On the contrary, it was generally believed that Jews had been placed in the camp system for the same reasons as all other prisoners – because (in the words of a report that appeared in the American press from late April 1945) they 'refused to accept the political philosophy of the **Nazi party**' (quoted in Lipstadt, 1986: 255).

It took many years of historical research to demonstrate that that description overlooked what most observers today regard as a vital feature of the Jews' experience – that Jews (along with the Sinti and Roma and the disabled) became victims for reasons having nothing at all to do with what they believed or how they behaved. Historians now realize that Jews could have been the most ardent exponents of Nazi ideology, the most fervent advocates for the Third Reich in the disputes that led to the Second World War, yet their fate would have been the same. They have learned that at a certain point in its history the Nazi regime began actively to seek the death of each and every man, woman, and child within reach whom they claimed belonged to the Jewish group. And they have come to understand that the camps in Germany that so shocked their liberators in 1945 (like Dachau, Buchenwald, and Bergen-Belsen) were *not* the primary sites where the murder of European

Sinti and **Roma:** The two largest European Gypsy groups, distinguished by language. Sinti were more numerous in Germany, Roma throughout Europe. The origins of both groups can be traced to India, and their presence was noted in Europe from the fifteenth century. There are many similarities between the treatment of Jews by the Third Reich and the treatment of Gypsies. Gypsies were victims of mass murder; estimates of the number killed range from 200,000 to 1,000,000.

Nazi party: Common name of the National Socialist German Workers Party, founded in 1919 (known as the German Workers Party until 1920). Led by Hitler, it became the largest German political party in the July 1932 parliamentary elections. In January 1933 it took control of the government with Hitler as chancellor (premier); two months later it altered the German constitution and inaugurated the Third Reich.

Killing centres: Term referring to six German-established locations (Chełmno, Bełżec, Sobibór, Treblinka, Majdanek, and Birkenau) to which Jews were transported from across Europe to be killed.

Concentration camps: Camps employed for incarcerating political prisoners, 'asocials', and others deemed undesirable by the Third Reich because of their beliefs, behaviour, or presumed racial inferiority. They were not killing centres of the type used for mass murder of Jews (although concentration camps were located next to the killing centres at Auschwitz and Majdanek).

Genocide: Term coined by Raphael Lemkin in 1944 to refer to the destruction of a nation or ethnic group. The United Nations Genocide Convention of 1948 determined that genocide could occur through killing, torture, deprivation of adequate living conditions, or prevention of reproduction.

Jewry took place. On the contrary, millions of Jews were shot to death close to home or asphyxiated upon arrival in specially designed **killing centres**; most Jewish victims of the Third Reich never made it to a **concentration camp**.

Those discoveries about the encounter between the Third Reich and the Jews made that encounter stand out in the minds of many from other instances of Nazi persecution and encouraged observers to assign it its own special name. Yet other observers have questioned just how unusually horrific those features of the Jews' mass death at Nazi hands really were. After all, the encounter between the Third Reich and the Jews was not the only instance of premeditated mass murder in human history. In fact, it was neither the largest nor proportionally the most extensive case. Estimates of the number of Soviet civilians who died as a result of their government's deliberate actions against them between 1929 and 1950 vary widely, but all vastly exceed the number of Jews killed by the Third Reich. The losses sustained by the Sinti and Roma under the Third Reich may also have reached or even exceeded two-thirds of their pre-1933 population in many parts of Europe. Some historians have argued that perhaps 95 per cent of the indigenous population of North and South America prior to European settlement – anywhere between 50 and 100 million people – died between the sixteenth and the nineteenth centuries because of the determination of Europeans to annihilate them; others have disputed the reasons for this massive loss of life, but they have affirmed its extent.

Noting these facts, some scholars have insisted that thinking about the killing of Jews by the Third Reich in isolation from the many other instances of mass murder throughout the ages actually impedes understanding of a broader phenomenon, often called '**genocide**'. This term was invented in 1944 by legal scholar Raphael Lemkin, a Jewish refugee from German-occupied Poland who, while serving as an advisor to the US War Department, wrote a book entitled *Axis Rule in Occupied Europe* [*Doc. 1*]. Lemkin defined 'genocide' as 'the destruction of a nation or of an ethnic group' (Lemkin, 1944: 79). Later he stated that although he originally coined the word to designate mass German killings of Jews, he eventually realized that not only Jews, but members 'of all peoples, religions, and nationalities', had been or could become victims of the same crime (Lemkin, 1952: 98); for 'genocide does not necessarily mean . . . mass killings of all members of a nation . . . [but] the destruction of essential foundations of the life of national groups' (Lemkin, 1944: 79). Echoing this view, some have contended that the expression 'the Holocaust' ought to refer not only to the encounter between the Third Reich and the Jews but also to 'the horrors that Poles, other Slavs, and Gypsies endured at the hands of the Nazis' (Lukas, 1986: 220). Others have extended the term to encompass the Third Reich's treatment of homosexuals, the mentally ill or infirm, and Jehovah's Witnesses, speaking of eleven or twelve million victims of the Holocaust, half of whom were Jews. Still others have employed the word 'holocaust' also when referring to cases of mass murder not perpetrated by the Third Reich.

Against this position, some historians have pointed to certain features of the encounter between the Third Reich and the Jews that, they claim, render it 'unique' among instances of mass murder. Most often, they hold that 'only in the case of Jewry under the Third Reich' did 'a state set out, as a matter of intentional principle and actualized policy, to annihilate physically every man, woman, and child belonging to a specific people' (Rosenbaum, 1996: 19–20). They often contrast this 'total murder of every one of the members of a community' with 'a policy of selective murder designed to destroy . . . nations as such, but keep most of their members alive to become a Helot working force', which is what they understand by the term 'genocide' (Bauer, 1978: 34–35). Their assertion that such a programme was implemented only once in history, against the Jews by the Third Reich, has been challenged, often angrily, by scholars who have discerned a similar drive toward total murder in the Third Reich's treatment of the Sinti and Roma or of the Poles and other Slavic peoples, in the Turkish massacres of Armenians in 1915, or in European actions against the native peoples of the Americas. Although today almost no serious historian denies that the leaders of the Third Reich did indeed hope to kill each and every Jew within their reach, the basic facts of these other cases are still being disputed, and the issue of 'uniqueness' remains one of intense debate.

The strong feelings that often accompany this debate indicate that it involves more than an academic controversy. Some evidently believe that if Jews can be said to have been victims of a type of persecution *sui generis*, they will have a greater claim to special consideration than other peoples who have also suffered horribly from crimes committed against them. In response to this suspicion, some proponents of the 'uniqueness' argument have stressed that they are '*not* . . . endorsing the injudicious claim that the Holocaust is *more evil* than alternative occurrences of . . . mass death' (Katz, 1994: 31). But they continue to insist that the encounter between the Third Reich and the Jews is best understood as a historical singularity and that the phrase 'the Holocaust' be reserved for that encounter alone.

WHO IS RIGHT?

Is there any way to resolve this debate? Not really. After all, historical events don't come pre-packaged with ready-made labels: it is historians and other observers who identify, classify, and name events after they occur. Sometimes they agree about these matters; sometimes they disagree. But there is no single correct way to assign boundaries or designations to any particular past occurrence.

Moreover, all historical events are unique in the sense that they involve distinctive individuals at particular points in time. But by the same token it is also difficult to imagine a historical event that does not share at least some characteristics with other events. One can argue about whether the similarities between two sets of events are more significant than the differences between them; but doing so merely begs the question: significant for what purpose? And because different people are likely to have different ideas about what is significant or meaningful for them, no single, definitive answer to this question is possible.

In other words, in order to determine how we might want to interpret the encounter between the Third Reich and the Jews, we need to think about why we might want to study it in the first place. At bottom, the purpose of any study in the humanities is to learn about human beings – how they think, feel, and behave, and why they do as they do. This aim surely constitutes a sensible reason for studying what befell European Jewry at Nazi hands. Hence it seems appropriate to ask first of all what things of importance we might learn about human beings in general (and thus about ourselves) by doing so.

One way to answer this question is to examine what people who have confronted that encounter have found to be most noteworthy about it. Sociologist Zygmunt Bauman has written that 'the Holocaust was born and executed in our modern rational society, at the high stage of our civilization and at the peak of human cultural achievement, and for this reason it is a problem' (Bauman, 1989: x). Indeed, the story of the Third Reich and the Jews has surprised many people because it runs counter to what they might intuitively have expected from a 'modern rational society' like that of twentieth-century Germany. As will become clear in the following pages, the leaders of the Third Reich looked at the world in a way that made no sense to the rest of Western civilization: in particular, they believed that Jews were (literally) not human, that they were actually a pathogen that threatened (again, literally) to destroy all humanity, and that therefore, by killing all Jews, the Third Reich was actually saving the entire human world from mortal danger. As far as the leaders of the Third Reich were concerned, killing Jews was one of the most important reasons for their state's very being, and they devoted considerable resources – scientific, economic, and human – to carrying it out. Yet while the Third Reich was in existence, hardly anyone outside of Germany understood that this was so: such thinking, it was believed, may have been possible in earlier times or in other parts of the world still mired in irrational superstition, but not in modern, rational

Europe. Only after extensive study did this fundamental feature of the Third Reich become clear to scholars, who had to overcome their most basic assumptions about the effects of modernity upon human beings in order to do so. In other words, studying the Third Reich and the Jews stretches our self-understanding as human beings; it forces us to rethink fundamentally what it means to be human, especially in the modern world.

Perhaps it will eventually be shown and widely agreed that the leaders of the Third Reich (or of another modern state) thought similarly about other peoples. If so, then studying the histories of those peoples' victimization would no doubt serve a similar purpose, and those histories would invite the same attention as that presently given the history of Europe's Jews during the Second World War. Nevertheless, the case of the Third Reich and the Jews offers a wealth of documentation that has been compiled and analysed for over half a century; it is thus at present more easily accessible to most people than other similar cases that might exist. In this light, the question of whether the term 'the Holocaust' ought to be restricted to the encounter between the Third Reich and the Jews or extended to encompass other instances of deliberate mass murder becomes insignificant: the phrase can be used however one wishes, but the manner in which it is used has little bearing upon what the encounter between the Third Reich and the Jews stands to teach us about the meaning of modern human existence.

In what follows, 'the Holocaust' will refer, as a convenient shorthand, solely to the systematic mass murder of European Jews by the Third Reich, without prejudging the issue of possible equivalents.

STUDYING THE HOLOCAUST HISTORICALLY

Because it was rooted in a view of the world that seemed so alien to the one that prevailed in the modern West, the Holocaust has often been said to be incomprehensible. The novelist Yehiel De-Nur, a camp survivor who wrote under the pseudonym Ka-Tzetnik, has called **Auschwitz** (the largest of the Nazi killing centres) 'another planet', where people 'breathed according to different laws of nature' (State of Israel, 1993, vol. 3: 1237). This perception has led many people to claim that the encounter between the Third Reich and the Jews cannot be discussed in the same way that it is possible to describe and analyse other sets of historical events. Such people have argued that the Holocaust can be apprehended at best only partially, through the individual memories of survivors or through artistic representations. In works of these types greater emphasis is often placed upon evoking strong emotions than upon conveying strict factual precision; frequently they produce a feeling of

Auschwitz: German camp complex near the town of Oświęcim, in occupied Poland, 50 km west of Kraków. The main camp (Auschwitz I) was opened in June 1940 to house Polish political prisoners. A larger satellite camp, Birkenau (Auschwitz II), was built in late 1941, and a labour camp in the nearby village of Monowice (Monowitz or Auschwitz III) was operated by the IG-Farben chemical concern from May 1942. The Auschwitz complex became the largest and most notorious of all Nazi camps. Because almost 1.5 million Jews were put to death in the killing centre at Birkenau, Auschwitz has become a primary symbol of the Holocaust.

shock, mystery, and bewilderment over how the horrors that characterized the encounter could ever have taken place.

The chapters that follow, while not negating this manner of dealing with the subject, take a different approach. They try to offer first of all a dispassionate look at the basic facts of the encounter between the Third Reich and the Jews. Then they attempt to place those facts in a historical context, reconstructing the thoughts of participants in the encounter, Germans and Jews alike, along with witnesses who were neither Germans nor Jews, in a way that, it is hoped, will allow bewilderment to yield to a sense that events unfolded as they did for intelligible reasons. They appeal, in other words, not to readers' emotions but to their intellects; they demand of them a mental effort to enter into the minds of people whose way of looking at the world was very different from their own, and at times even altogether alien to it. In the end, readers will decide for themselves to what degree their effort and the book's have rendered the Holocaust comprehensible.

2

The Jews

The leaders of the Third Reich defined millions of Jews out of humanity. They viewed Jews as their mortal enemies and on that basis justified their systematic mass killing, no matter what any individual Jew said, did, or believed.

Who were these Jews who so bedevilled and frightened them?

JEWISH ORIGINS

The word 'Jew' is derived from the name Judah, who was one of the sons of the Biblical patriarch Jacob. Judah (or in its Greek variant, Judea) was also the name of a political entity that existed in the eastern Mediterranean region from perhaps a thousand years before the birth of Jesus to more than a century thereafter. At times Judea was a fully independent country; at other times it was a province of a foreign empire (Babylonian, Persian, Greek, or Roman). Its boundaries varied, but its centre was in the hill country south of Jerusalem between the Mediterranean coast and the Jordan River. Originally the word 'Jew' was used to designate what might be called today a citizen of Judea – someone whose right to reside in that country was inalienable and could be passed on from generation to generation. It was, in other words, primarily a political term.

Already in ancient times, though, the name was employed in other senses as well. As early as the sixth century BCE Jews had settled outside Judea, and by Hellenistic times they had established communities throughout much of the eastern Mediterranean area. These Judean emigrants and their descendants continued often to be referred to as Jews, on the grounds that initially they or their ancestors had come from Judea; their communities came to be referred to collectively as a 'diaspora' – a word of Greek origin meaning 'scattering'. In this way, the word 'Jew' was used as what might be called an ethnic designation. Such usage was facilitated by the fact that Jews in the diaspora generally continued to observe a set of laws that they believed their God had revealed to their ancestors long ago and that were binding upon Jews alone. Their continued observance of these laws in addition to local laws set them off as a distinct group among the peoples in whose midst they lived. Thus the term 'Jew' acquired religious as well as political and ethnic associations.

In the ancient world it was not unusual for states, provinces, or ethnic groups to have their own particular religions. Religion and ethnicity, in other words, were not easily separated in ancient times. During the Hellenistic era, however, a tendency emerged among members of various ethnic groups to develop a common religious core that transcended ethnic origins. This movement was reinforced with the appearance of Christianity, which claimed the status of a universal religion, one that all people could accept and practice no matter to which group or country they belonged. Jews, however, remained by and large an exception to this trend. The polytheistic peoples of the ancient world were amenable to religious syncretism largely because each people perceived fundamental similarities between its gods and those of its neighbours. In contrast, most Jews believed that their God was the sole omnipotent lord of the entire universe, who demanded that the Jewish people serve that God and that God alone; hence they could not join other peoples in any religious endeavour that would require them to acknowledge the reality of other gods or to compromise the manner in which they carried out their God-given law. Although some Jews disagreed with this approach, an internal struggle in the middle of the second century BCE effectively put an end to open syncretistic tendencies among them.

This refusal to be merged into a universal religion often made Jews an object of intense curiosity in the ancient world. Sometimes it even led to violent clashes between Jews and their neighbours. But it also helped them to preserve their identity as a distinct people after the Romans eliminated Judea as a political entity in the year 135.

THE JEWS IN CHRISTIAN EUROPE

Jews had established diaspora communities in Mediterranean Europe already in pre-Christian times, but not until the tenth century are Jews known to have established permanent settlements north of the Alps. The most important of these early communities were located in German-speaking regions, mainly in the Rhein valley. Jews referred to these regions by the Hebrew name Ashkenaz; Jews who lived there came to be known as Ashkenazic Jews, to distinguish them from Jews in the Mediterranean countries and the Middle East, who were called Sefardic Jews. In the early Middle Ages Sefardic

Jews were far more numerous, but over the centuries Ashkenazic Jews increased in number, until by the early twentieth century they made up almost 90 per cent of world Jewry.

Although in ancient times Jews were largely an agricultural people, the Ashkenazic communities were based mainly on commerce. Initially European rulers welcomed the Jews' contribution to their economies; in the highly localized feudal system, in which most of the population worked the land, Jews (along with other foreign minorities) played a significant role in promoting exchange among far-flung territories, especially between Christian Europe and the Islamic world. To encourage them in this endeavour, rulers, in accordance with the common medieval practice of decentralizing political authority, granted Jews special charters of rights that allowed them to establish their own autonomous institutions and live according to their own laws. However, by the twelfth century a growing native Christian merchant class came into conflict with the Jews. This clash contributed to a concomitant spread throughout Europe of stereotypes portraying Jews as a serious danger to Christian society; indeed, many historians have pointed to the twelfth and thirteenth centuries as a time when European society was especially intolerant not only of Jews but of minorities in general. Another expression of popular hostility towards Jews during this period came in the form of repeated attacks upon Ashkenazic communities that accompanied the Crusades. In the wake of these attacks many Jews migrated from the Germanic lands to Poland, where conditions resembled those of the earlier Middle Ages farther west. By the sixteenth century Poland became a major centre of Ashkenazic Jewry.

Contrary to a common misperception, the medieval Church leadership generally did not encourage violence against Jews. Officially its position was that Jews must be allowed to live among Christians, although their status must be visibly degraded in order to remind Christians of the dire consequences of denying the divinity of Jesus. In accordance with this principle, Church leaders protested at times against the relatively beneficent treatment Jews often received from secular rulers who valued their commercial services. They demanded that Jews wear special types of clothing to mark them as different, and they called for measures to segregate them from Christian society as much as possible. But they also tried to restrain the common people who, under the influence of hostile stereotypes, lashed out physically every so often against their Jewish neighbours, and they opposed efforts to convert Jews by force. Still, the extent to which Church teachings, especially as transmitted to the common people by various segments of the Church hierarchy, helped to foment an ongoing climate of violent hostility towards Jews in Christian Europe remains a matter of controversy among scholars.

Church requirements that Jews be visibly marked off from Christians were not always enforced. Nonetheless, Jews were often easily distinguishable from Christians by their dress and grooming customs, dietary habits, educational practices, and social networks, as well as by their heavy involvement in commerce and virtual absence in many places from agriculture and artisanry. Jewish religious law, especially prohibitions on consuming certain foods and beverages, helped reinforce social separation. Moreover, in many Ashkenazic communities Jews spoke their own distinct language, called Yiddish. This language was based upon the Germanic dialect spoken in the Rhein valley when Jews first settled there, with vocabulary added from Hebrew, the Slavic languages, Latin, and old French. For written communication, Ashkenazic Jews employed mainly Hebrew; gradually they developed a written form of Yiddish as well, using the Hebrew alphabet.

As popular and clerical pressure against Jews mounted, secular rulers often concluded that the Jewish communities in their territories were more a liability than an asset. King Edward I of England expelled all Jews from his realm in 1290. Expulsions from most French territories followed during the fourteenth century, from Spain in 1492, and from many of the German states during the next two hundred years. In other places, beginning in sixteenth-century Italy and later in Central Europe, Jews were confined to closed neighbourhoods, often called **ghettos**. In general, the later Middle Ages were a period in which European Jewish existence was less secure than it had been in earlier centuries. Nevertheless, in most places where Jews lived they enjoyed considerable autonomy, governing themselves largely according to their own laws.

Ghetto: An urban area where Jews were compelled by law to reside. Between the sixteenth and eighteenth centuries ghettos were common in Italy and central Europe; the last such ghetto was dissolved in 1870. The Nazis revived the institution in occupied Poland and extended it to the Soviet territories conquered in 1941.

IN MODERN TIMES

The precariousness of the Jewish situation began to recede in the late seventeenth century. The appearance of capitalism with its emphasis upon individual freedom and initiative, the spread of rational philosophy and the notion of religious tolerance, the emergence of centralized state administrations in place of the medieval system of corporate estates – all of these led various elements of European society to rethink their attitudes towards Jews. Some began to argue that if states treated them on the same basis as all other subjects, Jews would become productive and loyal members of the larger society. Such thinking was evident in Oliver Cromwell's effective suspension of the ban upon Jewish settlement in England during the 1650s. However, others maintained that the non-universalistic nature of the Jewish religion prevented Jews from identifying with the peoples among whom they lived. They claimed that Jews would always be a distinct people, more concerned with the welfare of their fellow Jews in faraway lands than with that of their closest non-Jewish neighbours.

In the late eighteenth and early nineteenth centuries, several European countries decided to test which view was correct. In 1782 Emperor Joseph II of Austria issued an Edict of Toleration, which removed many medieval restrictions upon Jewish residence and economic activity. It was widely understood, though, that in return Jews were expected to dress and groom themselves like their neighbours, speak the language of the country, educate their children according to the demands of the state, expand their range of occupations, and renounce all claims to autonomy or special group status. Revolutionary France granted Jews civic equality on similar terms, as did many of the countries that fell under French influence as a result of Napoleon's conquests. By 1871, Jews had been 'emancipated' – made equal citizens of all of the European states west of the Elbe River, with the expectation that they view themselves as Frenchmen, Germans, or Englishmen of the Jewish religion instead of as members of a single historic people scattered throughout the world. Most Jews in these countries welcomed this bargain; they declared that the term 'Jew' now referred to a religious group only and no longer had any ethnic significance. They worked hard to eliminate the economic, social, linguistic, and cultural distinctions that had visibly separated them from their surrounding societies in medieval times. Some, known as Reform Jews, even proposed far-reaching changes in Jewish religious law, including elimination of dietary prohibitions, in order to facilitate social integration. By the end of the nineteenth century, most western European Jews had done much to make themselves superficially indistinguishable from their neighbours in many respects, speaking the same language, attending the same schools, reading the same books and newspapers, wearing the same clothes. And as the economies of their countries prospered, they prospered too. Their numbers grew accordingly, rising from about 700,000 throughout Europe in 1750 to upwards of 9 million by 1930. That growth was more than four times the overall increase of the European population during the same interval.

However, the processes of emancipation and social integration affected only a minority of Europe's Jews. The majority, more than 5 million in 1880, lived in the Russian Empire, which had taken over most of Poland between 1772 and 1815. Tsarist Russia did not offer Jews civic equality; hence a major impulse towards integration was absent among Russo-Polish Jewry. Moreover, the country's relative economic underdevelopment kept the bulk of its Jews in poverty. Most of these Jews continued into the twentieth century to be distinguished from the surrounding society in language, culture, social organization, and occupational structure as well as in religion. Many eastern European Jews, influenced by ideas of nationalism, began to define

Zionism: Modern Jewish political and ideological movement arguing that Jews constitute primarily a national group (comparable to Germans or Poles) instead of a religious one (comparable to Catholics or Muslims) and that as such they are entitled to political sovereignty over their historic homeland. During the early twentieth century the World Zionist Organization, established in 1897, encouraged Jewish migration to Palestine, where, it hoped, a large Jewish settlement would serve as the basis for a Jewish national home. Zionism was a controversial idea among Jews from its inception; nonetheless, from the end of the First World War it was one of the principal forces in European Jewish life.

themselves as members of a Jewish nation and to demand national rights. **Zionism**, which emerged during the 1880s, claimed that Jews had a right to establish their own nation-state in the historic Jewish homeland. Other Jewish nationalist movements sought autonomy for Jews within multicultural European bourgeois or socialist states.

From the late 1870s through to 1914, almost 3 million eastern European Jews, seeking better economic and political conditions, migrated westward, increasing the Jewish populations of Germany, France, and England and turning the United States, with 4.4 million Jews in 1930, into the world's largest Jewish community. Especially in Germany, the influx of these foreign Jews helped strengthen the hand of those who opposed Jewish civic equality. During the 1880s these German opponents formed political parties and pressure groups with the goal of curtailing Jewish rights; calling themselves 'antisemites', they demanded that Jews be removed from the civil service and free professions, denied citizenship, taxed discriminatorily, and forbidden from migrating to Germany. Similar groups emerged in other European countries. Yet although they attracted much attention, nowhere did they achieve their legislative goals. In Germany they were an insignificant political force before the First World War.

With the overthrow of the tsarist regime in 1917 and the establishment of new states after the First World War, the Jewish masses of eastern Europe gained formal civic equality. However, their strong Jewish national identity often clashed with the equally strong nationalist feelings of the Poles, Lithuanians, Romanians, and other eastern European peoples who had acquired state power. Such clashes impeded social integration and the redefinition of Jews as a religious group along western European lines. Particularly in Poland, which regained independence in 1918 and became home to Europe's largest Jewish population (3.3 million in 1931), Jews retained many attributes of a distinct national group: they spoke mainly Yiddish (although their use of Polish increased steadily); maintained their own schools, theatres, health and welfare organizations, and political parties; published their own daily newspapers; and lived in compact Jewish neighbourhoods. Many Poles looked upon Jews as alien competitors for jobs and hoped to see their country's Jewish population substantially reduced through emigration. The same was true in other eastern European countries with large Jewish populations – particularly Romania, with 750,000 Jews in 1930, and Hungary, with 450,000. The 3 million Jews of the Soviet Union were subjected to intense governmental pressure to merge into that country's socialist economy and society. As a result, integration proceeded more rapidly there than elsewhere in eastern Europe, but the size of the Jewish community and its nationalist heritage helped many Soviet Jews preserve a measure of cultural uniqueness. Also, although only a relatively small number of Jews were attracted to communism, Jews had been prominent among the leaders of the Bolshevik revolution. Hence Jews were often identified invidiously with Bolshevism by the eastern European peoples who had fallen under Soviet domination or who feared the spread of communism into their own countries.

Yet even though their numbers had grown prodigiously over the nineteenth and early twentieth centuries, Jews remained for the most part a small minority in their countries of residence: in no country did they make up more than 10 per cent of the population. In Hungary, Latvia, Lithuania, Poland, and Romania Jews comprised between 4 and 10 per cent of the country's inhabitants. In Austria, Czechoslovakia, Greece, the Netherlands, and the European areas of the Soviet Union their proportion was between 1 and 4 per cent, while in more than half of the countries within the Nazi orbit (Albania, Belgium, Bulgaria, Denmark, Estonia, Finland, France, Germany, Italy, Luxembourg, Norway, and Yugoslavia) they constituted less than 1 per cent of the total. In cities, however, especially in eastern Europe, they were more visible: in Poland between the two world wars they made up one-quarter or more of the population in six of the country's twelve largest urban centres, as they did in Iaşi (Romania), Kaunas (Lithuania), Odessa (USSR), and Thessalonike (Greece). Their proportion in the capitals of western and central Europe at the same time was much less: 9.4 per cent in Vienna, 8.7 per cent in Amsterdam, 6.1 per cent in Paris, 4.1 per cent in Berlin, and 3.8 per cent in Prague. In those places Jews stood out mainly in the free professions: in Germany in 1933, 16 per cent of lawyers, 9 per cent of dentists, and 11 per cent of physicians were Jews. In the arts and in journalism their percentage was greater than their proportion in the overall population but still quite low: 5.6 per cent of stage directors in Germany in 1933; 5.1 per cent of newspaper editors and reporters; 3 per cent of stage actors; 2.4 per cent of painters and sculptors; 2 per cent of musicians. And – perhaps surprisingly, considering their widespread medieval role as moneylenders – the proportion of Jews in banking and finance dropped precipitously between 1870 and 1930. In the early twentieth century most European Jews were small-scale merchants, clerks, artisans in petty production, and factory labourers.

A reasonable assessment of the Jewish situation in Europe around 1930 would thus have placed Germany's 525,000 Jews among the continent's most prosperous and secure. Comprising only around 0.8 per cent of the country's population, German Jews were on the whole economically well off. Their civic equality, which appeared untouchable, had allowed them to become well integrated into German cultural and political life. Socially they were gaining acceptance as well; by the 1920s one of every four German Jews was marrying into a non-Jewish family. In fact, some German Jewish leaders saw intermarriage as a much greater threat to their community's survival than the hostility of the surrounding society, which appeared far milder and less extensive than in eastern Europe. That a German government would shortly seek to kill not only all German Jews but millions of Jews beyond the country's borders was not a possibility that any observer anywhere in the world could reasonably be expected to have entertained.

3

Hitler, Nazis, Germans, and Jews

The German government that undertook the systematic mass killing of Europe's Jews was dominated by the National Socialist German Workers (Nazi) Party, led by Adolf Hitler. Historians of Germany continue to debate whether the Third Reich is best understood as Hitler's personal creation, as a product of programmes generated out of the broader ideas and goals of the Nazi party, or as the outcome of historical developments, within Germany or beyond, whose origins predate the Nazi period. The same questions animate academic discussions about the origins of the Holocaust. In 1996 Daniel Goldhagen aroused great controversy among scholars with his statement that the idea of killing Jews had been 'immanent in the conversation of German society' for over a century (Goldhagen, 1996: 449). To his mind, Hitler and the Nazi party were not central to the development among the German people of the notion that Jews were dangerous enemies who deserved to die; that notion, he claimed, was an integral part of modern German culture.

Most historians have rejected Goldhagen's thesis. Many have pointed out that the major features of what Goldhagen termed 'eliminationist anti-semitism', which he argued was a uniquely German idea that predated the rise of Nazism, were in fact present in other European societies in the nineteenth and twentieth centuries no less than among the Germans; but in the absence of Nazi-like leadership they did not lead to systematic mass murder. Others have identified similar ideas in the teachings of the medieval Church or in writings from pagan antiquity. Hence the question of how a *German* government, and not that of another people, came during the 1930s and 1940s to launch what Lucy Dawidowicz called a 'war against the Jews' (Dawidowicz, 1975), on the pretext that Jews were non-human pathogens who threatened human survival, continues to perplex scholars and non-scholars alike.

THE JEWS IN HITLER'S WORLD VIEW

One thing is certain: Hitler himself repeatedly expressed the view that Jews represented a deadly menace to all people on earth. In one of his earliest recorded political speeches, on 13 August 1920 [*Doc. 2*], he called Jews 'parasites', claiming that 'from early on [the Jew] felt the need to rule over the peoples among whom he lived, which meant first of all to destroy the inner fabric of their countries' (Phelps, 1968: 409, 411). And in his final political testament, dictated on 29 April 1945, the day before he died, he called upon the Germans to continue 'to fight mercilessly against the poisoners of all the peoples of the world, international Jewry' (Arad *et al.*, 1999: 162).

This perception was not simply the result of blind hatred, nor does it appear to have been merely an unthinking repetition of ancient, medieval, or modern anti-Jewish calumnies. Rather it was a conclusion derived from a complex (though preposterous) general world view. In his autobiographical work, **Mein Kampf**, written between 1924 and 1926, as well as in an untitled, unpublished second book written in 1928, Hitler hinted at how his view of Jews flowed logically, to his mind, from more fundamental ideas about the nature of human beings and human history.

Mein Kampf: Hitler's autobiography and main ideological tract, published 1925–28. Among other things, it is a principal source for the reconstruction of Hitler's ideas and plans concerning Jews.

Indeed, in retrospect that view seems clearly to have been rooted in Hitler's central conviction that 'all occurrences in world history are only the expression of the races' instinct of self-preservation, in the good or bad sense' (Hitler, 1943: 296). This statement indicated first of all that, like many people in his time, Hitler divided humanity into distinct biological groups, each supposedly displaying a unique, genetically derived essence or spirit. Following common usage of the day, he often termed these groups 'races' – a word that suggested less skin colour than a gene pool. Sometimes he used the words 'peoples (**Völker**)' or 'nations' to describe them as well. The behaviour of individual members of these 'races' or 'peoples', according to Hitler, could be understood as manifestations of shared hereditary tendencies; people acted as they did because they were genetically ('racially') inclined to do so. Hence, Hitler deduced, if individuals appear to demonstrate an inborn will to live, then the various races to which they belong must also naturally possess a collective instinct for self-preservation.

Volk (*pl. Völker*): German word literally meaning 'people'. Hitler used it as a substitute for the term 'race', indicating a fundamental genetic division of humanity. *Völker*, in Hitler's view, were the repositories of all values.

Hitler claimed that this collective instinct could be observed, as in individuals, in two fundamental human drives – for food and for reproduction. Each race, to his mind, naturally sought to maximize both its food supply and the number of its offspring. To accomplish these goals, he reasoned, each race required land, where it could grow food and raise progeny. However, as he observed in his second book, although 'the population grows incessantly . . . the soil as such remains stationary' (Hitler, 1961: 15), meaning that the more successful a race was in producing offspring, the greater the difficulty it faced in feeding them. The only way for a race to escape this dilemma, according to Hitler, was constantly to increase the amount of land at its disposal; yet by doing so it would inevitably clash with other races seeking to do the same thing, because the total amount of land in the world was finite. Each race's attempt to satisfy its instinct of self-preservation, in other words, had, to Hitler's mind, necessarily to lead it into conflict with all other races. Hitler regarded this eternal conflict as the basic motive force in human history; hence 'all occurrences in world history are only the expression of the races' instinct of self-preservation'.

Jews presented an obvious problem for this theory. Hitler identified them initially as a race, not a religious community. According to his central conviction, this racial character ought to have made them struggle for land throughout their history. But in fact Jews had controlled no territory of their own for many centuries. If Hitler's view of human history was correct, this lack of territory should have caused the Jews to disappear many years before. Yet instead of concluding that his theory was flawed, Hitler decided that Jews must have found a secret way to survive without land. In the culminating passage of his second book he observed that 'as a support of its own existence [the Jewish people] needs the work and creative activities of other nations'. An organism that cannot survive on its own but must attach itself to another organism in order to ensure its food supply is a parasite; hence Hitler concluded that 'the existence of the Jew himself becomes a parasitical one within the lives of other peoples' (Hitler, 1961: 212).

Others had portrayed Jews as parasites before, but none seems to have taken the analogy nearly as literally as Hitler did. During his youth in Vienna Hitler had been influenced by occult racist circles that – despite all common sense data to the contrary – posited the existence of non-human creatures in human bodies and called them an evil principle that destroyed life itself. Hitler's theory of history allowed him to infer that Jews were in fact such creatures. Because the way in which they struggled for survival was fundamentally different from that of all other peoples, he reasoned, they could not be a true human race; rather 'their apparently great sense of solidarity is based on the very primitive herd instinct' of animals (Hitler, 1943: 301). They could survive, he concluded, only through a planned, coordinated effort to weaken all genuinely human peoples; they were genetically compelled to insinuate themselves slowly into other societies, mating with non-Jewish young women in order 'to destroy the racial foundations of the people [they] have set out to subjugate'. 'Just as [the Jew] systematically ruins women and girls', he wrote, 'he does not shrink back from pulling down the blood barriers for others, even on a large scale. It . . . is Jews who bring the Negroes into the Rhineland, always with the same secret thought . . . of ruining the hated white race by the necessarily resulting bastardization, throwing it down from its cultural and political height, and . . . rising to be its master' (Hitler, 1943: 325). Ultimately, he declared, 'wherever [the Jew] appears, the host people dies out' (Hitler, 1943: 305). 'The Jew . . . cannot possibly be human in the sense of God, the Eternal's own likeness', he asserted. 'The Jew is the likeness of the devil' (quoted in Bucher, 2011: 76).

It follows from such a literal conception of the Jew as noxious parasite that Jews were mortal enemies not of Germany alone but of all humanity; indeed, Hitler stated clearly that 'if . . . the Jew is victorious over the other peoples of the world, his crown will be the funeral wreath of humanity and this planet will . . . move through the ether devoid of men'. This belief, in turn, gave Hitler's proposed struggle against the Jews a messianic quality: 'I believe that . . . *by defending myself against the Jew, I am fighting for the work of the Lord*' (Hitler, 1943: 65). Historian Saul Friedländer has called this 'distinctive aspect of [Hitler's] world view "redemptive anti-Semitism"' and concluded that 'it was this redemptive dimension . . . that led to Hitler's ultimate decision that the Jews were to be exterminated' (Friedländer, 1997: 3).

JEWS IN THE IDEOLOGY AND PROGRAMME OF NAZISM

Other historians, though aware of Hitler's thoughts about the Jews, question whether they are the most important facts to note in explaining the German war against the Jews. After all, a single individual could not have launched such a war unless his proposed anti-Jewish struggle made sense to many others in his country. Hence they have asked who those other Germans were and how they came to the conclusion that Jews everywhere ought to be killed.

One of the earliest attempts to explain the systematic mass killing of Jews claimed that such killing was an essential consequence of a broader German ideology called national socialism or Nazism, which the Nazi party was organized to implement and spread. Nazism, according to this view, taught 'that all traditional doctrines and values must be rejected . . . whether liberal or absolutist, democratic or socialist', in order to establish Germany as the world's foremost power (Neumann, 1944: 38). National socialists justified their demand for world domination by claiming that Germans constituted a genetically ('racially') superior people whose biological supremacy entitled them to political pre-eminence. No existing political doctrine, whether of the right or the left, recognized the possibility that such a claim could ever be valid; hence, it was asserted, national socialists were compelled to eliminate those doctrines altogether, along with anyone who persisted in espousing them. To those who viewed national socialism in this way, Jews appeared to be the first people slated for elimination, both because they were convenient symbols of such non-racially based ideas as liberalism, socialism, and Christianity, and because their social situation suited them uniquely to serve as 'guinea pigs for testing the method of repression'. According to this perception of Nazi ideology and practice, however, 'not only Jews [were bound to] fall under the executioner's axe but . . . countless others of many races, nationalities, beliefs, and religions . . . ; the extermination of the Jews [was] only the means to the attainment of the ultimate objective, namely the destruction of free institutions, beliefs, and groups' (Neumann, 1944: 550–51]. In other words, national socialism demonstrated murderous potential towards a variety of enemies; it felt no special enmity towards Jews per se.

The author of this interpretation, Franz Neumann, himself a Jewish refugee from the Nazi regime, did not attribute these national socialist ideas to Hitler; in fact, he did not ascribe them initially to any specific individuals or groups. In his opinion, 'the ideologies [that national socialism] uses or discards are mere . . . techniques of domination' (Neumann, 1944: 467). Persecution of Jews, he suggested, had a long history in Germany and elsewhere, and it was strongly rooted in popular anti-Jewish stereotypes and prejudices; thus it could easily be employed to unify the German people against 'one enemy who can easily be exterminated and who cannot resist' (Neumann, 1944: 125). From this premise it followed that the roots of the Holocaust were not to be found in any new idea or world view – Hitler's own thoughts notwithstanding – but simply in the desire of national socialists to consolidate their rule: Jews were persecuted, and eventually killed, because it made good political sense to do so.

The theme that the war against the Jews was designed to facilitate the broader nihilistic war against all of Western civilization preached by national socialists had been sounded even before the onset of mass killing by Hermann Rauschning, a Nazi senator from Danzig who quit the party in 1934 [Doc. 3]. Variations of it were put forth by several important scholars during the first three decades following the Nazi defeat. Studies of what Nazis other than Hitler thought about Jews seemed to strengthen this conclusion: relatively few appear to have joined the party primarily in order to strike against the Jewish enemy as conceived by Hitler. Nazis who later played key roles in the killing of Jews, including Heinrich Himmler, Hermann Goering, Hans Frank, and Adolf Eichmann, evidently acquired their radical animus towards Jews after becoming Nazis, not before.

However, other historians have noted several facts that this view does not easily explain. For example, the question has been raised why it was necessary for the Third Reich not merely to *persecute* Jews but to *kill* them. The enormous distance between persecution and murder was revealed dramatically at a meeting between Hitler and his ally, the Hungarian regent, Miklos Horthy, on 17 April 1943. Discussing how to control the social damage Jews were allegedly causing in his country, Horthy asked what he ought to do about them. The Hungarian leader explained that he had already moved to destroy the Jews economically; the only remaining measure that could be taken against them was to kill them, but that, as far as he was concerned, was unthinkable [*Doc 4*]. In other words, the Hungarian ruler could oppress Jews with little compunction, but he could not conceive of murdering them *en masse*. A mental gulf appears to have separated him from the leaders of the Third Reich, who had already accomplished the leap from persecution to total, systematic murder. Enslaving the Jews – including selective killing of Jewish leaders, the destruction of Jewish social and cultural institutions, and the elimination of the basis of their economic life (what Raphael Lemkin called 'genocide') – ought to have accomplished the instrumental goals that Neumann, Rauschning, and others ascribed to the anti-Jewish aspect of national socialism. Indeed, Neumann had predicted in 1942 that 'the internal political value of Anti-Semitism will . . . never allow a complete extermination of the Jews', because 'the foe . . . must always be held in readiness as a scapegoat for all the evils originating in the socio-political system' (Neumann, 1944: 125). Systematic total killing did not unambiguously advance those goals. Why, then, did it take place?

Nor is it clear that the leaders of the Third Reich ever had serious plans to visit the fate of the Jews upon other groups. To be sure, the thought was raised from time to time that Poles and other Slavic peoples ought to disappear from the face of the earth; Hans Frank, head of the part of occupied Poland called the **Generalgouvernement**, even declared that 'once we have won the war, for my part all the Poles and Ukrainians and the rest that are roaming around here can be made into mincemeat' (quoted in Tal, 1979: 39). However, Third Reich policymakers seem to have been reluctant to act on such ideas. Erhard Wetzel, head of the Department of Racial Policy in the Ministry of the Occupied Eastern Territories, explained that 'it should be obvious that the Polish question cannot be solved by liquidating the Poles as we are doing with the Jews', as 'such a solution of the Polish question would weigh upon the German people into the distant future . . . and cause our neighbours to figure that at some point they will be treated the same way' (Heiber, 1958: 308). And Hans Frank noted in his diary on 14 December 1942 that it would be impossible to kill even all those Poles who were unfit for labour service, because 'the extirpation of millions of human beings depends upon certain preconditions that at present we cannot fulfil' (*Trials of the Major War Criminals*, 1949, vol. 29: 565).

Generalgouvernement: German-controlled territory carved out of Poland, incorporating the districts of Kraków, Lublin, Radom, and Warsaw (and Galicia after 1941), but excluding the western Polish provinces, which were annexed directly to Germany.

When Frank wrote those words, more than two million Jews had already been murdered by the Third Reich. Evidently he thought about Poles and Jews not as similar obstacles to the goals of national socialism but in fundamentally different terms: Poles were human beings, Jews were not. Hence, whereas Nazi officials could ask whether mass murder of Poles would be an effective means to the Third Reich's basic ends, it does not seem to have occurred to them to ask the same question regarding Jews. Wetzel's apprehensions about how Germany's good name would be affected and how other peoples might react to the killing of Poles were not at issue in the case of the Jews. Murder of Jews thus appears to have been considered more as an end in itself than as a means to some other goal; it was an action that the Third Reich felt compelled to take no matter what the immediate consequences. It could not, then, have been simply a by-product of national socialism.

JEWS IN GERMAN PUBLIC OPINION

Similarly, the idea that the mass killing of Jews helped the Nazi party solidify its standing among the German people assumes that most Germans supported the killing. However, studies of German public responses to Nazi anti-Jewish practices at various stages in the history of the Third Reich have shown that those practices did not always enhance the party's popularity and often were more extreme than mainstream popular opinion found acceptable. In 1929–33, when the Nazis were competing with increasing success in democratic elections (they grew from a mere 2.6 per cent of the vote in May 1928 to 33.7 per cent in July 1932 before falling off a bit to 33.1 per cent three months later), their propaganda usually did not stress how they proposed to deal with Jews; party spokesmen tended to refer to the Jewish theme only in abstract terms, toning down anti-Jewish rhetoric, integrating it into the discussion of broader political and economic concerns, and obscuring specific plans for anti-Jewish action. Indeed, there were many reasons for Germans to vote Nazi – reasons having to do with Germany's increasingly difficult economic situation during the years of the Great Depression, with growing fears of communism, and with the overall impression the Nazis gave of a colourful, dynamic, youthful movement with new ideas and the ability to get things done. All of these factors appear to have swayed about a third of German voters in the Nazis' direction much more than the promise of specific measures to be taken against Jews. In his work on the Nazi rise to power in Bavaria, Geoffrey Pridham found that 'the majority of voters did not . . . realize how seriously the Nazis meant to put their [anti-Jewish] ideas into practice' (Pridham, 1973: 244). Likewise,

W.S. Allen's study of a small town in Hannover found that 'many who voted Nazi simply ignored or rationalized the anti-semitism of the party, just as they ignored other unpleasant aspects of the Nazi movement'. In his famous formulation, the townspeople 'were drawn to anti-semitism because they were drawn to Nazism, not the other way around' (Allen, 1966: 77).

After the Nazi party came to power in 1933, it found a public highly ambivalent about how the regime ought to relate to Jews. Although feeling seems to have prevailed among Germans that their Jewish neighbours exercised excessive influence in the administration of their country and in its cultural and economic life, few evidently regarded that situation as one of Germany's most serious problems. Hence even some opponents of the regime initially accepted discriminatory laws aimed at reducing that influence, like the April 1933 dismissal of Jews from the civil service; and many more were indifferent, preferring not to trouble themselves with the Jews' legal status. Similarly, the 1935 **Nuremberg Laws**, which effectively revoked Jews' German citizenship and outlawed marriages between Jews and non-Jews, met with widespread public acquiescence. On the other hand, considerable public dissatisfaction was recorded whenever the regime engaged in anti-Jewish violence. In particular, the so-called **Kristallnacht** riots of November 1938, with their countrywide looting of Jewish shops and homes and burning of Jewish public institutions, aroused revulsion among significant segments of the German populace – although many Germans seem to have been bothered more by the pogrom's disorder and wanton brutality than by any sense of obligation towards their Jewish countrymen [*Doc. 5*]. Brutal physical attacks upon Jewish life, limb, and property thus might not have called forth vigorous public protest against the regime, but they were hardly an effective way to mobilize public support. Indeed, when the regime finally embarked upon its programme of systematic mass killing in 1941, it took pains to keep information about the murders from the public, evidently convinced that 'it could not rely on popular backing for its extermination policy' (Kershaw, 1981: 289; *Doc. 6*).

Hence many historians have rejected the notion that the Holocaust can be satisfactorily explained as an essential product either of national socialism or of widespread popular German hostility towards Jews. Instead they have directed their attention to the processes that might have made at least a minimum critical mass of Germans receptive to the idea that Jews were noxious parasites who needed to be killed. Some have examined a relatively small circle of 'true believers' in Hitler's world view – estimated by Saul Friedländer at about 10 per cent of the adult German population (approximately 4 million people) – in order to explore 'the formation . . . of a collective consciousness governed by total inversion of the most widely accepted human moral values' (Friedländer, 1971: 146).

Nuremberg Laws: Name for two German laws promulgated on 15 September 1935. The Reich Citizenship Law stated that only people with pure German blood could be German citizens; all others were classified as 'subjects'. The Law for the Protection of German Blood and Honour outlawed marriages between citizens and subjects. In November 1935 a third category, *Mischlinge*, was added.

Kristallnacht: Nazi-organized anti-Jewish riot of 9–10 November 1938, in which synagogues were burned and Jewish property looted throughout Germany and Austria.

TRUE BELIEVERS AND THE FIRST WORLD WAR

One detailed study, based on the autobiographies of 600 Nazis who joined the party before 1933 and recorded their life histories shortly after the party came to power, showed slightly over half seriously believing that Jews represented in some way a significant threat to Germany. Of these, almost 60 per cent suggested that Germany's defeat in the First World War and the political revolution that followed had shocked them into this conviction. The finding was not surprising, for the aftermath of the defeat had witnessed a sharp upsurge in German expressions of anti-Jewish antipathy. That upsurge could be explained by recalling the strange circumstances in which Germans learned that their country had lost the war: no foreign troops had yet set foot on German soil, while German soldiers continued to occupy large sections of enemy territory. Thus many Germans concluded that they had won the war on the battlefield, only to be 'stabbed in the back' by enemies within. Some were inclined to identify those internal enemies as Jews. During the war, Jews as a group had been accused of shirking military service and of profiteering, and Jews had been prominent among those calling for an end to the fighting through a negotiated peace. When, in the days following the imperial German collapse, radical socialists, including the Jews Kurt Eisner and Rosa Luxemburg, threatened to establish a new government based upon workers' and soldiers' councils, many recalled the association of Jews with Bolshevism, concluding that Jews wished to enslave Germany to the communist yoke. The postwar **Weimar Republic**, regarded by many Germans as an Allied imposition against the will of the German people, featured many Jews among its architects, so it was not long before opponents branded it the 'Jew-Republic'. In this context, a line portraying Jews as potential destroyers of Germany found readier acceptance among Germans than it had in less troubled times.

Weimar Republic: Name commonly used to designate the German republic established in February 1919. Fourteen years later it gave way to the Third Reich.

In *Mein Kampf*, Hitler played heavily upon the associations between Jews and the German defeat, Bolshevism, and the Weimar Republic. He presented Marxism and Bolshevism as the Jews' main weapons in their perverted struggle for survival: by preaching international working-class solidarity across racial lines, these doctrines deflected people's loyalties from their own racial groups, thereby weakening each nation's ability to mobilize its members in the constant battle for land. Hence, he explained, 'for every hero who had volunteered and mounted the steps of Valhalla after a heroic death . . . there was a slacker who had cautiously turned his back on death' in order to establish the Weimar regime (Hitler, 1943: 521). Such slackers were, to his mind, 'Marxist gangsters', while 'the *real* organizer of the revolution and its actual wirepuller' was 'the international Jew' (Hitler, 1943: 522–23). Thus he reasoned that 'in exact proportion as, in the course of the War, the German worker and the German soldier fell . . . into the hands of the Marxist leaders, in exactly that proportion he was lost to the fatherland'; and he concluded that 'if at the beginning of the War and during the War twelve or fifteen thousand of these Hebrew corrupters of the people had been held under poison gas . . . the sacrifice of millions at the front would not have been in vain' (Hitler, 1943: 679). To be sure, Hitler was not the only German to express such ideas; after the war a number of groups organized to combat the alleged Jewish-Marxist conspiracy that had created the Weimar Republic. Yet Hitler's analysis may have been especially credible to some because it was rooted in a comprehensive, seemingly scientific world view – one that could show not only *that* Jews were dangerous but *why* they were so and suggest effective action for removing the danger.

Still, that analysis appears to have made sense at first to only a few Germans. Before 1930, the Nazi party never received more than 6.6 per cent of the vote in any parliamentary election, and evidently most Nazi votes were not cast mainly because of Hitler's ideas about Jews. Some scholars have thus asked whether Hitler's true believers shared any special characteristics that made them respond to the First World War and its aftermath precisely as they did and differently from other Germans. Efforts to answer this question have centred on constructing a common social or psychological profile of the group; but aside from the generalization that members of the middle class, broadly defined, were more receptive to Hitler's message about the Jews than members of other social strata, such a profile has proven elusive. In any case, the German middle class was far more extensive than the circle of Nazi true believers, so scholars must still explain why only a part of this group fell so completely under Hitler's sway. Moreover, even if a clear profile could be established, it would not explain how over time the number of Germans prepared to play a role in the systematic mass killing of Jews came to extend beyond this limited circle. Indeed, as the researches of Raul Hilberg and Christopher Browning, among others, have shown, the Holocaust could not have happened without the participation of many other Germans – soldiers, civil servants, doctors, lawyers, industrialists, clerks, railway workers, even clergymen – who were not ideologically committed Nazis of long standing yet who helped locate Jews, identify them, imprison them, and kill them without protest or attempts at evasion. If, as studies of German public opinion have suggested, most Germans did not display especially violent inclinations towards Jews even after the Nazi regime came to power, where did these participants in the killing process come from?

ORDINARY MEN OR ORDINARY GERMANS?

Aside from Goldhagen and a handful of others who continue to posit a unique German national character, arising out of the peculiarities of German history since the Reformation, which – public opinion studies notwithstanding – ostensibly made the German people as a whole especially receptive to the notion that Jews were their mortal enemies, attempts to answer this question have taken two approaches. One has stressed general psychological factors – careerism, peer pressure, deference to authority – that under the brutalizing influences of modern warfare might have turned virtually anyone into a killer. As Browning, who studied a German reserve police battalion involved in killing operations in Poland, noted:

> there are many societies afflicted by . . . racism and caught in the siege mentality of war . . . Everywhere society conditions people to respect . . . authority . . . Everywhere people seek career advancement. In every modern society . . . bureaucratization and specialization attenuate the sense of personal responsibility of those implementing official policy. Within . . . every social collective, the peer group . . . sets moral norms. If the men of Reserve Police Battalion 101 could become killers under such circumstances, what group of men cannot?
>
> (Browning, 1992: 188–89)

In this way of looking at things, the perpetrators and facilitators of the Holocaust were ultimately 'ordinary men' (indeed, there were few women among them), and their behaviour was but marginally influenced by a specific ideological conception of Jews. The Holocaust, in this view, thus appears not so much as a massive hate crime (in the sense that many key perpetrators were not motivated mainly by hostile feelings toward Jews as such) but as the product of certain normal social and psychological processes exploited by a regime that knew how to harness them to its own horrible ends.

The other approach has accorded more weight to ideology, suggesting that the specific Nazi environment in which they lived was ultimately decisive in eroding the perpetrators' natural human aversion to killing. A proponent of this view has argued that appeals to universal behavioural patterns have inadequately considered 'the broader background, the larger contextual and mental structures that *shaped the choices made*, guided action and created the atmosphere in which decisions proceeded and the [killing] machine operated' (Aschheim, 1994: 144). Killers, in other words, were less 'ordinary men' than 'ordinary Germans' – not, in Goldhagen's sense, as bearers of a longstanding German cultural tradition but as people gradually imbued after 1933 with the basic values of *Nazi* Germany. Scholars inclined to this position have thus emphasized the importance of indoctrination, exploring the social and educational channels – the **Hitler Youth**, the League of German Girls, the **Reich Labour Service**, and the Army, among others – through which Nazi leaders and true believers might have persuaded ever greater numbers of Germans that Jews everywhere deserved to die. But even this notion does not necessarily suggest wide-scale hatred of Jews: just as homeowners who set out mousetraps cannot be presumed to hate mice (or parents who vaccinate their children against chickenpox cannot be presumed to loathe the virus that causes the disease), so too non-Jews could be taught that the Jewish parasite had to be eliminated even in the absence of any strong emotions against them.

Hitler Youth: Nazi organization for boys aged 15–18; membership was compulsory from 1936. Along with the League of German Girls, it provided a principal avenue of indoctrination for the Nazi regime.

Reich Labour Service: German government labour battalion to which German men and women aged 19–25 could be conscripted for six months. It served as an important indoctrinatory vehicle for the Nazi regime.

The best answer to the question of how the Nazi regime managed to recruit a sufficient number of German citizens to carry out the mass murder of Jews probably lies somewhere between these poles, in 'a combination of ideological and situational factors that allowed a popular, ideologically driven, dictatorial regime and its hardcore followers to mobilize and harness the rest of society to its purposes', including the systematic mass murder of Jews (Browning, 1996: 108). As Saul Friedländer put it, 'the Nazi system as a whole had produced an "anti-Jewish culture", which "Ordinary Germans" . . . may have internalized . . . without recognizing [it] as an ideology systematically exacerbated by state propaganda and all the means at its disposal' (Friedländer, 2007: xx). Indeed, the Holocaust was clearly born in the first instance out of the interaction of a German leadership viewing Jews as noxious parasites with a German public potentially animated by motives rooted both in universal psychology and in the German historical, social, and cultural environment. The nature of that interaction and the relative weight of the motives, however, remain matters for debate.

4

1933–41: A twisted road?

The controversy over whether the participation of Germans other than longstanding Nazi true believers is best explained through deliberate indoctrination or universal human psychology is only part of a broader historiographical discussion. That discussion asks whether Nazism as a whole should be represented as a unique incursion of evil into history or as a phenomenon that, no matter how horrible, grew out of normal historical processes and human behaviours. In the mid-1980s German historian Martin Broszat issued a 'plea for the historicization of national socialism', by which he appears to have meant that historians should not presuppose that the Third Reich took decisions and formulated policies any differently than other modern governments, whatever their ideological orientations. Broszat charged that scholars of the Third Reich often explained Nazi actions in terms that they would not employ for other regimes, because they were more concerned with condemning Nazi atrocities than with understanding them. Thus, he held, they were unable to see Nazi leaders as anything but criminals. Broszat did not deny or make light of Nazi criminality, but he suggested that Nazis did not set out from the beginning to do evil for evil's sake.

Broszat's position was widely criticized. Saul Friedländer, while agreeing that 'during the Nazi era, few domains – with the exception of direct criminal activities – can be considered as entirely abhorrent', insisted nevertheless that 'very few domains can be considered as entirely untouched by some of the . . . criminal aspects of the core' (Friedländer, 1992: 73). Because of the Third Reich's 'criminal core', he argued, 'writing about Nazism [cannot be] like writing about sixteenth-century France' (Friedländer, 1992: 80). In explaining the behaviour of 'ordinary' participants in the killing process, then, historians who stress the importance of ideological indoctrination might be applying Friedländer's approach. Universal psychological explanations, in contrast, seem to chime more with Broszat's method of 'historicization'.

A DIABOLICAL PLOT OR THE WORK OF 'ONLY MEN'?

There is yet another area of controversy that has pitted those who concentrate upon the horrific features of Nazi ideology against those who appeal to general propositions about human behaviour. That debate concerns the interpretation of the actions that the Nazi regime took towards Jews between the time it came to power in 1933 and the actual beginning of systematic mass murder of Jews in 1941, as well as of the circumstances in which the decision actually to begin mass killing was taken. After all, even if Hitler personally held radical and unprecedented ideas about Jews which, if carried to their logical conclusion, demanded that each and every one of them be killed, and even if a hard core of true believers was disposed to accept that inference, it still does not necessarily follow that a campaign to murder all Jews was inevitable once the Nazi party assumed power in Germany in 1933. In the event, the Nazis had been in power for well over eight years before they actually set out upon such a campaign during the latter half of 1941. True, that campaign, once launched, could easily be justified by reference to Hitler's world view. But the rationalization offered for an action after the fact is not necessarily the same as the spur that led to the action in the first place. Noting the difference between the two types of explanation has prompted a series of questions about the long interval between the Nazi takeover and the onset of mass killing that have engaged historians for many decades: How and to what extent might developments during that interval have made the killing easier to carry out once it began? Did the encounter between the Third Reich and the Jews during its first eight years lay the groundwork in any significant way for the horrors that were to follow? If it did, were Nazi actions toward Jews during that interval consciously designed to do so? Did the Nazis come to power already armed with a mass murder plan? Or, Hitler's personal world view notwithstanding, did the regime as a whole decide upon mass murder only after concluding on the basis of experience that other, less violent approaches to controlling the danger Jews allegedly posed to Germany and to humanity as a whole wouldn't work?

For the first three decades or so following the end of the Second World War, most historians maintained that, even before taking control of Germany, Hitler, with malice aforethought, had formulated a coherent programme of action intended from the start to bring about the death of each and every Jew within the Third Reich's reach. According to this interpretation the succession of anti-Jewish measures undertaken by the Nazi regime between 1933 and 1941 was carefully calculated in advance to facilitate the ultimate goal of total murder. Hitler himself is supposed to have laid out a clear path that would lead Europe's Jews inexorably from social marginalization, political disenfranchisement, and economic ruin to death, while the officials and soldiers of the Third Reich, totally subservient to their sole leader and thoroughly imbued with his fiendish vision, executed that plan flawlessly at every stage.

Beginning in the 1970s an alternative interpretation developed. Several historians, noting that the Third Reich was generally torn by internal strife among its central figures and that policy decisions in many key areas were subject to ongoing conflict, contended that when the Nazi regime came to power none of its leaders had any clear idea how they were going to act towards the Jews. In the opinion of these scholars, the idea of systematic mass murder evolved only gradually, a result of the failure of Nazi leaders to find a less radical way to eliminate the supposed Jewish peril. Some of them have presented mass killing as the product of a process of 'cumulative radicalization', born of individual initiatives by Nazi party, government, and military officials undertaken in an administrative climate in which Hitler himself provided little concrete direction. According to this view, Hitler's role in the formulation of the Third Reich's Jewish policies was confined to setting broad guidelines: Reich officials knew that their leader wanted the danger allegedly represented by Jews to be controlled, but they were never told explicitly how they ought to accomplish that goal. As a result, various agencies of the regime, seeking to 'work towards the **Führer**' – to carry out what they thought to be his will (Kershaw, 2008: 29) – experimented with several different anti-Jewish strategies, not always consistent with one another, before the idea of mass killing surfaced. This situation created, in the words of one historian, not a straight path but a 'twisted road to Auschwitz' (Schleunes, 1970).

Although it was first advanced well before Broszat's plea for historicization, this latter argument (of which Broszat was a leading exponent) clearly accords with his call. As Léon Poliakov, one of the earliest to adumbrate this position, wrote, 'to say that the Nazis arrived at genocide as it were in spite of themselves . . . reminds us that the Nazis, however criminal they may have been, were only men' (Poliakov, 1954: 3). That suggestion, however, has been difficult for many observers to accept; some have perceived in it a morally offensive tendency to trivialize the radical evil in Hitler's exclusion of Jews from the ranks of humanity, claiming that it reduces the diabolical, premeditated, ideologically driven murder of millions to the almost accidental outcome of mundane bureaucratic processes, in a way that places 'the behaviour of the criminals themselves beyond the realm of personal responsibility' (Gutman, 2008: 195).

Ultimately, though, no matter what the moral implications of each stance, the test of their relative merits must be in the historical record. Is there any

Führer: German for 'leader'. It was used as Hitler's title in the Nazi Party beginning in 1931. In 1934, when Hitler combined the offices of president and chancellor of Germany, *Führer* became his official designation as head of the German state and government.

documentary trace of a Nazi master plan for mass murder? Or is there any concrete evidence that the idea was first generated from somewhere within the Nazi administration and not with Hitler?

THE STATE OF DOCUMENTATION

The only formal public statement by the Nazi party of its intentions regarding Jews was contained in the party programme, co-authored by Hitler and adopted in February 1920. That programme, which was reissued unchanged in 1933, called for legislation that would revoke the German citizenship of all Jews; prevent them from voting or holding public office; expel them from Germany if full employment could not be achieved for members of the German race; bar the immigration of Jews from other countries and expel Jewish (and other) immigrants who had entered Germany after August 1914; and prohibit Jews from publishing, investing in, or editing German-language newspapers. It also pledged in general terms that the party would 'fight against the Jewish-materialistic spirit' and declared that 'persons committing base crimes against the People, usurers, profiteers, etc., are to be punished by death without regard to religion or race' (Arad et al., 1999: 15–18).

In light of subsequent events, it is tempting to read into these latter statements a hint of an early design to kill all Jews: usury and profiteering were precisely the sort of 'base crimes' that, according to Hitler, Jewish 'parasites' were racially compelled to perpetrate. Some scholars who incline to this reading have pointed to remarks that Hitler made privately even before writing *Mein Kampf* that seem to have hinted at or spoken explicitly of mass killing. On 16 September 1919 Hitler wrote in a letter that the 'ultimate goal' of state Jewish policy must be not merely 'the elimination of the prerogatives of the Jew which he alone possesses in contradistinction to all other aliens living among us' but 'the elimination of the Jews altogether' (quoted in Jäckel, 1981: 48). And in 1922 he reportedly told a journalist that 'once I really am in power, my first and foremost task will be the annihilation of the Jews'; he promised to 'have gallows built in rows' upon which 'the Jews will be hanged indiscriminately . . . until all Germany has been cleansed of Jews' (quoted in Fleming, 1984: 17).

On the other hand, Karl Schleunes, the historian who first proposed the 'twisted road' metaphor, has wondered whether it is 'not possible that hindsight allows us to see [in such statements] a clarity and a design where they did not exist' (Schleunes, 1989: 56). Did 'elimination of the Jews altogether' (*Entfernung* in German, which could also be translated as 'removal' or 'sending away') necessarily imply killing in 1919, or could it have meant expulsion? Indeed, the party platform spoke explicitly of this measure, which, if implemented successfully, would have obviated the need for gallows. Perhaps the 1922 comment about indiscriminate hanging was only hyperbole? After all, in 1935 with the Nazis firmly in power, Hitler told party leaders that he sought merely the enactment of legislation that would ensure 'a tolerable relationship with the Jews living in Germany' and would afford Jews 'opportunities to live their own national life in all areas' (Arad *et al.*, 1999: 82). Was Hitler being disingenuous in one or the other instance? Perhaps his thinking fluctuated over the years. Without appealing anachronistically to the period after 1941, it is difficult to know what any of these statements really meant when they were made or how seriously they were taken.

Besides the 1920 party programme and Hitler's scattered and perhaps inconsistent statements about practical measures that would eliminate the Jewish danger as he perceived it, a number of Nazi officials devised their own plans for dealing with the Jews. One was put forward in April 1933 by a 'working group' of eight administrators and advisors, chaired by jurist Rudolf Becker and including the head of the Prussian Gestapo, Rudolf Diels. This proposal called for the compulsory enrolment of all German Jews in an Association of Jews in Germany, to be governed by a Jewish Council (*Judenrat*) and supervised by a state-appointed 'people's guardian' (*Volkswart*), whose job was both 'to protect the German people from the danger posed by Jewry' and 'to protect the Jews and secure their rights'. In discharging the former function the *Volkswart* was 'empowered to take any measures that seem necessary for the protection of German citizens against Jewish abuse of laws and economic power'. Jews were to be excluded from the military and civil service; denied the vote; restricted in access to the free professions; and forbidden from serving as directors of large banks, public utilities, or cultural institutions, as editors of German periodicals, or as schoolteachers. Marriages and extramarital sexual relations between Jews and non-Jews were to be banned. Jews who had become naturalized in Germany after August 1914 were to lose their citizenship and be expelled from the country, as were all foreign Jews. All German Jews were to be 'officially obliged to add the letter J to their surnames' (Adam, 1976: 45, 47, 53). This plan, then, looked to legislation to isolate Jews from German society without necessarily doing them physical harm.

Another statement of policy was prepared in January 1939 by the German foreign ministry. This document declared that 'the ultimate aim of Germany's Jewish policy is the emigration of all Jews living in German territory'. According to the statement, emigration was to be induced through the forced liquidation of Jewish businesses and expropriation of Jewish property, which would make it impossible for Jews to survive in Germany economically. However, the document noted that 'the Jewish question will not be solved when the last Jew has left German soil'. It anticipated that an influx of Jewish

Judenrat (pl. Judenräte): Official Jewish administrations established at German behest in most east European ghettos and in several other occupied countries.

[handwritten: nazi's saw jews as a "national threat"]

refugees into other lands would 'waken the interest in . . . the Jewish danger in many countries', so that 'the Jewish question will develop into an international political problem'. Eventually, it was hoped, all the nations of the world would allocate a small part of the globe for a **Jewish reservation**, where Jews, isolated from the rest of humanity, would no longer threaten 'the national character of the nations' (Arad *et al.*, 1999: 127, 129, 131). Germany, in other words, would not eliminate the putative Jewish threat to mankind by its own action but would merely spark other governments to move against it. *[handwritten: source packet]*

Yet another indication of the regime's thinking about what to do with Jews was contained in an 'express letter' by Reinhard Heydrich, chief of the Security Service (**SD**), issued on 21 September 1939. Written three weeks after the German invasion of Poland that launched the Second World War, this memorandum discussed the disposition of the more than two million Polish Jews about to fall under German rule. It outlined three fundamental measures to be taken immediately: concentration of Jews from the countryside into larger cities near rail lines; establishment of a Jewish Council in each community, to be responsible for implementing all future German directives and for conducting a census of all Jews by age, sex, and occupation; and expropriation of Jewish businesses and property to the extent local economic conditions permitted. However, it spoke of these measures merely as means to a 'final aim' (*Endziel*), which would 'require extended periods of time' for completion and was 'to be kept strictly secret' (Arad *et al.*, 1999: 173–78).

Initially many historians interpreted the reference to a secret 'final aim' as proof that 'a master plan for annihilating the Jews had already been conceived, though only the preliminary stages were now to be implemented' (Dawidowicz, 1975: 116). In their view, it was no coincidence that Heydrich issued his memorandum almost simultaneously with the outbreak of war: Hitler had long intended to kill all Jews, but he needed the chaos of war to camouflage his murderous acts. They argued that Hitler closely associated the war against Poland with the war against the Jews in his own mind: indeed, in a speech to the Reichstag on 30 January 1939 he had warned that 'if the international Jewish financiers in and outside Europe should succeed in plunging the nations . . . into a world war, the result will be . . . the annihilation of the Jewish race in Europe' (Arad *et al.*, 1999: 134–35).

Increasingly, however, scholars have placed greater emphasis upon the fact that Heydrich's memorandum did not mention killing explicitly. By the beginning of the twenty-first century most historians interpreted the 'final aim' as a reference to the 'Jewish reservation' that the foreign ministry had discussed seven months earlier. They have noted that when Heydrich issued his 'express letter', and for over a year thereafter, high officials in both the

---

Jewish reservation: Idea floated within the Nazi regime in 1939–40, involving mass concentration of Jews in a single location. Proposed locations were Nisko (Poland) and Madagascar.

SD: Acronym for *Sicherheitsdienst* (Security service). Domestic espionage arm of the Nazi Party, led by Heydrich. Its principal function was to gather intelligence concerning so-called internal enemies of the party and the German state. In 1939 it was subordinated to the RSHA.

[handwritten margin: F- Germany invaded Poland which ignited WW2 in 1939]

[handwritten margin: view — Hitler's view WW2 would be the means to kill Jewish population]

[handwritten margin: although]

foreign ministry and Heydrich's own security service were developing two plans to create such a reservation, one in the area around the Polish city of Lublin, the other on the island of **Madagascar**; that some Jews from Austria, the Czech lands, and Poland were actually deported to the former in late 1939; and that some of the deportees were quickly expelled further, into the Soviet Union [*Doc. 7*]. On 25 May 1940 Heydrich's superior, Heinrich Himmler, the person in charge of all security forces throughout the Reich (later to become the chief supervisor of mass killing), wrote that he hoped that 'Jews will be completely extinguished through . . . large-scale emigration . . . to Africa or some other colony' (Arad *et al.*, 1999: 198). On 3 July 1940 several government departments approved a plan by which Madagascar would be made available 'for the solution of the Jewish question', holding Europe's Jews 'in German hands as a pledge for the future good behaviour of the members of their race in America' (Arad *et al.*, 1999: 217–18). Hence one historian has concluded that, far from being 'indicative of a mass-murder plan', Heydrich's memorandum actually contained 'a brutal plan . . . to facilitate a later massive expulsion' (Bauer, 1980: 42).

Lucy Dawidowicz, an exponent of the earlier view, argued against the later reading that 'everything we know of National Socialist ideology precludes our accepting . . . a Jewish reservation as the last stage of the Final Solution'. In her view, that ideology required that all Jews be killed; hence 'a reservation could have been conceived of only as a transitional stage' on the road to mass murder (Dawidowicz, 1975: 118). On the other hand, Yehuda Bauer has suggested that 'although mass murder of the Jews was the logical consequence of Nazi theories . . . that logical conclusion was not drawn until 1941' (Bauer, 1980: 45). In the end, though, neither position can be proved conclusively by reference to the documentary record alone. To date no document has been found that refers explicitly to a mass murder plan in a way that leaves no room for conflicting interpretations. For this reason, it is also impossible to determine with certainty when mass murder became the regime's preferred course of action towards Jews or where within the regime the initiative for mass murder originated.

Madagascar Plan: Nazi plan to create a Jewish reservation on the east African island of Madagascar. Developed by the SS and the German foreign ministry, it received much attention within the Nazi regime in 1940, but it was abandoned late in the year, when the decision was taken to invade the Soviet Union.

A STEP-BY-STEP PROCESS?

Because of the lack of unambiguous documentation, much of the discussion about the origins of mass killing and the role of the 1933–1941 interval in its evolution has focused upon whether a preconceived murder plan can be inferred from the specific actions the German regime took towards Jews before the beginning of systematic killing operations during the second half of 1941.

The idea that those actions constituted a step-by-step 'destruction process' was first advanced by Raul Hilberg in 1961. Hilberg identified four sequential stages in this process: definition, expropriation, concentration, and annihilation, each implemented by professional bureaucrats doing a job assigned by their superiors.

Definition of Jews, according to Hilberg, began in April 1933. On 7 April the Reich enacted a **Law for the Restoration of the Professional Civil Service**, which provided that 'civil servants who are not of Aryan descent are to be retired' (Arad *et al.*, 1999: 40). Four days later, an amendment to the law declared that 'a person is to be considered non-Aryan if he is descended from non-Aryan, and especially from Jewish parents or grandparents. It is sufficient if one parent or grandparent is non-Aryan. This is to be assumed . . . where one parent or grandparent was of the Jewish religion' (Arad *et al.*, 1999: 41). The definition was refined following the September 1935 enactment of the Law on Reich Citizenship and the Law for the Protection of German Blood and Honour – the so-called Nuremberg Laws (Arad *et al.*, 1999: 77–79). According to the First Regulation to the Reich Citizenship Law, proclaimed on 14 November 1935, 'a Jew is a person descended from at least three grandparents who are full Jews by race' (Arad *et al.*, 1999: 80). The regulation also provided that persons descended from only two Jewish grandparents would be considered Jews if they were members of a Jewish religious community, married to a Jew, or born of one Jewish parent after the Nuremberg Laws had been promulgated. Persons with one or two Jewish grandparents who did not meet any of these conditions eventually became known as *Mischlinge* (people of mixed blood); although technically non-Aryans and subject to some legal discrimination, they were not placed under the sentence of death that eventually befell Jews.

Expropriation involved measures that stripped Jews of their livelihoods, property, and financial reserves. This process began in 1933, with the civil service law and the dismissal of many Jews from positions in German academic and cultural institutions. It continued sporadically through 1937, as many Jewish business owners were pressured (often under threat of physical force) to sell their enterprises to non-Jews at a fraction of their value. In 1938 concrete steps were taken towards full-scale removal of Jews from the German economy. On 26 April 1938 all German Jews were compelled to register their assets. Jewish doctors were forbidden to treat non-Jewish patients on 25 July; Jewish lawyers were disbarred on 27 September. On 12 November all Jewish retail businesses were ordered liquidated; proprietors were forced to sell their stock to government-approved buyers at fixed prices. Finally, a law of 3 December empowered the government to appoint trustees for Jewish-owned industrial enterprises, whose function was to dissolve Jewish establishments or transfer them to non-Jewish hands. Jews'

Law for the Restoration of the Professional Civil Service: The first major piece of Nazi anti-Jewish legislation. Adopted in April 1933, it removed Jewish government employees from their positions.

Mischling (*pl. Mischlinge*): Category defined in the wake of the Nuremberg Laws, consisting of people with one or two Jewish grandparents who did not adhere to the Jewish religion and were not married to Jews. Because of their 'mixed blood', they were subject to certain restrictions in marriage and employment, which increased in severity in accordance with the percentage of Jewishness in an individual's pedigree.

remaining savings were placed in blocked accounts from which they could draw only a fixed subsistence allowance.

Concentration meant, in the first instance, visibly separating Jews from non-Jews. Separation measures commenced with the 1935 Law for the Protection of German Blood and Honour (the second Nuremberg Law), which forbade marriage or extramarital sexual relations between Jews and non-Jews. As with expropriation, however, the process began in earnest only in 1938. Beginning in July, Jews' identity papers and passports were marked with a special sign. On 17 August an ordinance required all Jews without identifiably Jewish first names to add a middle name of Israel or Sarah. In November new laws barred Jews from receiving medical treatment except in Jewish hospitals and expelled Jewish children from state schools. The following month housing restrictions were imposed, with Jews permitted to live only in specially designated apartment buildings.

Concentration took on an additional meaning in Poland following Germany's conquest of that country in September 1939. On 23 November 1939, the German governor general of occupied Poland, Hans Frank, ordered 'all Jews . . . to wear on the right sleeve . . . a white band . . . with the Star of David on it' (Arad *et al.*, 1999: 178). Moreover, the Heydrich memorandum of 21 September 1939 called for 'Jewish communities of less than 500 persons . . . to be dissolved and transferred' to 'cities located on railroad lines'. It also suggested that 'the concentration of the Jews in the cities will probably call for regulations . . . which will forbid their entry into certain quarters' and require them 'not [to] leave the ghetto' (Arad *et al.*, 1999: 174–75). Indeed, between October 1939 and April 1941 special closed areas, called 'ghettos' or 'Jewish residential quarters', were established in most occupied Polish cities and towns. Most ghettos were surrounded by high walls and gates that could not be crossed without special permission; they both constrained Jews' physical ability to manoeuvre and isolated them from the surrounding Polish population.

It seems logical to assume that each of the first three steps in Hilberg's 'destruction process' brought the final step of annihilation closer. But the ability to discern a step-by-step destruction process in hindsight has not resolved the debate over the origins of the Nazi murder programme. For one thing, definition, expropriation, and concentration do not represent everything done to Jews under Nazi rule. From the time the Nazis came to power Jews were subjected to periodic street violence and terror. Newspapers constantly published vituperative articles about Jews. Schoolchildren were taught that Jews were a danger to humanity. Pickets regularly stood outside Jewish shops, warning customers not to buy from Jews. On 1 April 1933 the regime proclaimed a nationwide boycott of Jewish businesses. On 9 June 1938 German authorities ordered the main synagogue in Munich destroyed;

the Nuremberg synagogue was demolished on 10 August. On 9–10 November 1938, the so-called 'night of the broken glass' (*Kristallnacht*), Nazi party leaders instigated riots throughout Germany, in which 1,400 synagogues and 7,500 Jewish-owned shops were attacked and looted and 91 Jews killed.

Historians continue to differ over how to interpret these brutal Nazi anti-Jewish actions (which Hilberg excluded from his destruction process on the grounds that they did not materially advance eventual mass killing), just as they differ over how to interpret measures aimed at definition, expropriation, and concentration. Daniel Goldhagen, for one, has represented brutality, boycott, legislation, and ghettoization all as parts of a single campaign, orchestrated by Hitler, 'to turn the Jews into "socially dead" beings' before murdering them (Goldhagen, 1996: 135). Increasingly, however, scholars have tended more towards the view that the wide variety of anti-Jewish actions demonstrates that Jewish policy was controlled by no single clear authoritative vision, of Hitler or of anyone else: 'the gruesome efficiency of the . . . death camps came only after the voices of numerous contestants for control over Jewish policy had been silenced' (Schleunes, 1970: 260). Most now hold that the idea of a step-by-step destruction process represents one scholar's retrospective imposition of order upon a situation that contemporaries experienced as chaotic.

Moreover, as Hilberg himself recognized, the steps of definition, expropriation, and concentration could have served the goal of expulsion just as easily as they eventually served the goal of murder. Thus he himself did not infer a prior murder plan from his analysis. The decision to begin systematic mass killing of Jews, he suggested, was not taken until the destruction process had already reached an advanced stage; until that time the German government retained a number of possible options for dealing with the ostensible Jewish threat.

JEWISH POLICY AND GLOBAL STRATEGY

These conflicting interpretations are not entirely irreconcilable, though, and the possibility of significant centralized planning still cannot be disproved conclusively. There is, after all, a fundamental difference between long-term strategic aspirations and immediate policy. For example, it *can* be documented conclusively that a consistent aim of the Third Reich's geopolitical strategy from its inception was to conquer the Soviet Union in order to enlarge Germany's 'living space' and to eliminate the spectre of Bolshevism. Still, that long-term goal did not prevent the Reich from entering into a nonaggression pact with the Soviet government in August 1939 in order to

goul: conquer soviet union

facilitate a successful military operation later on. In other words, even though Hitler and other Reich leaders had, from the time they took power, envisioned the German army's invasion of the Soviet Union that they eventually ordered in June 1941, the road to the invasion was nonetheless twisted. Similar considerations may well have been at work in aligning strategic aims regarding Jews with actual conditions that German planners encountered at different points in the Third Reich's history. Thus it is possible that even before coming to power Hitler believed that the only effective way to remove the threat to humanity that Jews represented in his world view was to kill them all, and he may have aspired to this long-range goal. But even so, he may not have had any clear idea about when or how the goal might be achieved. It is also possible that not many others shared the goal initially and that Hitler was not able to impose it unilaterally on the Nazi regime. Perhaps at first he regarded his aspiration as utopian and thus not worth formulating as an immediate policy aim.

One reason that Hitler might have thought this way is that in 1933 fewer than 4 per cent of the world's Jews and fewer than 8 per cent of the Jews of Europe were under Nazi control; 2.3 million Jews in Austria, the Czech lands, and western Poland came under German occupation only in 1938–39; 300,000 in occupied France, the Benelux countries, and Norway in 1940, and 4.4 million in eastern Poland, the Soviet Union, the Baltic states, Serbia, and Greece in 1941. Another 1.8 million Jews lived in countries that became allied with Nazi Germany between 1939 and 1941: Slovakia, Vichy France, Italy, Romania, Hungary, Bulgaria, and Croatia. In other words, even had he wished, Hitler had no chance to eliminate the Jewish threat even in Europe (let alone throughout the world) until 1941. Until then, Nazi Jewish policy could pursue only more limited, palliative objectives, like eliminating contact between Jews and Germans, plundering Jewish assets, or providing psychological release for fanatical Jew-haters, while reserving the option of total murder for a time when Germany controlled many more Jews.

too vast or few establishm. eisenhwe man under nazi control

At first glance, the policy of emigration enunciated in the January 1939 foreign ministry memorandum appears to contradict this reasoning, because it implied removing Jews from Germany's control. Indeed, pushing Jews out – now more and more by force – was the policy Germany most actively pursued following the March 1938 annexation of Austria. On 26 August 1938 Reich authorities established a **Central Office for Jewish Emigration** in Vienna, whose purpose was to streamline procedures for obtaining passports and visas. A similar office was opened in Prague after Germany overran Czechoslovakia in March 1939 and in other Reich cities thereafter. Simultaneously the Jews of those countries were subjected to ongoing violence and terror to frighten them into leaving; some Jews were even threatened with imprisonment if they did not emigrate. As a result, some 290,000 Jews left

jews were threatened + terrorized into emmigrating

Central Office for Jewish Emigration: Nazi-sponsored bureau established in Vienna in August 1938 to increase the pace of Jewish emigration from Austria. A similar bureau was established in Germany in January 1939 and in the Protectorate of Bohemia and Moravia in July 1939.

Reich-controlled territories in 1938–39, in addition to the 129,000 who had left between 1933 and 1937. If Hitler intended ultimately to kill these Jews, why did he let them go?

One answer, suggested by Eberhard Jäckel, is that there was a basic contradiction in Hitler's thinking: 'as a German he wanted the elimination of the German Jews before all others', even as in the long term he wished to 'do . . . humanity a service by exterminating' all Jews everywhere (Jäckel, 1984: 48). Another possibility may lie in Hitler's foreign policy, whose key aim was to destroy the Soviet Union. Achieving that aim required Germany to build up its economic and military power and to expand its territorial base eastward. The economic-military build-up began in earnest with the launching of the **Four-Year Plan** in 1936, territorial expansion with the Austrian annexation in 1938. However, both actions involved violations of the Versailles Treaty that Germany had signed after the First World War. Germany thus needed to take care lest Britain or France, the other major parties to the treaty, intervene militarily to punish its infractions and nip its global strategy in the bud. Keeping the western powers at bay while Germany became the dominant force in continental Europe was a serious challenge for German politicians, and they employed many sophisticated devices to meet it.

Four-Year Plan: Economic programme announced by Goering in September 1936, aimed at augmenting German industrial and armaments production and reducing its dependence on imports. It is widely viewed as a preparatory step towards an eventual invasion of the Soviet Union.

One way of discouraging western military intervention against Germany was to portray intervention as serving nefarious Jewish interests. Indeed, from 1933 the Nazi regime strove to isolate Jews in world public opinion, depicting 'international financial Jewry' as determined to plunge Britain and France into war against a Germany that had no aggressive intentions towards them. The emigration policy might well have been part of this strategy. As the January 1939 foreign ministry memorandum indicated, 'the greater the burden [the Jewish immigrant] constitutes for the country [of immigration] . . . the stronger the reaction . . . and the more desirable the effect in support of German propaganda' (Arad et al., 1999: 131). By arousing fear in western countries of a massive influx of penniless Jewish refugees, Germany may have hoped to induce western governments to turn away Jews from their domains. German propagandists could then warn the public in those countries against going to war in the interests of people whom they themselves did not want as neighbours. Hitler himself spoke in this fashion in his Reichstag speech of 30 January 1939: 'The nations are no longer willing to die on the battlefield so that this unstable international race may profiteer from a war' (Arad et al., 1999: 135). And if some German Jews should manage through emigration to escape the Nazis' reach, the boon to Germany's global strategy that the emigration policy stood to yield by cultivating western public reluctance to stop German rearmament and eastward expansion may have more than compensated for this loss.

This analysis, which permits the notion of Hitler's constant intention to kill Jews *en masse* to be reconciled with the picture of the 'twisted road', is hypothetical; no documents uncovered to date can prove or disprove its validity. Nonetheless, it has become increasingly clear that without Hitler's insistence that a way be found to eliminate what his world view taught him was the mortal danger Jews posed to humanity, the destruction process that can be identified in hindsight would never have been set in motion. Whether Hitler or other elements of the Nazi regime first set it in motion and propelled it along its course, whether the end of that course was always clear to those who maintained it, whether it was the product of evil design or of the normal workings of a bureaucracy – these are problems of interpretation about which scholars will remain uncertain in the absence of definitive documentation.

controversy still exists.

by pushing Jews to west, encouraged western military action against germany

5

Responding to persecution

[handwritten annotation: period of power before this # holocaust actually began]

I f historians have found it difficult to ascertain precisely how the Nazi regime planned to deal with the Jews within its reach at any given moment between 1933 and 1941, how much more challenging must it have been for contemporaries to do so. Hindsight easily creates the impression that the encounter between the Third Reich and the Jews had to unfold as it ultimately did, prompting the question of why observers did not see the writing on the wall until it was too late. For two decades and more following the Holocaust such hindsight informed much of the writing on responses to Nazi rule. The Jews of Germany in particular were often chided for their alleged 'psychological predisposition against contemplating any alternative to the favourable and seemingly promising situation' they enjoyed on the eve of the Nazi era (Morgenthau, 1961: 8). Also, the actions of bystanders to the encounter between the Third Reich and the Jews in the 1930s have been interpreted in light of the systematic mass killing that characterized that encounter only after 1941. More recently, though, many historians have rejected this approach, noting that it assumes that there was always a clear message on the wall to be read, that the message always spelled death, and that any alert and reasonably intelligent observer should have been able to read it at any time. In the event, the first two assumptions have already been shown to be questionable. The third is no less problematic.

[handwritten annotation, left margin: can't assume that it was clear my Nazi's intended to do this]

PERCEIVING THE THREAT

Even if a master plan for systematic killing of all Jews within the Third Reich's reach had been set in motion from the time the Nazis acceded to power, the existence of such a plan was never made public. Thus all those not privy to the regime's internal, behind-the-scenes discussions of Jewish matters could only try to infer its long-range intentions indirectly, from what they were able to observe of its actual behaviour towards Jews. And what was observable – especially before the pace of expropriation and concentration measures and of government-sponsored violence surged in 1938 – was subject to many possible, thoroughly plausible interpretations.

To be sure, the economic and social conditions of day-to-day life for German Jewry deteriorated steadily from 1933 on. Mounting unemployment resulting from job dismissals and expropriation measures brought widespread poverty. By 1936 over 20 per cent of German Jews were dependent on welfare; another 20–25 per cent lived on savings, while only 10–15 per cent were estimated able to earn a comfortable living. Out of 1600 Jewish communities in Germany in 1933, 200 had dissolved by 1937, and another 600 were able to remain solvent only with outside assistance. Landlords increasingly refused to rent to Jews, storekeepers to sell them food and clothing. Many Jews' relations with non-Jewish friends became increasingly strained, and Jewish schoolchildren, though initially permitted to attend German state schools, were subjected to constant harassment by teachers and fellow students.

But there were also mitigating facts to be observed. True, for several months following Hitler's appointment as German chancellor on 30 January 1933, units of Nazi storm troopers (**SA**) perpetrated numerous acts of violence against Jews; but state authorities often suppressed these actions, fearing the general threat to public order they posed, and violence subsided between 1934 and 1938. Concentration camps had been built beginning in 1933, but until 1938 they were used mainly against political dissidents; communists, in particular, seemed to bear the brunt of the regime's most brutal repressive measures, not Jews. Jews had been excluded from the German army in early 1934, but as late as August 1935 Jewish veterans were receiving decorations for past service. Jewish newspapers continued to be sold in public and even to challenge the regime until October 1935. In 1936 the government promised unrestricted freedom to Jewish artists as long as they confined themselves to 'Jewish' themes. Random kindnesses and quiet expressions of sympathy for Jews by Germans were not uncommon. As late as 1939 Jews were sometimes able to find redress for their grievances against non-Jews in German courts. Many Germans, including Nazi party members, continued to do business with Jews well into the 1930s, ignoring widespread admonitions against such behaviour; some top Nazi officials were even patronizing Jewish-owned hotels until 1938. In the same year, five Jews were still directors of at least one major German bank. And for a number of Jews who owned large businesses and factories, the general upswing in the German economy during the mid-1930s actually proved a financial boon.

German Jews could also compare their situations with those of their fellow Jews in other European countries, and the comparison did not always appear to their detriment. Immediately to the east, in Poland, whose government

SA: Acronym for *Sturmabteilung* (Storm division). Nazi party activist formation, often known as 'storm troops' or 'brownshirts'. More than 500,000 Germans had joined its ranks by the time the Nazis took power, and it became a major pressure group within the party, sometimes challenging Hitler's direction. It urged more radical, violent action against Jews than the Nazi government wished at first to undertake. It was purged of radical elements in 1934, after which it lost political significance.

had signed a ten-year nonaggression pact with Nazi Germany in January 1934, economic policies helped undermine the livelihoods of Jewish artisans and merchants, until by 1937 a major Jewish newspaper described the Jews of that country as 'a helpless minority sunk in squalid poverty and misery such as can surely be paralleled nowhere on the face of the earth' – presumably not even in Nazi Germany (*Jewish Chronicle*, London, 8 January 1937). Indeed, between 1935 and 1938 popular violence against Jews was significantly more pronounced in Poland, where some 150 mob attacks killed at least several dozen Jews and wounded nearly 1,300. In Romania, too, with increasing intensity beginning in 1937, Jews faced a government-led campaign to 'Romanianize' the economy and to revoke the citizenship of at least a quarter of a million Jews said to have entered the country illegally. The leader of a major Romanian political party even declared the Jews to be his country's 'archenemies' and promised that 'we shall destroy the Jews before they can destroy us' (quoted in Mendelsohn, 1983, 204). Before the end of 1938 German Jews had few signs that their peril might well be more acute than that of their brethren elsewhere.

Moreover, the first years of Nazi rule were experienced differently by different Jews, depending upon their age, sex, class, occupation, place of residence, and political affiliation. Small-town Jews often became victims of economic pressure, social ostracism, and violence earlier and more consistently than city dwellers. Wealthier Jews often had the means to circumvent restrictions or to compensate for them in ways unavailable to their less well-to-do coreligionists. Women tended to suffer less abuse by state officials than men, but they were often more exposed to hostile interactions with non-Jews in the private sphere. Jews active in left-wing political movements confronted the most brutal aspects of the regime from the outset, whereas others could at first feel themselves relatively safe from arbitrary search and arrest.

What could be deduced from such conflicting and confusing signals about German long-range plans? Understandably, Jewish assessments were mixed. Most agreed that the situation represented an 'end of emancipation', in which Jews would no longer be regarded as equal citizens of Germany or as rightful members of German society. But where some perceived rightlessness from the start as a prelude to what Jewish banker Georg Solmssen called 'the economic and moral annihilation of all members, without any distinctions, of the Jewish race living in Germany' (quoted in Friedländer, 1997: 35), many more took comfort in the thought that 'Jewry has long undergone a process . . . of constant fluctuation between the poles of emancipation and ghettoization' (Kellermann, 1933: 174), suggesting that Jewish rights and status would eventually be restored. As the popular German Jewish novelist Lion Feuchtwanger wrote after the promulgation of the Nuremberg Laws,

'through the . . . study of history I have reached the . . . conviction that . . . we
cannot consider an eruption of madness such as the one in Germany as
something that can last more than a generation' (quoted in Friedländer,
1997: 174). In the early years of Nazi rule some thought they saw signs that
the regime was on the verge of collapse, and with it all official discrimination
and persecution. Others interpreted Hitler's 1935 statement that he sought
'opportunities [for Jews] to live their own national life in all areas' as indicating that the regime intended merely to regulate Jews as a minority while
allowing them broad internal autonomy, according to the model that had
prevailed in medieval Europe [*Doc. 8*].

In the end, German Jews could never be completely sure of the government's intentions. In November 1933 the Organization of Independent
Orthodox Communities sent a memorandum to Hitler asking him to 'tell us
the truth openly' about what lay in store. On the one hand, the memorandum explained, 'the position of German Jewry must be perceived as altogether desperate . . . and . . . the German National Government might all too
easily be suspected of aiming deliberately at [its] destruction'. On the other
hand, it declared, 'Orthodox Jewry is unwilling to abandon the conviction
that it is not the aim of the German Government to destroy the German
Jews'. Thus, it stated, 'if we should be mistaken, if you . . . have indeed set
[yourself] the ultimate aim of the elimination of German Jewry . . . then
we do not wish to cling to illusions any longer and would prefer to know
the bitter truth' (Arad *et al.*, 1999: 61). Hitler offered no response; the
uncertainty remained.

Some outside observers, like the popular American radio correspondent
William L. Shirer, thought German Jews 'unduly optimistic' (Shirer, 1941:
31). But even the most pessimistic commentators, Jewish and non-Jewish
alike, foresaw no more than economic ruin and spiritual breakdown, which
might eventually force Jews out of Germany altogether. This is what phrases
like 'destruction', 'elimination', and 'annihilation' meant to virtually everyone
at the time, not systematic mass killing. A careful reading of *Mein Kampf*
might, perhaps, have led to a more radical prognosis; but, as historian
Jacob Katz observed, 'an essential difference exists between announcing an
intention and resolving to act upon it. Nobody, including Hitler himself,
could know whether he would ever have the opportunity to carry out his
intentions and how far he would go [if he did]' (Katz, 1975: 43).

TO LEAVE OR NOT TO LEAVE?

However varied their perceptions of the threat facing them, virtually all
German Jews acknowledged that life under the Nazi regime would be hard.

which is what H wanted

In theory it was possible to avoid hardship altogether through emigration. Indeed, many German Jews left: 37,000 in 1933, 23,000 in 1934, 21,000 in 1935, 25,000 in 1936, and 23,000 in 1937. But these represented only about one quarter of the 525,000 Jews living in Germany in 1933. It was only after the German government placed emigration at the centre of its Jewish policy following the annexation of Austria in 1938 and stepped up economic and physical pressure accordingly that a majority of German Jews sought to flee the country. Thus it is often asked why more did not seek to leave sooner.

the costs of emigration

not as simple as it sounds

"difficult to adapt to an entire new environ"

The answer is that emigration had serious costs. Some were literal: even before the Nazis came to power the German government, hoping to mitigate the effects of the depression of the early 1930s by stemming the outward flow of capital, had imposed a steep 'flight tax' on the property of those who sought to leave, and the transfer of assets abroad was severely restricted. Others were less tangible. Emigration meant the pain of leaving behind family, friends, and a familiar environment to which most German Jews felt a deep attachment. It also meant economic insecurity. Migrants often arrived at their destinations without means of support or skills that could be transferred easily to their new environment, and with much of the world still suffering from economic depression, employment opportunities were scarce. Migrants unable to work in their professions or to support themselves at all lost social status as well, and their sense of personal identity was often shaken. Such difficulties led some 10,000 Jews who had fled Germany in the first months after the Nazis took power to return by early 1935; only a government threat to incarcerate returnees in concentration camps put an end to this reverse migration.

Whether these costs were worth bearing depended both upon how severely individual Jews were likely to feel them and upon how they assessed the severity of the Nazi threat. Research by historian Marion Kaplan suggests that women, whose status was less defined by their jobs than men's and who viewed the situation more from the perspective of everyday life than from that of high politics, tended more towards pessimism than men and were more willing to uproot themselves [Doc. 9]. But with the increasing tempo of expropriation, concentration, and terror during 1938, and especially after the *Kristallnacht* riots in November, differences in perception narrowed, and the desire to emigrate became virtually universal. 40,000 German Jews fled the country in 1938; 78,000 in 1939; thousands more wished to leave but found they had no means to do so or no place to go. Migration and natural decrease lowered Germany's Jewish population to under 200,000 by the outbreak of war; those who remained were disproportionately elderly or ill.

COMMUNAL LEADERSHIP: COPING AND RESISTING

Because emigration was not immediate and total, German Jews, even those who remained under Nazi rule only a short time before fleeing, needed help coping with their situation. The burden of helping fell largely upon German Jewish welfare organizations. In April 1933 a coalition of Jewish groups created a country-wide Central Committee for Aid and Reconstruction. This Committee tried to find jobs for Jews who had lost them and offered interest-free loans to help shopkeepers remain afloat. In October 1935 a Jewish Winter Aid campaign provided food, clothing, and shelter for almost 85,000 Jews – 20 per cent of German Jewry at the time. A Jewish Cultural Association, founded in 1933, offered employment to many Jewish artists and intellectuals who had been dismissed from their positions soon after the Nazi takeover. Ismar Elbogen, a Jewish scholar and communal leader, summarized the spirit that underlay these activities: 'They can condemn us to hunger, but they cannot condemn us to starvation' (quoted in Friedländer, 1997: 60).

attempts @ unifying Jews

Additionally, a central Jewish political representation, the *Reichsvertretung*, formed in September 1933, sought to provide Jews with a unified voice in the public arena. Besides supervising welfare work, this body interceded with state authorities on behalf of individual Jews and lobbied for the most lenient application possible of anti-Jewish laws. It vigorously protested defamatory statements made in the press and by public officials, hoping to defend 'the honour of the Jewish name' (Arad *et al.*, 1999: 59). And, as the situation for Jewish children in state schools became untenable, the *Reichsvertretung* organized Jewish schools. By 1937, some 24,000 elementary and secondary school pupils, representing 61 per cent of the Jewish school-age population, attended 160 *Reichsvertretung* educational institutions.

Reichsvertretung: Central organization of German Jewry under Nazi rule, established in 1933. The *Reichsvertretung der deutschen Juden* (Reich Representation of German Jews) was a voluntary social welfare organization; in 1935 it was ordered to change its name to the *Reichsvertretung der Juden in Deutschland* (Reich Representation of the Jews in Germany) – the Nuremberg Laws having made the term 'German Jews' untenable. In 1939 the *Reichsvertretung* was converted by government action into the *Reichsvereinigung der Juden in Deutschland* (Reich Association of the Jews in Germany).

Historians are divided over how effectively the *Reichsvertretung* provided leadership to German Jews. Some have suggested that its perception of the Nazi threat was as flawed as that of most German Jews and less accurate than that of many; had it been otherwise, the organization would have actively encouraged immediate mass emigration instead of concentrating upon palliative measures. Others contend that the *Reichsvertretung* understood by 1935 that any tolerable existence for Jews under Nazi rule was impossible and accepted 'the necessity for emigration on a large scale' (Lamberti, 1997: 146). In the event, the *Reichsvertretung* actively assisted many Jews who wished to leave Germany in paying the flight tax, and it conducted training courses to help would-be emigrants learn the skills they would need for successful relocation; but it never recommended formally that German Jews should leave *en masse*. This does not mean that its prognosis was more optimistic than the observable facts warranted. German Jewish leaders faced a conundrum over emigration. They were troubled not only by the regime's anti-Jewish actions but by its constant branding of Jews as enemies of Germany. For German Jews who had worked assiduously during the previous century to eliminate the cultural barriers that had set them off from the surrounding society and had cultivated a strong sense of themselves as Germans, this was an especially painful – sometimes even a psychologically unbearable – charge [*Doc. 10*]. In this context, active official Jewish encouragement of mass emigration could have been understood as confirming the regime's position that Jews had no place in Germany's future. In other words, emigration *en masse* was easily interpreted as abandoning the battle for Jewish rights. Joining that battle, in contrast, could be taken as the path of heroic resistance; it meant trying defiantly to thwart what even the most pessimistic contemporary observers saw as the Nazis' ultimate aim – the banishment of Jews from German life. Hence the Central Committee for Aid and Reconstruction publicly proclaimed that 'there is no honour in leaving Germany in order to live untroubled on your income abroad, free of the fate of your brothers', urging German Jews to 'do your duty here' (Arad *et al.*, 1999: 49–50).

Frequently the public proclamations of German Jewish leaders also stressed the necessity to show pride in Jewishness. That attitude chimed well with the belief that the persecutions associated with the Nazi regime represented the backward swing of a historical pendulum that would sooner or later oscillate forward in the direction of greater freedom. For decades German Jews had absorbed an interpretation of Jewish history according to which 'unprecedented suffering and constant martyrdom in which each century brought new depths of abuse and humiliation' had instilled in their forebears 'a great, noble pride in bearing a teaching that reflects eternity' (Graetz, 1866: 1). That pride, in turn – so their leading historian explained to them – had enabled Jews in every era to outlive their tormentors without 'sinking to the level of brutal vagrants' (Graetz, 1866: 3). Accordingly, following the anti-Jewish boycott of 1 April 1933, in which Jewish-owned shops were marked with a yellow Star of David, a leading Jewish newspaper urged Jews to remember that this symbol had once adorned the shield of King David and thus to turn the derogatory sign into 'a badge of honour' (Arad *et al.*, 1999: 46). That understanding of their people's past also suggested to many German Jews that they would profit from learning how their forebears had withstood earlier periods of hardship. In order to foster such knowledge, the *Reichsvertretung* encouraged Jewish adults to learn more about their Jewish heritage and history. Under its auspices the philosopher Martin Buber opened a Central Office for Jewish Adult Education, whose purpose was to 'groom a community that will stand firm, that will prevail, that will guard the spark' of Jewish culture (Dawidowicz, 1976: 161). These efforts appear to have found considerable response among German Jews, who felt that since they had been 'singled out for persecution . . . solely because they were Jews, it was necessary that their Judaism be invested with powerful meaning and sufficient inspirational power to enable them to endure the burden of hate and hardship' (Margaliot, 1971: 105, *Doc. 11*).

[handwritten margin note: believed their pride & honour of being a Jew would allow them to endure the Nazi's.]

Yet sponsoring such 'spiritual resistance' did not necessarily work against emigration, as some have charged. On the contrary, the widespread 'return to Judaism' among German Jews led in many cases to increasing identification with Zionism and interest in the possibility of resettlement in Palestine. Indeed, almost 30 per cent of the Jews who left Germany between 1933 and 1935 went to that country, many as a result of newfound Jewish ethnic consciousness and nationalist convictions. Membership in Zionist organizations also increased exponentially during those years.

[handwritten margin note: ↑ zionism]

ZIONISM, GERMAN JEWRY, AND WORLD JEWRY

Although before 1933 Zionism had attracted only a small minority of German Jews, and most German Jewish leaders had regarded its nationalist message as inimical to the idea of emancipation, after the Nazi rise to power Zionists became part of the *Reichsvertretung*, and even Germany's largest Jewish organization, which had long insisted that Jews constituted a religious group only, acknowledged that 'Palestine holds a special place among the countries of immigration' and that 'Palestine is an essential factor in [Jewry's] survival' (Dawidowicz, 1976: 167). This development was eventually to off-set much of the reluctance of non-Zionist Jewish leaders to encourage Jews to leave.

[handwritten margin note: Jews encouraged by publist. to emig. to palistine (zionists)]

Zionists, both in and out of Germany, were among the first to call upon German Jewry to make emigration (to Palestine) a communal priority. Chaim Arlosoroff, head of the Political Department of the **Jewish Agency for Palestine**, who visited Germany in April 1933, argued that although Palestine might not provide the sole solution to German Jewry's predicament, it had the advantage of permanence. Arlosoroff also suggested that Zionists might actually be able to reach an agreement with the Nazi regime that would allow Jews emigrating to Palestine to take a significant portion of their assets with them; he proposed that departing Jews be allowed to use the value of the assets they left behind to purchase German-made goods exported to the Middle East. Such an agreement, he thought, could help resettle large numbers of German Jews within three or four years [*Doc. 12*].

Jewish Agency for Palestine: Body created in 1929 to represent the Jewish community of Palestine in political matters. Though including non-Zionists, it was closely associated with the Zionist movement.

There were several bases for this optimism. First, many Zionists thought that their movement and the Nazis – for all their fundamentally polar attitudes towards the Jewish people – shared a common interest in seeing Jews leave Germany. Second, they understood that the German economy, hard-hit by the depression of the early 1930s, was in dire straits; indeed, the German government needed desperately to develop export markets for German industries, in order to build foreign currency reserves and provide jobs for millions of unemployed Germans. Finally, they knew that, unlike much of the world, the economy of Jewish Palestine was booming and that there was significant demand there for heavy machinery, which could be obtained from manufacturers in several countries, not only Germany. They believed, therefore, that they possessed both ideological and economic leverage that they, alone among Jewish leaders, could exercise to Jewish advantage.

As it happened, individual Zionists from Germany and Palestine had been speaking informally with certain German officials along these lines even before Arlosoroff had broached his idea publicly. Negotiations were institutionalized in May 1933, and on 17 August a formal agreement was actually concluded between the German Zionist Federation and the German Ministry of Economic Affairs. Known (even in German) by the Hebrew name *Haavara* (transfer), the arrangement permitted prospective emigrants to invest in a new export company, which would buy German merchandise and market it in the Middle East. Payments for merchandise sold would be sent to a special account in a Palestine bank. When emigrants who had invested in the export company reached Palestine, they could redeem their shares at the bank and receive cash out of the special account. The agreement was actually implemented, too: by 1939, 50,000 German Jews had transferred £8 million to Palestine.

Haavara was widely supported by German Jews, Zionist and non-Zionist alike. In 1937 the *Reichsvertretung* even reached agreement with the government to make similar arrangements for Jews departing for other countries. But many Jews outside of Germany, Zionists and non-Zionists, opposed it. In March 1933, before the negotiations that led to *Haavara* had begun, Jews in several countries had adopted a radically different response to the threat of Nazi persecution of their German coreligionists: they had organized a boycott of German products, hoping to thwart Nazi efforts to solve Germany's economic problems and thereby encourage internal German opposition to the Nazi regime. Nazi officials feared that such a boycott could do Germany real economic harm, and they resolved to fight it: on 25 March 1933, Interior Minister Hermann Goering ordered German Jewish leaders to tell their counterparts in Britain and the United States that continuation of the boycott or other anti-Nazi agitation would be met with reprisals against

Haavara: (Hebrew: transfer) 1933 agreement between the Nazi government and agencies of the Zionist movement allowing German Jews migrating to Palestine to transfer a portion of their assets with them.

German Jews. In fact, the German anti-Jewish boycott of 1 April 1933 was represented as retaliation for the Jewish anti-German boycott abroad. German Jewish leaders delivered the message, urging that the boycott cease. Nevertheless, over the next several months the boycott movement gained strength among world Jewry.

Haavara, which favoured negotiation over confrontation, clearly represented the antithesis of the boycott strategy and threatened to defeat it. As a result, it was attacked vigorously by many non-German Jews. It was also opposed on moral grounds: by promoting German exports, the agreement helped strengthen a regime that was persecuting Jews. This controversy has continued in retrospect, with historians and others hotly debating whether Haavara undermined a real chance to nip the Nazi threat in the bud. Careful statistical analysis of both the boycott and Haavara suggest, however, that neither had more than a miniscule effect on the German economy. German officials may have feared the boycott at first, but it appears that they supported Haavara less because of its economic potential and more because it represented a way to rid Germany of many Jews. At least some agencies of the Nazi regime appear to have pursued this goal even in 1933, as long as it could be accomplished without disrupting the economy. Measures such as the 'flight tax' and restrictions on the removal of property were supposed to prevent disruption, but they also discouraged Jews from emigrating. Haavara thus removed both a source of discouragement for Jews and one of economic loss for Germany.

EXTERNAL OBSTACLES TO EMIGRATION

As time progressed, however, it became clear that there were other obstacles to emigration that neither Nazis nor Jews could eliminate. These were hurdles imposed by countries receiving German Jewish refugees.

By the early 1930s, virtually all countries possessed legal and administrative means of restricting immigration, and with much of the world suffering economic depression, most thought it wise to employ them. True, in a widespread outpouring of sympathy immediately following the Nazi takeover, several European states chose temporarily not to do so, thereby allowing almost 30,000 German Jews to enter their borders in 1933. That sympathy dissipated, however, as it became clear that the Nazi government was likely to last, and by 1935 officials in the most likely receiving countries were actively trying to hold the refugee flow to a minimum. Some governments expressed concern about setting a dangerous precedent: certain eastern European countries were, for their own reasons, pressuring their much greater numbers of Jews to emigrate, and if restrictions were relaxed for

German Jews, would not Jews from these other countries also demand similar consideration?

Until 1936 Palestine represented an exception to this thinking. Britain governed Palestine under a League of Nations mandate that required it to promote the development of a Jewish national home by facilitating Jewish immigration. In theory Britain limited the number of immigrants according to the country's 'economic absorptive capacity', but with the Palestinian economy growing, this restriction meant little in practice. For this reason, too, Palestine was an attractive destination, not only for German Jews but for Jews leaving eastern Europe as well. Where in 1932 fewer than 10,000 Jews had migrated to Palestine, the number rose to 30,327 in 1933, 42,359 in 1934, and 61,854 in 1935, with the overall Jewish population of the country increasing 80 per cent in that interval. That growth worried local Arab leaders, who feared that Jews would soon become a majority. In April 1936 Palestinian Arabs launched a revolt against British rule and Jewish settlement, which eventually tied down nearly 20,000 infantry troops and two full Royal Air Force Squadrons (by some accounts as much as 40 per cent of Britain's battle-ready forces) in maintaining order. To free those troops for use in potential trouble spots elsewhere around the globe, Britain tried to assuage Arab grievances; in 1937 it began limiting Jewish immigration to 1,000 per month. As a result only half as many German Jews entered Palestine in 1937–38 as had in 1933–34.

Slowing the flow of refugees to Palestine merely increased demand for admission to other destinations, however – a phenomenon that led Britain, France, the United States, and other potential receiving countries to tighten immigration procedures even more. Germany responded with the stepped-up expropriation and concentration measures and acts of violence, that marked Nazi Jewish policy in 1938–39, especially following the annexation of Austria and the occupation of the Czech lands. This unambiguous pressure to leave meant that Austrian and Czech Jews showed little of the uncertainty that German Jews displayed during the beginning of Nazi rule: some 130,000 of 185,000 Jews from Austria and 35,000 of 118,000 from Czechoslovakia fled between occupation and the outbreak of war. Moreover, in July 1939 the regime replaced the *Reichsvertretung* with a new body, the **Reichsvereinigung**, whose explicit purpose was 'to further the emigration of the Jews' (Arad *et al.*, 1999: 140).

Vigorous protests against the Nazi terror were launched in the West; after *Kristallnacht* the United States even recalled its ambassador to Berlin. But the German policy of brutally prodding Jews into flight effectively challenged protesting countries to relax their barriers against refugees: German propaganda chided as hypocrites those who decried persecution while denying the persecuted a haven. To counter such arguments, even before *Kristallnacht*, US President Franklin Roosevelt convened a coordinating conference of 32

Reichsvereinigung: Legally recognized official administration of the German Jewish community, established in 1939, replacing the *Reichsvertretung*. The *Reichsvereinigung der Juden in Deutschland* (Reich Association of the Jews in Germany) was a compulsory organization to which all Jews under German rule were compelled to belong. Its leaders were selected by the Nazi government, and its principal task was to effectuate mass Jewish emigration.

potential receiving countries at Evian, France, in July 1938. Each country was asked to explain how it could contribute to alleviating the refugee crisis; however, it was stipulated in advance that no country would be asked to change any of its existing immigration policies.

Little came of the **Evian Conference**; almost all countries explained why they could do little more than they were already doing. The conference did create an **Intergovernmental Committee on Refugees**, which negotiated with the Nazi regime about broadening the *Haavara* principle so as to allow emigrants to transfer significant assets to any destination while stimulating German exports worldwide; but war broke out before an agreement could be implemented. In the meantime the confrontation between a German government bent increasingly upon forcing Jews out and countries reluctant to let them in continued. In 1939 German government agencies, together with German shipping lines, began purchasing visas wholesale from Latin American consular officials in Germany and reselling them to Jews together with steamship tickets. Sometimes, however, the issuing countries refused to honour them. In May 1939 this situation greeted 930 passengers on the SS *St Louis* who, holding Cuban tourist visas, tried to disembark in Havana: Cuban officials ordered them and their ship to leave. Petitions to the United States to relax its immigration laws so that the refugees could land there were ineffective. Finally, after two months of negotiations, Britain, France, Belgium, and Holland agreed to divide the passengers among them. ⤳ *finally, countries agreed to it fully*

Historians differ in their evaluations of the potential receiving countries' responses to Nazi persecutions of Jews. Some see in the application of immigration restrictions to Jewish refugees an expression of extreme callousness towards the Jewish plight, while others contend that the sheer size of the refugee flow overwhelmed well-meaning countries inadequately equipped to handle it. A controversial 1997 study argued that the successful resettlement of 290,000 German, Austrian, and Czech Jews in 1938–39 indicates that in those years 'the international reception of Jewish refugees was . . . generous' in light of most countries' policies of excluding virtually *all* immigrants (Rubinstein, 1997: 25). But in the event, although the majority of German, Austrian, and Czech Jews did find refuge in other countries, examination of consular records in several western countries has shown that refuge was often granted begrudgingly and with considerable resistance. More important, potential receiving countries consistently made it clear that whatever special efforts they might make on behalf of several hundred thousand refugees from Nazi persecution would not be extended to the millions of Jews simultaneously being pressured to leave Poland, Romania, and other eastern European countries. The German invasion of Poland in September 1939 and the extension of Nazi rule to two million Polish Jews thus complicated the implementation of Nazi Jewish policy immeasurably.

Evian Conference: International conference on refugees, July 1938. Representatives of 32 countries came together in an effort to coordinate plans to absorb Jewish and other refugees from Germany. The conference established the Intergovernmental Committee on Refugees, but it generated virtually no practical results.

Intergovernmental Committee on Refugees: Body established by the Evian Conference in 1938. In 1939 it negotiated an arrangement allowing German Jews leaving the country to take their assets with them. The arrangement was not implemented due to the outbreak of war. During the war it was largely inactive.

6

used from step 2-3 review [handwritten]

The transition to killing

*be German
was against
countries.
Jews were
to hard to
find another
find up.* [handwritten annotation]

Protectorate of Bohemia and Moravia: German administrative unit established in the Czech lands following the conquest of Czechoslovakia in March 1939. Though officially run by Czechs, sole political authority actually rested with the German Protector and his officials.

Nisko Plan: Nazi scheme to create a Jewish reservation in the eastern Generalgouvernement, to which Jews from throughout the Nazi realm would be deported. Several tens of thousands of Jews were deported there from the Protectorate and western Poland in late 1939, but the operation was abandoned in early 1940 in favour of the Madagascar Plan.

The outbreak of war and the conquest of Poland made it virtually impossible for Germany to continue pushing Jews out of the territories it controlled, as it had been trying to do ever more intensely since 1938. Now the sheer number of Jews under German rule – multiplied six times over the pre-war Jewish population of all German-controlled areas – frightened potential receiving countries. Moreover, for Britain, France, and other states at war with the Third Reich, Jews from Germany, Austria, and the Czech lands (known since March 1939 as the **Protectorate of Bohemia and Moravia**) were now legally enemy aliens. Thus, immediately following its declaration of war, Britain cancelled all visas granted previously to refugees seeking to leave those countries.

Realizing that the policy of extrusion could not continue, Germany began to think about unilaterally creating the 'Jewish reservation' that the foreign ministry, in its January 1939 policy statement, had hoped would be established by international action. This reservation would have to be located on territory Germany already controlled. Initially, thinking centred about a part of the Lublin district near the town of **Nisko**, at the south-eastern extreme of the Generalgouvernement. As early as October 1939, Jews from Vienna and the Protectorate were forcibly resettled in this region; transports soon followed from Germany and western Poland [Doc. 7]. By January 1940, 78,000 Jews had been moved into the area, with plans underfoot for transporting 400,000 more there shortly. Following the fall of France in June 1940, German attentions turned to the French African colony of Madagascar, highly preferable to Lublin in its distance from areas where Germans might settle. This idea was connected, however, with German efforts to reach a comprehensive agreement with Britain (which controlled the sea routes to East Africa) about the disposal of all African colonies. When those efforts failed, and Germany began preparing actively for the invasion of the Soviet Union, the Madagascar reservation project was abandoned.

Still, Germany did not immediately abandon its policy of eliminating Jews through emigration, expulsion, or deportation. During 1940 and early 1941 it continued to try to help Jews leave Reich territory. Adolf Eichmann, who had supervised the Central Offices for Jewish Emigration in Vienna and Prague and had assumed control of a similar Reich-wide agency in October 1939, actively assisted German Jews in using escape routes through Italy and Lithuania and worked with Soviet and Japanese authorities in arranging for thousands of Jews to travel via the trans-Siberian railroad to the International Settlements at Shanghai. He also cooperated with clandestine Jewish efforts to circumvent British restrictions on immigration to Palestine. On occasion German Jews were forcibly expelled westward; 6,504 were sent to unoccupied France in October 1940, hundreds more in sealed trains to Lisbon the following month. In all, 15,000 Jews left Germany proper in 1940, despite wartime difficulties; many times more left other German-controlled territories, including perhaps up to 300,000 Jews who fled Poland eastward into the USSR, often prodded by German troops.

But in the summer and autumn of 1941 German practice reversed itself. Orders given in August and October prohibited all further Jewish departures from German-occupied areas. Germany was now seeking not to drive Jews away but to keep them locked in. This reversal suggests a radical change in the Nazi regime's immediate plans for dealing with the Jews under its control. Indeed, it was precisely during the summer of 1941 that the first organized, indiscriminate mass killings of Jews took place. Such killings began shortly following Germany's invasion of the Soviet Union on 22 June 1941. Over the next five months, mobile killing squads, known as **Einsatzgruppen**, together with regular German army units, shot and killed half a million Jews on Soviet or Soviet-occupied territory. By November 1941 preparations were underway for the construction of special killing centres in occupied Poland, where over 3.5 million Jews from throughout Europe would be gassed to death by late 1944. In other words, the ban on emigration coincided with the transition to active systematic mass murder.

What brought about this transition? Was it connected in any way with the diminishing returns of the policy of extrusion?

[handwritten margin note: "ban on emigration transitioned to plans for mass murder"]

Einsatzgruppe (pl. Einsatzgruppen): Special task forces under SS supervision, deployed first in Poland and later in the Soviet Union for eliminating potential resistance to German rule. During the invasion of the Soviet Union in 1941, they bore a major part of the responsibility for carrying out mass shootings of Jews.

WHY BEGIN KILLING?

Predictably, there is much debate over these questions. For many years the most common view among historians was that the adjustment was one not of policy goals but merely of method and pace. According to this view, total physical annihilation of all Jews within Germany's reach had long been Hitler's aim, and all that the Nazi regime had done prior to the beginning of mass shootings and gassings had been planned to advance that end. In fact, some early historians argued that the beginnings of actual killing operations should be set not in 1941 but in 1939, when Nazi authorities began to mandate establishment of ghettos in occupied Poland.

This argument is based largely on the fact that the ghettos created throughout Poland in 1939–41 were often themselves sites of mass death. Indeed, many of them were set up so that they could hardly have been otherwise [*Doc. 13*]. Generally ghettos were located in poorer parts of town, where sanitary conditions were often substandard. Living space was often hopelessly overcrowded: in Warsaw, for example, 450,000 Jews were crammed into 1.3 square miles, with more than seven persons for each available room. Restrictions on food supplies often left daily rations for Jews at around 1,000 calories, sometimes even below 200. Such conditions produced extraordinary mortality. Perhaps half a million Polish Jews died before systematic mass killing began, 43,000 of them in Warsaw during 1941 alone. Had the Germans merely continued the harsh ghetto regime, Polish Jewry might well have died out altogether within less than a decade. Hence, it has been claimed, the changeover from 'indirect extermination' in ghettos to active killing reflected nothing more than Nazi dissatisfaction with the pace at which Jews were perishing (Esh, 1979: 259).

That dissatisfaction supposedly became acute during the winter or spring of 1941, when Germany began actively planning the invasion of the Soviet Union. At that time some 4,000,000 Jews inhabited Soviet-held territory, more than double the number already under German rule. Hitler's world view suggested that Soviet Jews must be especially dangerous, having successfully wielded their Marxist-Bolshevik ideology to subdue the Russian nation. Thus, noting that on 13 March 1941 German Chief of Staff Wilhelm Keitel defined the impending war against the Soviets as 'the decisive struggle that will have to be carried out between . . . two opposing political systems' (Arad *et al.*, 1999: 375), and that Hitler himself told his generals two weeks later that the war against communism was to be a 'war of extermination' (Burdick and Jacobson, 1988: 346), some historians contend that the decision to attack the USSR signalled that the time had come to complete the long-planned physical extirpation of the Jews. While the campaign was being planned, they argue, Hitler gave an oral order that all Jews should be killed.

 More recently, however, historians have increasingly tended towards the view that systematic killing did not become a policy goal until after the invasion of the USSR had begun. These historians implicitly or explicitly reject the notion that ghettos were intended from the start to produce mass death among Polish Jews, noting that it is a logical fallacy to infer the goal of an action from its outcome. Research by Christopher Browning and by Dan Michman on Nazi ghettoization practices has strengthened this opinion.

Soviet Union

[Handwritten annotations at top: "wanted to establish a Jewish reservation → but must / at any not / plan our" and "→ ghettos seen as / holding places"]

Browning found that local Nazi officials in occupied Poland set up ghettos on their own initiative, without orders from Berlin, as what they hoped would be a temporary solution to the problems created by the delay in establishing a Jewish reservation. He also showed that in Warsaw and Łódź, the two largest ghettos, senior officials tried to prevent Jewish attrition, hoping to exploit the ghetto population's labour. Michman reinforced this finding, noting that for most key Nazi planners in Berlin, including Reinhard Heydrich, who envisioned concentration of Polish Jews in his memorandum of 21 September 1939, the word 'ghetto' denoted nothing more than the sort of heavily Jewish residential neighbourhoods that already existed in dozens of Polish cities and towns. The only clear policy objective associated with the term was, he determined, to move rural Jews out of the countryside in order to clear land for settlement by German colonists – an aim that was only partially pursued by local commanders. In his words, 'we should refer to "Nazi ghettos" in the plural, rather than to "the Nazi ghetto" as a single uniform phenomenon'; in any event, 'the institution of the ghetto . . . was not a preliminary stage of the final solution' – the Nazi code-word that eventually came to signify systematic mass murder (Michman, 2011: 148, 154).

Thus, some historians reason, mass killing represented a totally new direction in Nazi policy throughout the ghetto period, and even during the first months following the Soviet invasion, the leaders of the Third Reich continued to hope that Jews could be deported en masse to some far-off locale. According to Martin Broszat, even as late as autumn 1941 Nazi leaders 'spoke only . . . of deportation "to the East"', meaning that they planned to concentrate Jews from Germany, the Protectorate, and Poland in territories they expected to conquer from the Soviet Union, probably in Siberia (Broszat, 1979: 85–86). Therefore, it has been argued, even though the Einsatzgruppen and German soldiers murdered hundreds and thousands of Jews on Soviet-held lands between June and November 1941 and placed even more in ghettos to await later slaughter, those killings should not be viewed as part of a comprehensive programme to annihilate all of European Jewry. Instead they were the product of a measured escalation growing out of the ideological war against 'Jewish Bolshevism': initially Jewish state and communist party officials were killed; then Jewish communal leaders and intellectuals; finally ordinary men, women, and children. Until the autumn, however, if not even later, the Germans had no concrete plans systematically to kill any other than Soviet Jews.

Those plans changed, according to this thesis, only after it became clear that the anticipated German conquest of Soviet territory was not proceeding as expected. In the wake of the invasion, plans had begun to be made to make major German cities 'Jew-pure (judenrein)' by deporting all their Jewish inhabitants 'to the east', but those plans were thwarted by the failure of the

German army to capture the necessary eastern dumping ground. Instead of changing course, however, top Nazi officials decided to send German Jews to ghettos in Poland or in occupied Soviet lands. Those ghettos were already filled to capacity, a fact that angered the local Nazi officials who had to receive the deportees. In response, local officials in certain ghettos concluded that in order to prevent intolerable overcrowding they would have either to shoot the newcomers as soon as they came or to kill some current ghetto inhabitants. Thus on 7 November 1941 a mass shooting of Minsk Jews cleared room for 1,500 Jewish deportees from Hamburg. On 25–29 November, deportees from five different German cities were shot upon arrival in Kaunas; on 30 November, the same fate befell 1,000 Jews deported from Berlin to Riga. These local initiatives are said to have indicated an escape from the 'blind alley into which the Nazis had manoeuvred themselves' when they deported German Jews eastward without being prepared to receive them. Hence, in Broszat's words, 'the practice of liquidation . . . gained predominance and evolved . . . into a comprehensive "programme"' to murder all Jews throughout Europe (Broszat, 1979: 93). Some proponents of this thesis assume that Hitler ratified this development with an oral order for systematic Europe-wide mass killing in late 1941; others contend that although Hitler unquestionably approved and encouraged mass killing, he did not need to order it explicitly.

Historians' disagreements about when direct systematic murder of all Jews became the Third Reich's active official policy stem largely from a lack of clear documentation. No written order for a comprehensive killing programme, from Hitler or anyone else, has been found. Almost all scholars today believe that no such order was ever put in writing; at most there was an oral instruction 'or, more probably, a broad hint that everybody understood' (Friedländer in Fleming, 1984: xiii). But such a hint is virtually impossible to trace. Moreover, most extant documents that seem to reflect the transition to killing are maddeningly ambiguous. German officials typically employed euphemisms to avoid speaking directly about killing, to the point where, in one scholar's words, 'the best-kept, most organized files are not necessarily the key to [understanding the genesis of] . . . mass murder on an unprecedented scale' (Breitman, 1991: 32). For example, on 31 July 1941 Hermann Goering commissioned Reinhard Heydrich 'to carry out all necessary preparations . . . for a total solution of the Jewish question . . . in Europe' [Doc. 14]. However, this order did not state explicitly that that 'total solution' (or 'final solution', a phrase also used in the document) was to involve mass killing. On the contrary, it represented itself as a 'supplement' to a January 1939 instruction 'to solve the Jewish question by emigration and evacuation'. Did the order mean that the 'final solution' was to be sought through 'emigration and evacuation' (perhaps to Siberia, which in July 1941 the Germans still thought they would soon conquer)? In earlier Nazi documents the phrase had been used in this sense. Or did it mean that a new 'final solution' was now to replace 'emigration and evacuation'? There is no way to be certain.

The volume of such tantalizing but imprecise documents is enormous. Moreover, new documentary discoveries take place regularly. With more and more evidence brought into the historiographical debate, historians have recently staked out a range of positions between the poles of mass murder as premeditated or improvised. Browning, for example, while dating the decision to begin mass killing on a continental scale to autumn 1941, has rejected the local initiative argument, ascribing the impetus for the decision primarily to Hitler and suggesting that the possibility of mass murder had been on the dictator's mind even earlier in the year. Philippe Burrin has claimed that Hitler had long regarded either extrusion or killing as acceptable approaches to dealing with Jews, although he decided firmly upon killing only in autumn 1941. Saul Friedländer has written similarly that 'during the early months of the new campaign [against the Soviet Union] Hitler . . . decided to leave the fate of the Jews of Europe in abeyance until final victory in the East', only to change his mind abruptly in September 1941, when he ordered all Jews deported from Germany in preparation for what the Nazi leader, returning to his longstanding apocalyptic anti-Jewish rhetoric that had portrayed the disappearance of Jewry as the key to the redemption of all humanity, called 'the last powerful blow that will shatter this [Jewish] enemy before the onset of the winter' (Friedländer, 2007: 202, 272). Adam Tooze has called 'the destruction of European Jewry' the 'central objective' of the Nazi regime from its inception, but he has pushed the turning point towards a programme of continent-wide mass murder back even farther, locating it in late November 1941 (Tooze, 2006: xx). By contrast, Richard Breitman has maintained that the decision for murder was taken by Hitler in early 1941 in conjunction with the planning of the Soviet invasion, although at the same time he has contended that the Nazi leader did not even entertain the thought of mass killing until the eve of war, much less systematically lay the groundwork for it from the moment he came to power. The scholars disagree over what sparked the decision: for Browning it was euphoria over the initial victories against the Soviets, for Burrin anxiety over Germany's military position once the Soviet invasion had stalled. Friedländer, Tooze, and Breitman, for all of the differences among them, have emphasized broader geostrategic concerns, especially the realization that a world conflagration, in which both the USSR and the United States would join Britain against the Axis, was about to begin. In fact, Christian Gerlach has argued that Hitler did not officially sanction a continent-wide mass murder programme until after he declared war on the United States on 11 December 1941. Based largely on an entry in the diary of Nazi Propaganda Minister Josef Goebbels from 13 December [*Doc. 15*], he has concluded that once 'the war [became] a world war' Hitler, 'with complete logical consistency . . . proclaimed his decision to exterminate all Jews in Europe' (Gerlach, 1998: 784).

Still other historians have tried to reconceptualize the issue altogether by connecting the decision to kill Jews to broader goals and policies of the Third Reich. Studies by Michael Burleigh, Wolfgang Wippermann, and Henry Friedlander have argued that Jews were murdered as part of a general programme to create a German racial utopia, in which all who threatened the Nazi vision of an ideal 'Aryan Germanic race' – not only Jews, but Sinti and Roma, the handicapped, and (for Burleigh and Wippermann) the so-called 'asocials' (habitual criminals and derelicts) and homosexuals – were deemed 'life unworthy of life' and condemned to eventual death. Noting that many techniques employed in the mass murder of Jews after 1942 were tried out on a smaller scale against the handicapped by the so-called **T4** organization in 1939–40 and that T4 personnel were later heavily involved in slaughtering Jews and Gypsies, Friedlander argued that 'one cannot explain any one of these Nazi killing operations without explaining the others' (Friedlander, 1995: 295). Thus, he implied, the anti-Jewish murder campaign had always been intended, and the timing of its onset depended less upon circumstances surrounding the invasion of the Soviet Union and the failure of the extrusion policy than upon the success of T4 in perfecting methods that could be used against larger population groups as well.

Similarly, Götz Aly and Susanne Heim have maintained that the Holocaust can be understood only against the background of Nazi Germany's overall economic and population policies in eastern Europe. In their view, the Nazis hoped to colonize millions of Germans in the conquered eastern territories but saw overpopulation in those areas as a primary impediment to achieving this goal. Killing off large segments of the local population, including certain categories of Slavs as well as Jews, was supposed to overcome this problem, thereby stimulating economic modernization in a backward part of the world. According to Aly and Heim, this idea was formulated around 1938–39 by a group of young social scientists working for the Nazi regime and made such good sense to policymakers that it was implemented during the occupation of Poland. In opposition to Browning, they believe that ghettos and Jewish reservations were indeed meant to serve as instruments of mass death by starvation, with active killing beginning once it became clear that the ghettos represented a severe economic burden. However, they claim that it was not any particular animus towards Jews but cold-hearted, rational economic thinking that underlay the intention of mass murder.

The Aly–Heim thesis attracted much critical comment, and most historians have rejected it. In general the historiographical mainstream continues

Asocials: Nazi term referring to habitual criminals, vagrants, and beggars. Believing that criminality and vagrancy were hereditary, the Nazi regime incarcerated and sterilised many whom they branded 'asocial' without reference to any specific crime.

T4: Code name for a Nazi programme to kill mentally retarded and physically deformed individuals believed to present a danger of corrupting German racial stock. Operating in 1939–41, it was responsible for the development of techniques (including mass killing by asphyxiation) that were later employed in the murder of Jews. Some T4 workers were instrumental in the initial operation of the killing centres.

to separate the killing of Jews analytically from Nazi persecutions of other groups, believing that fundamentally different sets of considerations were at work in each case. That conclusion has been reinforced by a series of studies of the origin of mass killing in specific districts and towns in regions wrested by Germany from the USSR in the second half of 1941. Those studies have suggested that, in some places at least, wholesale murder, like ghettoization before, was initially undertaken by local German military commanders and civilian officials looking to solve ad hoc problems that surfaced in their areas of responsibility during the months following the invasion of Yugoslavia in April 1941 and of the Soviet Union two months later. Foremost among those problems was the need to feed, clothe, and house German troops and administrators in the newly conquered territories, where supplies were scarce. For some officials that situation required that the number of people who competed with Germans for scarce resources be reduced as quickly as possible. Nazi ideology held that Jews had the least legitimate claim upon resources of any people. Hitler's portrayal of Jews as nonhuman also provided justification for killing them in order to make sure that they would never be able to take food, clothing, or shelter from Germans. Hence, for example, in July 1941 the German commissar of the Šiauliai region in Lithuania, Hans Gewecke, issued an order for all Jewish women and children in his area to be shot. In Belarus, **SS** General Erich von dem Bach-Zelewski argued *up* the chain of command for similar action, eventually obtaining from Himmler, on 31 July 1941, an 'explicit order' that 'all Jews [in Bach-Zelewski's area of responsibility] must be shot' (quoted in Browning, 2004: 281). Thus, some historians reason, it may have been the success of such locally initiated killing operations – operations that are perhaps best described as wildcat actions, because they went *against* the grain of the then dominant thinking within the bureaucratic hierarchy, which still envisioned mass deportations of Jews to the Soviet interior – that eventually encouraged a later decision in Berlin to make systematic indiscriminate total murder a policy for all of Nazi-dominated Europe once it became clear that a quick and decisive victory over the Soviets was not forthcoming.

Recent studies have also suggested that German officials in the Soviet, Polish, and Yugoslav territories occupied by Germany in 1941 may have been assisted in imagining wholesale killing of civilians by observing violent acts perpetrated by local Lithuanians, Estonians, Belorussians, Ukrainians, Romanians, Croats, and Poles against their Jewish neighbours in cities and small towns throughout the occupied regions. Attacks against Jews were also carried out by local residents, along with military and police units, in Croatia and Romania, which were independent allies of the Third Reich. Sensing that Jews could now be attacked with impunity, some non-Jews in these countries took advantage of what seemed to them a chance to settle

SS: Acronym for *Schutzstaffel* (Protection squad). Nazi police force and Hitler's personal bodyguard corps, transformed under Himmler's leadership into the principal police agency in the Third Reich. Its primary task under Himmler was to survey and eliminate all activity that might threaten the Reich. In this capacity it supervised most of the German concentration camps and took on primary responsibility for controlling (and eventually killing) the Jewish population in German-occupied territories.

Bessarabia: Romanian–
Soviet border region
between the Prut and
Dniester Rivers. Mostly
under Russian rule during
the nineteenth century,
it was awarded to
Romania by the Paris
Peace Conference in
1919. Soviet forces
annexed the area in June
1940, but Romania
reclaimed it in the wake
of the German invasion
of the USSR a year later.
In anticipation of the
reconquest, Romanian
dictator Antonescu
secretly ordered mass
killings of the province's
more than 200,000 Jews,
who were charged with
disloyalty. Well over half
were killed in combined
Romanian–German oper-
ations during July–
August 1941. The
remaining Jews were
deported to Transnistria,
beginning in September
1941; many thousands
died en route.

Bukovina: Former duchy
of the Habsburg Empire,
extending from the
northeast end of the
Carpathian Mountains
to the Dniester River,
awarded to Romania by
the Treaty of St Germain
(1919). The USSR
annexed the northern
half of the province in
June 1940; Romania
recovered it in June
1941. Like the Jews of
Bessarabia, Bukovinian
Jews were charged by
the Romanians with
supporting the Soviet
enemy and subjected
to revenge attacks by
the Romanian army
(together with German
forces). Local Ukrainians
also instigated pogroms
against Jews. Over
20,000 Jews were killed
in this fashion; another
57,000 were deported
to Transnistria.

old personal or communal scores. On the evening of 28 June 1941, for example, less than a week after the beginning of the German-Soviet war, residents of Iaşi, capital of the Romanian province of Moldavia, attacked Jews in their houses and on the street; the local police assisted, as Christians ironically marked their doorposts with crosses as a sign to the deadly mob to pass over their homes. The next day Romanian police and soldiers conducted a mass shooting of Jews outside police headquarters. An additional 4,300 Jews were rounded up and herded into closed boxcars; over the next seven days they were transported to a Romanian army camp 428 km distant, without food, water, or fresh air. By the time the train reached its destination 2,430 Jews had suffocated to death; half of the survivors died within the next six weeks. Altogether perhaps as many as a third of the city's 34,000 Jewish residents were murdered by their fellow townspeople, 8,000 in a single day.

Mass killing began shortly thereafter in Romanian-controlled **Bessarabia** and **Bukovina**, where in the space of two months local peasants joined Romanian soldiers and German SS units in shooting perhaps as much as half of the region's Jewish population. Virtually all of the remaining Jews from these provinces were deported to ghettos and camps in the new Romanian colony of **Transnistria**, carved out of the former Soviet Ukrainian area between the Dniester and Bug Rivers; 25,000 died en route during the forced march, while another 80,000 perished over the next three years. In Croatia local killing of Jews, without German assistance, began even earlier, with a riot in Zagreb on 22 June and an order by dictator Ante Pavelić four days later that all Jews in the country, without exception, be incarcerated. Incarceration began at the end of the month; Jews were taken to eight specially-constructed prison camps, where some two-thirds – about 35,000 Jews – were shot on arrival. In German-occupied eastern Galicia it is estimated that upwards of 10,000 Jews were shot in riots led by local Ukrainians during the first half of July 1941 alone. In Estonia a local militia shot over 95 per cent of the country's small Jewish community to death within two months of the German occupation, with SS approval but with little practical assistance.

Notably, much of the violence against Jews perpetrated by local populations was indiscriminate. Indeed, some Jewish communities lost from one-third to more than one-half of their number in the space of a few days. In a few cases virtually all Jews who were unable to escape met violent death at their neighbours' hands. In the Polish town of Jedwabne, on 10 July 1941, a mob, led by the mayor and members of the town council, first hacked and bludgeoned some 75 young and healthy Jewish men to death with axes and nail-studded clubs, then marched all of the town's remaining Jews who could not flee in time – probably about 400 people – into a barn owned by a local

Plate 1 Writer Yehiel De-Nur (Ka-Tzetnik) testifying at trial of Adolf Eichmann, Jerusalem, 1961

Source: United States Holocaust Memorial Museum

Plate 2 Heinrich Himmler (left) and Hans Frank (right), Kraków, 1940

Source: United States Holocaust Memorial Museum

Plate 3 Berlin, 1938: A Jewish department store defaced

Source: Centrum Judaicum Archive, Berlin

Plate 4 Boundary of Łódź ghetto, 1940

Source: United States Holocaust Memorial Museum, courtesy of Walter Genewein

Plate 5 Jews in Białystok move into the ghetto, August 1941
Source: Yad Vashem Photo Archive

Plate 6 Mordechai Haim Rumkowski, head of Łódź ghetto (in rear seat)
Source: United States Holocaust Museum, courtesy of Walter Genewein

Plate 7 A mechanized saddlery in the Łódź ghetto

Source: United States Holocaust Museum, courtesy of Walter Genewein

Plate 8 Civilians walk past bodies of Jews killed in Iaşi, Romania, June 1941

Source: United States Holocaust Memorial Museum

Plate 9 German soldiers force Jews to do gymnastics, Salonika, 1942

Source: United States Holocaust Memorial Museum, courtesy of David Sion

Plate 10 Employees of Jewish Council, Netherlands (*Joodse Raad*) manage records, 1942

Source: United States Holocaust Memorial Museum, courtesy of Eric Zielenziger

Plate 11 Jewish prisoners at Płaszów labour camp carry cloth for German uniforms

Source: United States Holocaust Memorial Museum, courtesy of Leopold Page Photographic Collection/Raimund Titsch

Plate 12 Abba Kovner enters Wilno after liberation, 1944

Source: United States Holocaust Memorial Museum, courtesy of Vitka Kempner Kovner

Plate 13 Bronia Klibański

Source: United States Holocaust Memorial Museum, courtesy of Bronia Klibański

Plate 14 Jan Karski (portrait taken during mission to United States, 1943)

Source: United States Holocaust Memorial Museum, courtesy of Jan Karski

carpenter who had volunteered his property for the purpose. The barn was doused with kerosene and set afire; all inside were burned alive. Here, quite literally, was a holocaust – the word comes, after all, from the Greek *olos*, meaning 'whole', and *kaustos*, meaning 'burnt'.

As with so many issues in the study of the Holocaust, no documents yet prove without question that the idea of total murder occurred to the Germans who initiated it in the field first as a result of watching the local populations under their rule or influence. Indeed, historians' views are constantly changing as new documents are brought to light and analysed from different perspectives. Documentary discoveries have led gradually to the widespread view that no single murder decision or single catalyst that led to it can be identified. Instead scholars increasingly view the transition from persecution to murder as a gradual one, accomplished incrementally and triggered by different combinations of factors in different locations. Yet scholars still debate the nature and relative influence of the various triggers and of the contexts in which they were set off. In short, the question of why the Third Reich began actively and systematically to murder the Jews of Europe in 1941 remains far from settled.

Transnistria: Ukrainian region between the Bug and Dniester Rivers, occupied by Romania from 1941 to 1944. The Romanian government deported some 150,000 Jews, mostly from Bukovina and Bessarabia, to Transnistria, where they were incarcerated in ghettos and camps and conscripted for forced labour. About 90,000 of the deportees died. In addition, some 185,000 Jews who had lived in the region before the Romanian occupation were murdered by German and Romanian forces.

THE MEANS OF MURDER

Whatever the case, it is clear that by the end of 1941 the phrase 'final solution' stood for mass murder. On 29 November Heydrich invited representatives of thirteen government, party, and police agencies to a conference, 'followed by luncheon', to discuss 'the remaining work connected with this final solution' [*Doc. 16*]. The meeting, known as the **Wannsee conference** (after the address where it was held) was set for 9 December, then postponed to 20 January 1942. According to the conference minutes, Heydrich noted that 'instead of emigration, the new solution has emerged, after prior approval by the Führer, of evacuating Jews to the East'. However, Heydrich explained, 'these actions are . . . to be seen only as temporary relief', but they are nevertheless 'providing the practical experience that is of great significance for the coming final solution of the Jewish question' (Roseman, 2002: 161–62). As part of that 'coming final solution' young, healthy Jews would be sent to forced labour, 'during which the large majority will be eliminated by natural causes'. The surviving remnant would 'have to be dealt with appropriately', for it would represent a physically resistant strain that could 'otherwise, by natural selection . . . form the germ cell of a new Jewish revival' (Roseman, 2002: 164–65). Virtually all historians agree that, in this context, 'deal[ing] with appropriately' meant killing. Indeed, as preparations for the Wannsee conference were being made, construction of six special

Wannsee conference: Meeting held in Berlin in January 1942 to establish a timetable and coordinate the logistics of the transportation of European Jews to the killing centres.

Chełmno: The first Nazi killing centre. Located about 50 km west of Łódź, it employed sealed lorries for killing Jews by asphyxiation from exhaust fumes. Between December 1941 and March 1943, 320,000 people were murdered there, mainly Jews from western Poland.

Bełżec: German killing centre on the Lublin–Lwów rail line. Some 450,000–500,000 Jews, mostly from ghettos in Poland, were killed there between March and December 1942.

Sobibór: German killing centre in eastern Poland. Some 200,000–250,000 Jews were killed in the Sobibór gas chambers between March 1942 and September 1943.

Treblinka: German killing centre midway between Warsaw and Białystok. About 870,000 Jews were killed there between July 1942 and July 1943, almost all from the Generalgouvernement.

Majdanek: Killing centre combined with concentration camp on the outskirts of Lublin. About 500,000 Jews, Poles, and Soviet prisoners were brought to the camp between October 1941 and July 1944; 150,000 Jews from many European countries were killed there in gas chambers.

centres for mass killing – **Chełmno**, **Bełżec**, **Sobibór**, **Treblinka**, **Majdanek**, and **Birkenau** (Auschwitz II) – was already underway. In these centres some 60 per cent of Jewish victims were to meet their deaths.

Building the killing centres signalled a change in German methods of murdering Jews. Jews in Soviet-held lands had been killed mainly by shooting: units of the *Einsatzgruppen*, police, or regular army would enter a town, seize some or all of its Jews, march them to a secluded location in a nearby forest, force the Jews to dig a pit, line them up at the pit's edge, and shoot them one by one in the back of the head [*Doc. 17*]. In 1941–42 some 1.4 million Jews from the USSR, Lithuania, Latvia, Estonia, and eastern Poland were murdered in this fashion. This method had several disadvantages, however. It was slow and often incomplete: for example, although shooting squads killed over 33,000 Jews in Kiev in late September 1941, another 120,000 remained in the city after this operation. Shooting also required considerable manpower, which was not easily spared from battlefield duty; eventually personnel had to be drawn not only from German forces but from native collaborators, whose number approached 300,000 by the end of 1942. Involvement of such large numbers made it difficult to keep the killing operations secret – a difficulty that, it was feared, could lead to unrest among the conquered non-Jewish populations, who were liable to wonder whether they might become the conquerors' next targets. And mass shootings generated undesirable psychological repercussions in some German executioners, who found the messy business of shooting – the screaming, the blood, the stench, and (perhaps most of all) the direct confrontation with their victims – emotionally devastating. Some killing squads reported problems with alcoholism; nervous breakdowns, albeit infrequent, were noted. A German commander grumbled after a shooting that his men were now 'finished for the rest of their lives'. 'What kind of followers are we training here?', he complained, 'either neurotics or savages!' (Hilberg, 1985: vol. 1, 332). Thus, for the murder of all European Jews, a method was required that could kill greater numbers faster, require less manpower, be kept hidden from the local population, and maximize the psychological distance between killer and killed.

Killing centres satisfied these requirements. They promised efficiency: instead of sending the killers after Jews, who were spread over a wide area, Jews from all over Europe would be brought to specially constructed central locations, which, by consolidating operations and processing the victims in assembly-line fashion, would demand the involvement of far fewer Germans than had mass shooting. In fact, the process could be designed so as to permit use of a relatively small number of non-German collaborators, and even some Jews, to perform the most gruesome tasks associated with the actual killing and subsequent disposal of corpses, thereby sparing Germans the

proposed set up ov killing centers

emotional strain of having to confront the results of their actions directly. Reducing the number of personnel involved and locating the centres in areas under direct German control also increased the chances of maintaining secrecy. Thus at Wannsee it was decided that 'Europe will be combed from west to east', with Jews 'first . . . sent, in stages, to so-called transit ghettos, from where they will be transported to the East' (Roseman, 2002: 165). The 'East' in this case meant Poland, where the six killing centres began operations between December 1941 and July 1942.

The centres killed their victims by asphyxiation. At Chełmno, the first to begin operation, Jews were loaded on to sealed vans whose exhaust fumes were channeled back into the cargo area. At Bełżec, Sobibór, Treblinka, and Majdanek, diesel engines sent carbon monoxide into specially constructed gas chambers, while at Birkenau the chambers employed the more efficient hydrogen cyanide, marketed under the trade name **Zyklon B**.

Sometimes the killing centres are called 'concentration camps', but this is a misnomer. Nazi Germany did erect many concentration camps – Dachau, Sachsenhausen, Buchenwald, and Mauthausen are among the most infamous – for incarcerating political prisoners and 'asocials', but they were not employed in the mass killing of Jews. To be sure, Majdanek housed both a concentration camp and a killing centre, and Birkenau was situated next to the concentration camp at Auschwitz. Jews brought to these locations underwent 'selection': those thought fit for labour were sent to the camp, while the others were killed immediately. Also at Birkenau several thousand Jews were chosen as subjects for medical experiments between 1942 and 1944. At the four remaining killing centres, however, Jews were killed upon arrival, except for the few chosen for the **Sonderkommando** (special command), whose job was to press the victims into the gas chambers and transport their corpses for incineration or burial [*Doc. 18*]. There was also a network of forced **labour camps**, including Płaszów, Janowska, and Trawniki, in which as many as half a million Jews (mostly from Poland) were incarcerated and where exhausted workers were often killed on the spot.

ORGANIZING THE TRANSPORTS

With the killing centres established, the Germans faced the task of bringing millions of Jews from throughout Europe to them. That task presented a logistical challenge of the first order. Transports of Jews had to be scheduled so that killing installations would be neither overloaded nor idle. Railroad tracks had to be cleared; cars, locomotives, and personnel allocated. Round-ups of Jews needed to be coordinated with local military and civilian

Birkenau: Satellite camp of Auschwitz, known also as Auschwitz II, about 3 km from the main Auschwitz camp. It also functioned as the largest of the Nazi killing centres: almost 1.5 million Jews, 16,000 Soviet prisoners of war, and 20,000 Sinti and Roma were killed there between January 1942 and November 1944. It was the primary killing centre to which non-Polish, non-Soviet Jews were deported.

Zyklon B: Trade name of prussic acid or hydrogen cyanide (HCN), a lethal substance used in the gas chambers at Birkenau.

Selection: Removal of young and healthy Jews from the ranks of those transported to killing centres, in order to exploit their labour or use them in medical experiments.

Sonderkommando: Name assigned to deportees selected upon arrival at killing centres to perform particularly gruesome duties associated with disposing of the bodies of the victims.

Labour camps: Camps where a minority of young, healthy Jews were exploited, along with non-Jews, as forced labourers instead of being killed immediately.

authorities. The agency that oversaw these operations was the SS. Led by Heinrich Himmler, the SS controlled all police functions in the Reich, including surveillance and repression of those deemed threats on ideological or racial grounds. This aspect of SS work, which encompassed Jewish matters, was supervised by Heydrich, head of the internal intelligence and secret police service, the Reich Main Security Office (**RSHA**). Heydrich in consultation with Himmler, in turn assigned responsibility for direct administration of the murder scheme to Adolf Eichmann.

RSHA: Acronym for *Reichsicherheitshauptamt* (Reich Main Security Office). Organized in September 1939 as a branch of the SS under Heydrich, the RSHA supervised the criminal police (Kripo), the secret political police (Gestapo), and the internal espionage service (SD).

At Wannsee, Eichmann had received the general instruction to 'comb Europe from west to east'. That guideline, though, proved difficult to follow. At the time, the westernmost country from which Jews were to be deported, France, with 350,000 Jews, was technically self-governing; Germany, needing to concentrate its manpower on the Soviet and African fronts, was thus heavily dependent upon French police and administrators to identify, concentrate, and hand over potential deportees. Similar situations prevailed in Denmark and Norway. Non-German officials also retained influence in Belgium and, to a lesser extent, Holland and Luxembourg. Italy and Finland were independent German allies that would have to be cajoled into cooperating in the murder programme. Such was the case too with Germany's allies to the southeast – Slovakia, Hungary, Croatia, Romania, and Bulgaria – while most of Greece was under Italian occupation. In contrast, Germany had virtually complete control over the Jews in Austria, the Protectorate, Poland, the Baltic states, the occupied Soviet areas, and Serbia, as well as Germany proper. Except for Serbia (where most Jewish men had already been shot between August and December 1941 in reprisal for the Serbian communist partisan revolt that followed the invasion of the USSR), these were the countries closest to the killing centres; deporting Jews from them thus presented the fewest logistical difficulties. Besides, they contained three-quarters of the Reich's intended victims. Small wonder that Jews from these countries became the first casualties of the continent-wide murder campaign, or that the percentage losses of their Jewish communities were, with few exceptions, greater than those elsewhere. Although as early as March 1942 tens of thousands of Jews were deported from France and Slovakia, the Germans placed primary emphasis in the year after Wannsee on making the countries under their direct control totally free of Jews.

Operation Reinhard: Code name for the construction of the Bełżec, Sobibór, and Treblinka killing centres and their use in the murder of over 2 million Jews from the Generalgouvernement.

The most elaborate such effort, to make the entire Generalgouvernement of Poland *judenrein*, was known as **Operation Reinhard** (after Heydrich). Under the direction of Odilo Globocnik, SS commander in Lublin and a confidant of Himmler, planning for it began even before the Wannsee conference. Globocnik and his staff designed both the gassing installations at Bełżec, Sobibór, and Treblinka and the process for bringing Polish Jews to them. Between March 1942 and October 1943 that process resulted in the liquidation of ghettos ⟶ shipment of Jews to killing centers ⟶ from cent to C.C.

The transition to killing   69

liquidation of ghettos in Lublin, Warsaw, Lwów, Kraków, Częstochowa, Białystok, and hundreds of smaller towns, and the death of over two million Jews. In all ghettos the process (known as an *Aktion*) was similar. The day before the scheduled deportation, posters instructed ghetto residents to report for '**resettlement in the east**'. The next day Germans and non-German collaborators sealed off the ghetto exits. If not enough Jews reported, searches were conducted house to house. Those caught in the search were brought forcibly to a railroad siding, where they were packed into freight cars and shipped to a killing centre [*Doc. 19*]. Sometimes these *Aktionen* lasted for months, as in Lublin, where 33,000 Jews were sent to Bełżec between 17 March and 20 April, or in Warsaw, where 265,000 were transported to Treblinka between 22 July and 12 September. Sometimes the pace of deportation was so great that not enough railroad cars were available; in those cases police units were despatched to kill small-town Jews by shooting.

For all of the brutality of the *Aktionen*, the Germans appear to have hoped that Jews would board the deportation trains voluntarily. To this end they engaged in elaborate tactics of deception. By presenting the deportations as 'resettlement', and by instructing the deportees to take baggage with them, they tried to persuade Jews that they would be moved to areas where there was plenty of room to live. Jews were told that they were important to the German war effort, that in their new homes they would put to work, and that they would have adequate food and shelter so that they could be most productive. 'Resettlement', in other words, was made to appear as a desirable alternative to the crowding, hunger, and disease of the ghettos. At the same time the Germans tried to weaken Jews' will to resist, both by acting with speed and surprise and by setting different segments of Jewish society against one another. Declaring certain categories of people immune from deportation encouraged Jews to compete with one another over the limited number of exemptions. Jews striving to obtain exemptions for themselves would be less inclined to demonstrate solidarity with the entire community, a prerequisite for effective resistance. Undermining solidarity was achieved also by compelling Jewish administrators in the ghettos to post the deportation orders and holding them responsible for supplying a daily quota of deportees. Indeed, ghetto administrators often found themselves in the position of selecting the deportees and using Jewish police squads (which the Germans had established in many ghettos for maintaining internal order) to force recalcitrant designees to the trains.

Such tactics pointed to a German understanding that, even in the territories under complete Nazi control, the ability to realize the 'final solution' depended partly upon German success in manoeuvring the designated victims into the most favourable position for taking their lives. In this sense, the architects of the murder campaign regarded the victims' behaviour as

Aktion (pl. Aktionen): An operation leading to the killing of Jews, most commonly involving a mass roundup and removal to a killing site.

'**Resettlement in the East**': German euphemism for deportation of Jews to killing centres.

critical to its outcome: victims who perceived a mortal threat might theoretically have taken action to avoid it, and those with the ability might have
tried to foil it. Similarly, they realized that bystanders – local non-Jewish
populations, underground resistance movements, governments of countries
fighting Germany, even people outside the Nazi orbit – might influence the
results of their crusade. In theory, under certain circumstances bystanders
could provide information to potential victims that could help them evaluate
their situation accurately, or they could even help victims escape or defeat
the threat. Hence the job of organizing the transports to the killing centres
necessarily involved careful consideration of the reactions of victims and
bystanders to the German machinations.

7

Responding to murder

Though the Nazis evidently believed that victims' and bystanders' behaviour might affect the eventual success of their murder campaign, it is a matter of considerable controversy whether their belief was well founded. Ever since the German defeat, scholars and non-scholars have debated intensely, often bitterly, whether Jews or anyone else, within the Nazi orbit or outside it, could have done anything that would have significantly altered the outcome of the murder programme once it was launched. Ultimately, of course, the question cannot be answered with any confidence: what might have happened if actions not taken had been taken is a matter for speculation, nothing more. Historians can, however, ascertain fairly reliably what sort of options were available to various categories of victims and bystanders in responding to the onset and progress of mass murder and record the choices different groups made as the campaign unfolded. They can also explore the reasons why certain responses were exhibited and others not.

INFORMATION AND IMAGINATION

In doing so, scholars and non-scholars must be aware that they observe the victims' and bystanders' actions with the benefit of hindsight. As historian Yehuda Bauer has noted, 'The post-Holocaust generation . . . already know[s] . . . that mass murder was possible; [Jews and non-Jews] who lived at the time did not. For them it was a totally new reality that was unfolding before their shocked eyes and paralyzed minds' (Bauer, 1978: 7). The extent of that mental paralysis was revealed starkly in July 1943, when Jan Karski, a Polish underground courier who had witnessed the killing of Jews in a labour camp, met with senior advisors to Franklin Roosevelt and related what he had seen. One of the advisors, Supreme Court Justice Felix Frankfurter (himself a Jew and ardent Zionist), reportedly responded that he was 'unable to believe' Karski's eyewitness testimony. Not that he doubted the truth of what he had heard: as Frankfurter is supposed to have explained, 'I did not say that this young man is lying; I said that I am unable to believe him. There is a difference' (quoted in Wood and Jankowski, 1994: 188). The inability to believe stories of behaviour seemingly incongruous with the image of modern civilized humanity was to retard the reactions of many who confronted the mounting holocaust.

Moreover, like German Jews following Hitler's accession to power, victims and bystanders throughout Europe had no direct access to German discussions of the murder campaign. They had to assess Nazi designs on the basis of indirect signals that were often vague, contradictory, and misleading. Such was the case both before and after systematic killing began. Different agencies of the Nazi regime often seemed to disagree about how Jews should be treated – as indeed they frequently did. Following the invasion of Poland, for example, when SS units had undertaken considerable gratuitous violence against Jews and Poles (hoping to terrorize the conquered population into submission), the German army command, believing that terror generated panic instead of order and made the job of controlling the civilian population more difficult, had voiced strong objections, even placing some perpetrators of violence on trial. Governor General Frank opposed the Nisko reservation project and interfered with the resettlement of Jews from outside the Generalgouvernement; as a result, resettlement transports were sometimes halted en route and returned to their point of origin. Ghettos were not formed according to a uniform schedule but at an uneven pace (and in some towns not at all); sometimes (as in Warsaw) there were false starts before ghettos were finally sealed. In some places practices changed literally from one day to the next: on 15 October 1941 a transport of Jews left Luxembourg for safety in neutral Portugal, but the following day a similar transport carried its Jewish passengers to the ghetto in Łódź, whence they would eventually be sent to their deaths.

Apparent contradictions persisted even after the onset of mass murder. In September 1941, after SS and Ukrainian militia units in Lwów (in newly conquered east Galicia) had already shot several thousand Jewish men, the local German governor issued travel documents to Jews who agreed to relocate westward to Kraków, capital of the Nazi Generalgouvernement, where a ghetto regime featuring several forced-labour projects (including the German Enamel Works headed by industrialist Oskar Schindler, who would eventually rescue upwards of 1,000 of his plant's workers) appeared to offer a more stable existence. That action, however, contravened the policy of the head of the Generalgouvernement, Hans Frank, who had sought for over a year to reduce the Jewish population of his capital to a minimum. Accordingly, Frank immediately returned the Lwów Jews to the place from which they had just arrived.

Inferring any consistent policy from such inconsistent behaviour was difficult at best, even if a consistent policy had been formulated behind the scenes. If anything, Nazi actions in occupied Poland and elsewhere initially appeared to sophisticated Jewish and non-Jewish observers to be aimed at plundering Jewish wealth, providing a psychological outlet for Germans convinced of their own racial superiority, and exploiting local antipathy towards Jews to endear the conquerors to the conquered, but not necessarily at implementing any single preconceived idea about how the so-called Jewish question ought to be solved [Doc. 20]. In an eyewitness report from March 1940 on conditions for Polish Jews under German occupation, for example, Moshe Kleinbaum, a leading Jewish journalist and political figure, spoke of the 'arbitrariness and treachery of the Nazi authorities', meaning that the regime was characterized by 'awful corruption' and that 'in exchange for gold everything can be gotten', including freedom from persecution (Engel, 1991: 278). That was an assessment based upon dozens of testimonies that Kleinbaum had gathered from Jews and non-Jews who related to him their actual day-to-day experiences with the occupiers – seemingly more reliable indicators of the future than Hitler's rantings in *Mein Kampf* or the rhetorical bombasts of Nazi politicians in Berlin. Mass killing contradicted those experiences and suggested that previous assessments of Nazi policy were no longer valid. Thus it necessitated a mental readjustment that was not easy to achieve.

thought
to be
an attack
upon
Jewish
wealth

Hence, when in the summer and autumn of 1941 the occasional survivors of mass shootings in former Soviet territories began to relate their stories to any who would listen, their accounts were often dismissed [Doc. 21]. Only after such stories were heard again and again could the natural and experiential resistance to believing them be overcome. Even then, it required both the collation of data from many different places and a radical leap of imagination to deduce that all Jews throughout Europe, and not merely some on the extreme eastern frontier of the Nazi orbit, were slated for death, no matter where they lived, what acts they had committed, or how much gold they could offer to annul the sentence. Collating the necessary data was impeded by the German determination to camouflage the murder campaign, by strict German control over information sources, and by the barriers the ghetto walls presented to communication, both between Jews and non-Jews and among the ghettos themselves. Imagination in the necessary degree was by nature the possession of only a gifted few.

Perhaps, then, it was no accident that one of the first people (and perhaps even the first person) to deduce that the Germans had decided to murder each and every Jew within their reach (or at least the first person to articulate such a deduction) was a young poet and Zionist youth movement leader from Wilno, Abba Kovner, who in late December 1941 announced to his movement comrades that 'a total system' existed for 'the annihilation of millions' of Jews [*Doc. 22*]. Jewish youth movement members had several advantages in overcoming the information blackout and isolation of the ghettos. Youth movements, a widespread feature of Jewish life in interwar Poland, were organized on a countrywide basis, so that members from different cities maintained regular contact with one another. They trained their members, usually in their teens or early twenties, to see themselves as part of an avant-garde, thereby reinforcing normal youthful adventurousness and daring. Many members had excellent command of the Polish language, which enabled them to pass as Poles when the need arose. These characteristics helped youth movements serve as primary vehicles for clandestine inter-ghetto communication [*Doc. 23*]. Nonetheless, Kovner's perception was initially exceptional even among youth movement members; indeed, once he made his announcement, some comrades questioned how he could be so certain. Kovner confessed that his deduction came mainly from 'a healthy instinct'; it was evidently his poet's sensibility, not any particular information, that brought him to it. Yet even that poet's sensibility did not produce his conclusion until almost six months after the first mass killings in his own town had taken place. How much more difficult would it be for less exceptional individuals, farther removed from the initial killing sites and facing ever greater German efforts at deception, to follow him.

Kovner made his deduction on the basis of information about mass shootings alone. Stories about killing centres began to filter back into the ghettos of the Generalgouvernement shortly after the centres went into operation. By April 1942 a clandestine Jewish documentation unit in Warsaw, led by the historian and activist Emmanuel Ringelblum for the purpose of collecting and distributing information about the condition of Polish Jewry under German rule and the ways in which Jews were coping with occupation, had learned of the killing centres in Chełmno and Bełzec and understood that the Lublin Jews recently deported had been sent to their deaths. The next month the leadership of the underground Jewish socialist party, the **Bund**, concluded that the Germans had formulated a plan to kill all the Jews of Poland. It incorporated that assessment into a comprehensive report on Polish Jewry, which it delivered through Polish underground channels to the Polish government-in-exile in London [*Doc. 24*]. This report constituted the first detailed statement about killing centres received in the West and the first document to suggest that a programme to murder all Polish Jews was being implemented.

The Bund report, however, represented only the first stage in the gradual unfolding of Jewish awareness of Nazi designs. It demonstrated that segments of the Jewish political leadership in Poland understood the danger that faced their community, but it did not prove that all members of the community shared their appraisal. Little research has been done on how

Bund: Jewish socialist party founded in 1897. In interwar Poland it was one of the largest Jewish political movements, and it played an important role in underground activities in the Polish ghettos. Its report of May 1942 included the first statement that the Germans had a programme to kill all Polish Jews.

ordinary Polish Jews perceived their situation, and that research has been inconclusive. Moreover, the Bund's evaluation emphasized Poland, not other European countries. Jews in western, central, and south-eastern Europe, far removed from the killing centres, had to gather information on their own concerning the fate of their brethren deported to Poland and to derive the appropriate inference themselves, in the face of Nazi deception efforts and their own psychological indisposition to do so. Many, especially in western Europe, thought that even if stories of mass killing of Polish and Soviet Jews were true, their own fate would surely be different, because of their supposedly higher cultural level and their greater degree of integration into the surrounding society. In the end, it appears that only a relatively small number understood that 'resettlement to the east' almost invariably meant death. Postwar testimonies of the proportionately few survivors of deportations from France, Holland, Greece, Hungary, and other Nazi-dominated countries outside Poland indicate that many had no idea where they were going until they arrived.

In other words, the choices Jews made in responding to Nazi domination were not always informed ones.

COMMUNAL RESPONSIBILITY AND STRATEGIES FOR SURVIVAL

Generally, those best able to assess Nazi intentions were associated with groups that took responsibility for Jewish communities. Yet even among those who could make informed choices there was much diversity of response to the German threat once it became clear.

In most occupied countries the Germans imposed an official governing body upon the Jewish population, charging it with registering Jews and Jewish property, enforcing German directives, and maintaining health, welfare, and order among the Jewish population. In western Europe these were usually countrywide organizations, like the *Reichsvereinigung* in Germany, the *Joodse Raad* (Jewish Council) in Holland, the *Union Générale des Israélites de France*, or the *Association des Juifs en Belgique*. In Poland and the former Soviet-held territories, in contrast, each ghetto had its own 'Jewish council' or 'Council of Elders' (*Judenrat* or *Ältestenrat*), with no superior body to coordinate among them. The imposed Jewish administrations, which were in closer contact with the German authorities than other segments of Jewish society, were often among the first to pierce the Nazi veil of deception. Theoretically they were thus in a powerful position to influence their fellow Jews' behaviour in the face of the German murder programme. In practice, however, the degree and manner of their influence varied.

Understanding the responses of the official Jewish administrations to mass killing depends upon recognizing that, except in the former Soviet-held territories, they were established before systematic murder began. Consequently, prior to the onset of deportations to the killing centres, each had already developed a relationship with the occupiers. For the most part that relationship was predicated on the assumption that Germany would sooner or later be defeated, as it had been in the First World War. This was a comforting thought. So too was the prevailing perception that the occupiers were interested primarily in extracting as much wealth from Jews as possible, for if such was the case, then the Germans were treating Jews rationally as an economic resource and could be negotiated with on a rational basis. From these premises it followed that Jews needed primarily to buy time, to do what they could to cultivate the Germans' favour sufficiently to guarantee themselves the minimum conditions required for day-to-day survival and to forestall the execution of any long-range evil Nazi designs. The sensible thing to do was to give the Germans whatever they requested – usually money, property, or labour service – as long as it was possible to do so. Resistance to German demands would be counterproductive, as it might anger the occupiers to the point where they would cease to deal with the Jews rationally and begin to give violent expression to their hostile emotions. On the other hand, cooperation might inspire German confidence in the Jewish administration, which could perhaps be exploited at crucial points in order to improve day-to-day conditions of Jewish life.

An early example of such thinking in action came from Warsaw. In October 1939 German press gangs began kidnapping Jewish passers-by for forced labour details, making Jews fear to leave their homes. Their lives disrupted to the point of paralysis, some Jews turned to the recently established Judenrat in the hope that it could persuade the authorities to mitigate the terror the kidnappings had sown. Led by chairman Adam Czerniaków, the Judenrat proposed to take upon itself the responsibility of supplying the occupiers with labourers if the Germans would stop the random abductions. The authorities agreed. From that time the Judenrat conscripted a regular labour battalion, although kidnapping did not cease entirely [Doc. 25].

This episode illustrated the equivocal position in which the official Jewish administrations stood as intermediaries between the German occupiers and Jewish communities. In its effort to ameliorate Jewish hardship the Warsaw Judenrat had voluntarily undertaken to cater to German desires. It had also assumed the role of selecting the Jews to be delivered to the Germans for forced labour and compelling them to serve. In this way, as the initial impetus to its intervention was gradually forgotten, the Judenrat increasingly appeared to Warsaw Jews more as an instrument of German oppression than as a body fighting for Jewish interests. Yet the regulation of forced labour was actually one of the Warsaw *Judenrat*'s most notable successes. More often its interventions on the Jews' behalf were for naught; and, as Czerniaków noted in his diary, 'when my efforts fail . . . [the Jews] blame me . . . as if the outcome had depended on me' (Hilberg *et al.*, 1979: 172). Indeed, not only in Warsaw but in every Jewish community administered by a German-imposed governing body, the appointed community heads had virtually no leverage with the occupiers except bribery, which they had increasingly to finance with levies upon their charges. The Germans meant them to be their functionaries, often holding them personally responsible for the behaviour of their communities. Ironically, therefore, without making their communities serve German interests in some way, often against their will, they could not hope to win meaningful improvements for them.

Once mass killing began, the only meaningful improvement to be won was suspension of shooting or deportation. Some administrators who sensed the German intention – Efraim Barash in Białystok, Moshe Merin in Upper Silesia, M. H. Rumkowski in Łódź, Jakob Gens in Wilno – thought this goal could be achieved by demonstrating their communities' productive capacities: the Germans, thinking rationally, would not destroy a resource that contributed to their economy and war effort [*Doc.* 26]. There was logic to this approach; indeed, the places where it was tried generally held on longer than those where it was not. 70,000 Jews actually remained in the Łódź ghetto as late as August 1944, with the advancing Soviet army only 120 km away. However, because the murder programme was ultimately driven by ideology instead of rational calculation of interest, the strategy could hope at most only to achieve delay. Moreover, it carried a terrible price. It meant using the power of the Jewish administration to cajole or even force Jews to labour long and hard to meet oppressive German production demands. It also meant that Jewish administrators had to be prepared to forsake ill and elderly Jews who did not enhance production. In Łódź in September 1942 the head of the ghetto, Rumkowski, even responded to a German order to supply 20,000 Jews for deportation by handing over children under 10, arguing that it was necessary to 'cut off limbs to save the body itself' [*Doc.* 27]. Inducing Jews to accept such bitter toil and sacrifice required, among other things, convincing them that the Germans did not intend to kill them all, that deportations were meant merely to satisfy capricious cruelty, and that deportees were not necessarily murdered. Jewish administrators who adopted the '**salvation through work**' approach thus tended to pass on to their communities only calming assessments of Germans intentions. Some even suppressed information that might have led to a more pessimistic conclusion.

Other ghetto administrations – Lublin and Warsaw are notable examples – appear to have had no strategy at all for confronting deportation. Indeed, the Jewish leaders in those ghettos seem to have been caught unawares when

Salvation through work: Survival strategy employed by several Judenrat heads. It involved intensive Jewish-initiated exploitation of the industrial and labour resources of ghettos for German war production, in the hope that the Germans would regard Jews as too valuable to the German war effort to be killed.

some ghetto leaders were more aware than others

the liquidation of their communities began; they themselves tended to dis-miss information that might have led to an accurate appraisal of the threat that faced them. In his diary entries for 16–22 July 1942, the week before the deportations from Warsaw began, Czerniaków spoke about rumours of impending doom sweeping the ghetto; he tried to rebut them. When he was finally commanded to post a deportation order, he responded by taking his own life. Although by doing so he may have drawn a personal moral line, he also did not share his perception of threat with the ghetto population. Some ghetto residents later criticized his action for leaving them leaderless in a time of crisis [Doc. 28].

Indeed, in only a few cases, such as Kaunas and Minsk, were ghetto administrators a source of reliable evaluations about the fate in store for their communities. And even there, that intelligence was passed on not directly but through the intermediary of a parallel, unofficial leadership.

THE UNOFFICIAL COMMUNITY AND RESISTANCE

Amidah is welfare program for Jews

The fundamental predicament of the official Jewish administrations as German-controlled bodies and the tension inherent in their relations with their communities frequently prompted the establishment of voluntary com-munal institutions not beholden to the Germans in any way. Before the onset of mass killing such institutions played prominent roles in the Jews' daily struggle against poverty, starvation, disease, and hopelessness. Self-help organizations ran public kitchens, children's centres, refugee asylums, and medical clinics. Theatre groups, libraries, culture clubs, and music societies tried to raise the spirits of the oppressed. Recent studies have noted wide variation from place to place in the extent of undertakings of this sort – often designated by the Hebrew word *amidah*, a term best translated as 'durability' or 'keeping one's feet'. *Amidah* tended to be more common in larger concen-trations of Jews than in smaller ones – not a surprising finding, since it involved group activity, which could be sustained only by a critical mass of people. But research on several smaller ghettos in the eastern parts of Poland has demonstrated that *amidah* was possible – though far from universal – even in towns with only a few thousand Jews. Self-help activities have also been noted in less populous, more dispersed communities in France, the Benelux countries, Italy, Hungary, Greece, and Slovakia. The growing body of research on *amidah* appears to suggest that a crucial factor in determining its extent and shape was the nature of the German regime in any particular location. Where local German commanders pursued attritionist policies by imposing food restrictions that bred widespread starvation *amidah* was limited or non-existent, but where Jews were provided sufficient rations to exploit their labour it became a notable feature of Jewish life.

In any event, *amidah* had to be undertaken surreptitiously, for the Germans effectively outlawed most unofficial Jewish public activity. Thus schools and synagogues functioned underground; newspapers were published and distributed in secret. Where food rations were at starvation levels, clandestine smuggling operations sprang up. All such activity represented a form of resistance in that it actively combatted the deleterious effects of Nazi policies. But as such it also stood to compromise the official administrations, who could not allow the German authorities to perceive them as unwilling or unable to implement their designs [Doc. 29].

Hence voluntary institutions bred an alternative leadership. Often that leadership was provided by youth movements. In addition to their advantages in gathering and analysing information about Nazi plans, youth movements were well suited in other ways to perform this role. They inculcated in their members a powerful sense of mutual attachment and commitment, often taking on the role of surrogate families. Each movement thus created its own self-help apparatus to look after its members' welfare. The energy and skill that youth leaders brought to their task made their movements among the most effective sources of material and psychological support. In consequence, non-movement members soon gravitated towards them, to the point where the movements found themselves assuming increasing responsibility for their communities as a whole.

In a few places official administrations realized that by themselves they could not provide their charges with the physical and spiritual sustenance they required; thus they covertly assisted the alternative leadership or at least did not interfere with its operation. In these locations – again, most notably, Kaunas and Minsk – *Judenrat* heads shared information about Nazi designs with underground groups, thereby helping make their communities more aware of the threat they faced. More often, however, official and alternative leaders clashed with one another to a greater or lesser degree. Such clashes became especially acute once mass killing began. Although both leadership groups were among the first to grasp that every Jew had been placed under a death sentence, the youth movements usually drew operative conclusions radically different from those of the official administrators. Kovner's assessment that there was no escape from the death sentence and that flight and rescue were illusions led him to reject the 'salvation through work' approach of the head of the Wilno ghetto, Gens, in favour of a call to armed resistance [Doc. 22]. Despite some initial hesitation, other youth movement leaders eventually agreed: Between 1942 and 1944 Jewish armed resistance units were established in well over a hundred ghettos in the Generalgouvernement, Lithuania, and former Soviet territories.

The call to armed resistance represented a dramatic change in the strategy of the unofficial leadership, for it was not aimed primarily at survival. The heads of the Jewish fighting organizations had no illusions of forcing the Germans to abandon their murder programme, nor did they believe that taking up arms would save many Jewish lives. On the contrary, many hesitated out of fear that armed anti-German actions would invite mass reprisals – as indeed they sometimes did. Thus they adopted this path only after they were convinced that death for all Jews was certain; they saw armed resistance merely as a way to choose how they would die. Their own heroic deaths in battle would, they believed, strike a blow for the honour of the Jewish people in the face of Nazi efforts to rob Jews of their humanity; they would cause Jews to be remembered not as pathetic victims but as proud defenders of their collective integrity. As Dolek Liebeskind, leader of an underground fighting organization in the Kraków ghetto, explained in November 1942, 'We are fighting for three lines in history. For this our youth has fought and not gone like sheep to the slaughter. For this it is worthwhile even to die' (quoted in Peled, 1993: 163).

That message proved psychologically impossible for most Jews to accept; it meant giving up all hope of escaping the occupiers or outlasting them. Moreover, armed resistance was inherently an option open only to those in the ghettos physically fit for it, a number already reduced sharply by the regime of hunger and disease. And, because of a chronic scarcity of weapons, even many potential participants could not take part in actual fighting. For these reasons armed resistance never became a mass phenomenon. Nevertheless, in April 1943 the **Jewish Fighting Organization** in the Warsaw ghetto engaged German forces in battle for nineteen days before the ghetto was destroyed; at the time this was the largest military action undertaken by any conquered European population, Jewish or non-Jewish. Smaller-scale acts of confrontation, sabotage, or reprisal occurred in dozens of other ghettos. Similar actions were carried out by Jewish military organizations in France and Belgium, and a number of Jews in most European countries were active in general armed resistance movements. Jews fought with partisan units in most countries where such groups existed, and in Poland, the Baltic countries, and the occupied Soviet territories some specifically Jewish partisan units were formed.

In the end, though, Jews throughout Nazi-occupied Europe had virtually no realistic options for inducing the Germans to abandon their murder programme through their own actions. Individual Jews might hide or disguise themselves as non-Jews, but only with enormous difficulty; and they were almost always dependent upon non-Jewish assistance in finding shelter, obtaining food, and avoiding betrayal [*Doc. 30*]. A 2002 study of Jews from Warsaw who tried to survive outside the ghetto estimated their number at

Jewish Fighting Organization: Armed resistance group established in Warsaw in July 1942; principal force behind the Warsaw ghetto revolt. Branches were established in Białystok, Kraków, and other ghettos as well.

about 28,000, of whom 11,000 (fewer than 40 per cent) remained alive at the end of the war. Hiding thus turns out in retrospect to have been the most successful survival strategy (at least in the one city that has been investigated in detail). However, until the Warsaw ghetto was actually liquidated in April 1943 the risks involved in leaving appeared to most Jews – quite reasonably – to have exceeded those of staying in the ghetto.

In some places Jews organized to help other Jews flee to areas not under Nazi occupation. Most notably, beginning in 1942 a semi-clandestine Jewish formation in Bratislava, capital of Slovakia, known as the Working Group, cooperated with a similar association from Budapest called the Aid and Rescue Committee and a coalition of Zionist youth movement cells from south-western Poland in operating a sort of underground railway that managed to smuggle some 8,000 Jews from Slovakia, 4,000 from Germany, and 1,100 from Poland into Hungary, where until March 1944 Jews were relatively safe. About 2,000 additional Jewish refugees from Nazi-occupied areas managed to make their way into Hungary on their own. When Germany occupied Hungary in 1944, the Aid and Rescue Committee joined local Zionist youth movements in an effort to move Jews out of Hungary into unoccupied Romania. About 7,000 Jews were rescued through this endeavour, which went by the codename *tiyyul* – Hebrew for 'excursion'. But these activities, too, could not have succeeded to even the minimal extent that they did without significant non-Jewish action. Indeed, most Jews who survived under Nazi occupation could not have done so without substantial non-Jewish assistance. Similarly, at least some who perished undoubtedly met their deaths because such assistance was not forthcoming in sufficient measure.

LOCAL NON-JEWISH LEADERS AND POPULATIONS: OPPOSITION AND COMPLICITY

That non-Jews, especially local non-Jewish leaders, could make a vital difference was demonstrated most graphically by the dramatic rescue of Danish Jewry in October 1943. In the face of intelligence concerning an impending deportation, Danes – spurred by clergymen and social democratic activists – spontaneously warned Copenhagen's 8,000 Jews and helped them find hiding places. As a result, during a raid on 1–2 October fewer than 300 Jews were caught. Danish underground units subsequently arranged to ferry the hiding Jews to neutral Sweden. In the end, fewer than 2 per cent of Danish Jewry perished in the Holocaust. No other Jewish community had such a high survival rate.

There were six other European countries under Nazi influence where the majority of Jews survived the war – Belgium, Bulgaria, Finland, France, Italy, and Norway. In each the Germans encountered effective local opposition, in one form or another, to at least some facets of their deportation plans, though all but Finland had previously enacted Nazi-style anti-Jewish restrictions. Except in Norway, native governments or officials played a role in disrupting the plans made at Wannsee. Finland refused categorically to initiate any anti-Jewish actions except handing over eight refugees to the Germans. The Belgian civil service interfered with the execution of measures for identifying Jews; the underground warned of scheduled round-ups and conducted reprisals against Belgians who assisted in deportation efforts (even going so far as to assassinate the official of the Jewish administration who had been posting deportation orders). As long as they were able, the Italian authorities prevented German forces stationed on their territory from taking control of local Jews, while Italian soldiers occupying parts of France, Greece, and Yugoslavia actively aided Jews seeking refuge. The Vichy French government, though it showed little compunction about despatching the many non-French Jewish refugees in the country to the killing centres, drew the line at deporting Jews who were French citizens. In Bulgaria, vigorous protests from church leaders and intellectuals led the king and his government to defy German demands to deport Jews (although they permitted the extradition of almost all Jews from Thrace and Macedonia, formerly Greek and Yugoslav territories that Germany had helped Bulgaria to annex). Similar protests by church leaders in Norway did not dissuade the Norwegian puppet government from initiating deportations, but the underground helped over half of Norway's Jews escape to neutral Sweden.

Total or partial opposition to the German murder programme was facilitated in these countries by the relative freedom of action enjoyed in them by local officials. Yet, as the case of Norway shows, relative local autonomy did not guarantee protection in high places. In fact, in two Nazi satellite states, Slovakia and Croatia, the native governments actually precipitated deportations on their own. Slovak authorities consistently pressed the Germans to remove Jews from the country, even offering to pay for each Jew sent away. In Croatia much actual killing was done by the **Ustaše**, a state-sponsored militia, which not only perpetrated pogroms with shocking brutality but erected special camps where incarcerated Jews (and Serbs) were shot, beaten, or hacked to death. Little wonder that in these two countries the percentage of Jews killed was among the highest.

In Romania, another independent ally of Germany, the government's Jewish policy varied over time and space. Jews in the outlying provinces of Bessarabia and Northern Bukovina suffered especially from official and popular vindictiveness. Romania had lost these regions to the Soviet Union

Ustaše: (Serbo-Croat: Insurgents) Units of a right-wing Croatian nationalist separatist paramilitary organization, led by Ante Pavelić. They came to power with Germany's creation of an independent Croatian satellite in 1941 and, without German assistance, initiated mass killings of non-Croatians, including 500,000 Serbs, 35,000 Jews, and 20,000 Gypsies.

in June 1940; the loss had been blamed partly on the alleged treachery of local Jews, who were associated stereotypically with communism. A year later Romania joined Germany in invading the USSR and recovered the lost provinces. Much of the populace assisted the Romanian army (together with the German *Einsatzgruppe* D) in taking violent revenge, killing upwards of 160,000 Jews, while the government made plans to deport the survivors of the massacre to Transnistria, the former Soviet territory between the Dniester and Bug Rivers now occupied by Romanian troops, as a prelude to their eventual transfer to German hands. The transfer to the Germans was never completed, but some 150,000 Jews were removed to Transnistrian camps, with 25,000 dying en route and another 80,000 dying over the next three years. On the other hand, the 250,000 Jews of the so-called Regat, or Old Romania, were for the most part not subjected to systematic violence, except for the June 1941 pogrom in Iaşi, which claimed the lives of perhaps a third of the town's 34,000 Jewish residents. To be sure, Regat Jews suffered from increasingly severe legal restrictions, expropriation measures, and forced labour, and Jewish males from certain towns were incarcerated in detention camps. Some historians have argued that these steps were undertaken in anticipation of eventual Romanian cooperation in the Nazi killing programme. However, from late 1942 dictator Ion Antonescu, with the support of much of the country's political and military leadership, resisted German deportation demands. This reversal was evidently caused by a growing sense that Germany would lose the war; Romania did not wish to be implicated any further in mass killing. Thus, whereas most Bukovinian and Bessarabian Jews perished, most Jews from Old Romania survived.

Regat: Area of Romania comprising the two original Romanian provinces of Moldavia and Wallachia, excluding outlying regions (including Bukovina, Bessarabia, and Transylvania) annexed from 1913 on. Despite German pressure, Romanian dictator Antonescu refused to turn Regat Jews over to the Germans for deportation.

Among other things, the Romanian example indicates that the behaviour of local leadership groups in German-allied countries could fluctuate with changes in the tenor of the alliance. So too does the case of Hungary, although the weakening of Hungarian confidence in a German victory affected the fate of that country's Jews rather differently than did the same development in Romania. Hungarian regent Horthy insisted upon retaining control over the 725,000 Jews of his realm, which included not only Hungary proper but extensive additional territories taken from Czechoslovakia, Yugoslavia, and Romania between 1938 and 1941. Between 1941 and 1944 his governments limited Jewish civic and economic freedoms severely and conscripted 50,000 Jews for labour service on the Soviet front (42,000 of whom lost their lives during the Soviet counter-offensive of January 1943). They were also prepared at one point to turn over 100,000 Jews from the additional territories to the Germans as forced labourers. But, aside from a single deportation of 18,000 such Jews in 1941, they did not contemplate participation in the murder plan. The situation changed abruptly, however, in March 1944: after Hungary, convinced that Germany was about to be defeated, sent out peace feelers to the West, German forces occupied the country, Horthy retired from active political involvement, and a new government, headed by the former Hungarian ambassador in Berlin and heavily influenced by German advisors, was established. This government ordered the immediate ghettoization and deportation of Hungary's Jews. Between 15 May and 9 July 1944, over 430,000 Jews were sent to Poland, mostly to the killing centre at Birkenau. A temporary respite was achieved in July, when Horthy, responding to entreaties from Western leaders and the Vatican, resumed his central role in politics, ordered a halt to the deportation of Jews from Budapest, and eventually removed the pro-German government. Two months later, though, the **Arrow Cross**, a Hungarian fascist party, toppled Horthy. By that time Soviet advances made deportation of Jews to killing centres impossible, but the Arrow Cross militia randomly shot thousands of Budapest Jews, placed thousands more in slave labour camps, and forcibly marched 70,000 overland to build defences for Vienna. In all, about 70 per cent of Hungarian Jewry was killed over a four-month interval.

No doubt the ability of local leaders in countries where local leaderships existed legally to protect or to harm Jews as they saw fit was enhanced by the Germans' relatively greater concern with the Jews in the countries that they controlled directly – most notably Poland, the Baltic states, and the Soviet regions. In these countries there was no Nazi-allied government or bureaucracy that could have affected the execution of the murder programme in any way; instead, the Germans recruited local sympathizers directly to serve as auxiliary policemen and guards at labour camps and killing centres and to assist in shooting operations. Indeed, Estonian, Latvian, and Lithuanian volunteers played a crucial role in locating Jews and handing them over to the *Einsatzgruppen*, while a German-sponsored Ukrainian militia launched pogroms on its own volition and later became an integral element in the liquidation of several ghettos. A native Polish police force also was often called upon – together with Jewish ghetto policemen enlisted by the Germans – to patrol ghetto walls, round up Jews for deportation, and hunt Jews in hiding. The participation of Poles in such actions, however, was roundly condemned by a highly ramified Polish civilian and military underground, which presided over what came to be called a 'secret state'. This clandestine leadership – whose size, range of activities, and popular support far exceeded that of underground formations in the other occupied countries under direct German control – was in a position to do much that could affect the fate of many individual Jews, even if it could not stop the German murder campaign to the extent possible in countries with legal local leaderships: it could locate hiding places for Jews seeking to avoid deportation; provide them with food, money, and false identity papers; help them across borders to countries where the danger was less immediate; and supply arms to Jewish

Arrow Cross: Radical right-wing Hungarian party founded by Ferenc Szálasi in 1939. It opposed the conservative Hungarian governments appointed by Miklos Horthy and was suppressed by them, even though those governments, like the Arrow Cross, favoured alliance with Nazi Germany. When Horthy sought to abandon the German alliance, the Arrow Cross militia, supported by German troops, staged a *coup d'état*. Once in control, the Arrow Cross began shooting, incarcerating, and deporting what remained of Hungarian Jewry. It is estimated that over 80,000 Jews fell victim to Arrow Cross violence.

resistance groups. It could also take direct action to sabotage deportation transports or killing centres, and it could transmit information about mass killing abroad in a way that might arouse bystanders outside the Nazi orbit to action.

The Polish underground and the London-based Polish government-in-exile that supervised it did many of these things, although usually to only a limited extent. In late 1942 a special Council for Aid to Jews, known by the cryptonym *Żegota*, was formed under Polish underground auspices to help Jews hide from their would-be executioners [*Doc. 31*]. This was the only such organization identified to date anywhere in Nazi-occupied Europe. On the other hand, it was founded only after half of Polish Jewry had already been killed, it was chronically underfunded, and it managed in the end to assist at most only 4,000 people. The Polish government-in-exile was a primary link in informing British, American, and other Western leaders about the Nazi murder programme; in fact, it was the first governmental body to confirm the programme's existence. However, it did not always transmit all the information in its possession, and it often subsumed the Jewish situation within the broader plight of the Polish people. The Polish military underground supplied some light arms to the Jewish Fighting Organization in Warsaw, but the supply represented only a small part of its available arsenal. Accounting for these actions and their limited nature is a matter of considerable scholarly debate, with some historians stressing objective constraints on the extent to which Poles could come to Jews' aid, others stressing subjective disinclination on the part of the Polish leadership to assist a people that it continued to regard as fundamentally alien. In the end, in the words of one scholar, it appears that the behaviour of the Polish leadership towards Jews 'was forged out of an entire range of factors, both of principle and of self-interest, both hereditary . . . and conjunctural' (Engel, 1987: 213).

A similar range of factors must be adduced to explain the variations in the behaviour of local non-Jewish leaders in all of the countries within the Nazi orbit. It is tempting to hypothesize a direct correlation between cooperation in the deportation of Jews and the pervasiveness of anti-Jewish prejudices among various populations, as sociologist Helen Fein did in 1979. Yet Romania and Hungary were countries where local authorities resisted deportation despite widespread popular dislike and suspicion of Jews. Moreover, these leaders' actions had much in common with those of the governments of France and Bulgaria, even though on the whole French and Bulgarian Jews enjoyed a significantly greater degree of social and political acceptance than did their Romanian or Hungarian coreligionists. In all four countries the authorities appear to have regarded retaining control over the fate of their Jews as symbolic of their own independence from Germany. But why did Slovak leaders not feel the same way? Why, too, did the Romanian dictator,

Żegota: Code name for the Council for Aid to Jews, established under the aegis of the Polish underground in December 1942. It assisted some 4,000 Polish Jews to maintain themselves in hiding or under cover of false identity during the German occupation.

like the leader of Croatia, countenance mass killing of Jews by forces under his control, while his Hungarian counterpart – a man of similar background and political beliefs – recoiled at the thought? And why did the government of Norway – a country with a miniscule Jewish population and virtually no anti-Jewish tradition – cooperate in deporting Jews almost as enthusiastically as did the authorities in Slovakia? Answers to these questions must no doubt take into account, among other things, the specific internal political and social conditions that prevailed in each country during the war years. Evaluating those conditions and relating them to the attitudes and actions of leadership groups towards Jews remains a largely unfulfilled task in contemporary Holocaust research.

But local leadership groups, whether legal or illegal, were not the only bystanders in a position to influence the fate of Jews. Individual victims and survivors, especially in the countries under direct German control, often were affected by the actions of non-Jewish neighbours acting on their own initiative. Virtually all Jews who survived in hiding or under cover of a false identity succeeded thanks to non-Jews who assisted them. Others survived because of the readiness of individuals with influence to protect them (like the German entrepreneur Schindler, who fought to prevent the deportation of his factory's Jewish workers). There were such 'righteous gentiles' in every country: over 8,000 have been recognized by **Yad Vashem**, the Israeli Holocaust memorial authority – most for hiding Jews in their homes for extended periods, usually risking their lives (and their families') to do so. One study of these individuals has suggested that they came from all social classes and walks of life but shared a strong ability to withstand social pressure and a sense that helping someone in need was the only course of action they could imagine taking. On the other hand, virtually every Jew in hiding lived under the constant threat of betrayal or blackmail. The case of Anne Frank and her family in Holland is probably the best known instance of the threat becoming real, but its extent was considerable in other countries as well. The Polish Council for Aid to Jews regularly called attention to the phenomenon, noting its continual increase despite efforts to suppress it and charging that it made the Council's work impossible [Doc. 32].

Assistance and betrayal were both atypical phenomena, however. Although the issue has not been systematically studied for any country, it seems likely that for the large majority of individuals within the Nazi orbit the fate of their Jewish neighbours was at most a matter of peripheral concern. Thus few were likely to go out of their way either to help or to harm Jews. Such disregard, however, ultimately played into German hands: if survivors owed their lives to the willingness of non-Jews to aid them, how many victims owed their deaths to the unwillingness of other non-Jews to do the same?

Yad Vashem: The official Israeli institution for studying and commemorating the Holocaust. Among other activities it maintains an extensive library and archive; it also honours and gathers information about non-Jews who risked their lives to assist Jews during the Holocaust.

BEYOND THE NAZI REALM

Another type of agent might have taken significant rescue action – the governments of Allied and neutral countries beyond the Nazi realm. Those governments had periodically protested persecution of German Jews before the beginning of mass killing, although on the whole they had shown only the most grudging willingness to provide sanctuary for those fleeing the Nazi terror and had taken little notice of the plight of Jews in other countries within the Nazi orbit. From late 1941 and throughout 1942 reports of mass killings reached the Soviets, the West, and outlying areas through a variety of channels. Recipients of those reports, however, faced even greater problems of imagination and analysis than did people who experienced the Nazi regime up close: officials in wartime London or Washington, working in the familiar, relatively tranquil surroundings of St James's Park or the Capitol Mall, could hardly grasp, as historian Bernard Wasserstein put it, that 'the agony of European Jewry was enacted in . . . a grim twilight world where their conventional moral code did not apply' (Wasserstein, 1979: 357). Thus the Bund report of May 1942 does not appear to have had much lasting effect upon the consciousness of Allied or neutral policymakers. Only in December 1942, following Polish underground courier Jan Karski's arrival in London, did the three principal Allies and the exile governments of nine occupied countries officially note and condemn the Germans' 'bestial policy of cold-blooded extermination'.

Karski brought to London and Washington a demand from Jewish resistance organizations in Poland to 'adjust [the strategy of war] to include the rescue of a fraction of the . . . Jewish people' (Karski, 1944: 328). On behalf of the Jewish leaders he asked the Allies to negotiate exchanges of Jews for German prisoners or for ransom, to drop leaflets from the air upon German cities informing the German people what their government was doing to Europe's Jews, and to send supplies (especially blank passports) that might help Jews escape or survive in hiding. Other Jewish spokesmen outside occupied Europe called upon Allies and neutrals to open their gates to Jewish escapees requiring temporary asylum, to warn Germans that the deportation and murder of Jews would be punished after the war, to create special government bodies to explore ongoing rescue opportunities, and to bomb the killing centre at Auschwitz-Birkenau and the rail lines leading to it.

For the most part, these demands were either ignored or rebuffed. Following their December 1942 statement, the Allies took no further official joint public notice of the German killing programme. An Anglo-American conference on refugees was held at **Bermuda** in April 1943, but no action stemmed from it. A February 1943 Romanian proposal to release 70,000 Jews from Transnistria in return for payment was rejected by the British and

Bermuda Conference: Anglo-American conference on refugees held on the Caribbean island of Bermuda, 19–30 April 1943. It was marked mostly by disagreements between the parties and the fear that concerted action to rescue Jews from Nazi-controlled Europe would interfere with the Allied war effort. The only substantive decision taken was to extend the mandate of the Intergovernmental Committee on Refugees that had been established at the Evian Conference of 1938.

US governments, as was an April 1944 German offer to exchange a million Jews, including all the Jews of Hungary, for 10,000 trucks and amounts of various foodstuffs. No Allied or neutral country expressed readiness to take in large numbers of Jewish exchangees or escapees (except Sweden with regard to Jews from other Scandinavian countries); in particular, British restrictions on Jewish immigration to Palestine were not lifted, and Jews attempting to make their way to the country were intercepted and imprisoned. Auschwitz was not bombed. To be sure, the US **War Refugee Board**, established in January 1944, catalysed the return of the survivors of the Transnistrian camps to Old Romania the following March and helped generate the international pressure that prompted Horthy's cessation of the Hungarian deportations in July. The Board was also active in searching for havens for the minority of Europe's Jews that remained alive in the last year of the war, and it underwrote the mission of Swedish diplomat Raoul Wallenberg to Budapest, through which some 20,000 Jews were rescued from deportation with the aid of special protective passports issued by the Swedish and other governments. However, even its chairman characterized the Board's activity as too little, too late.

War Refugee Board: US government agency established in January 1944 to explore possibilities for rescuing European Jews.

Historians have advanced various explanations for the relative paucity of significant Allied and neutral rescue action. Some have stressed faulty perception, reiterating that the enormity and unprecedented nature of the Nazi crime prevented real understanding of the threat facing Jews (even after reliable reports of mass killing had been confirmed) and suggesting that had the shock of the news not been so great, Allied and neutral policymakers would have accorded rescue high priority. Others, in contrast, have argued that Jewish matters would in any case not have been a central concern, whether because of the single-minded attention the combatants needed to devote to winning the war, the lack of Jewish political leverage in a situation where free-world Jewish groups would have to support the Allied cause enthusiastically in any case, or personal ill-will towards Jews on the part of certain officials in key positions. In fact, claimed historian Walter Laqueur, it was precisely the low priority that Allied bureaucrats gave the Jewish situation that allowed them to pass lightly over reports of mass murder without seriously considering their implications.

In the end, though, it appears that the Allied and neutral governments did not do more to extricate European Jews from their mortal peril because the only reason that could be adduced for them to do so was a moral one. Allies fighting a bloody and protracted war that demanded the full measure of their concentration and resources, and neutrals striving to avoid their own possible occupation, found accession to such a moral argument an unaffordable luxury. No country could see any compelling political, strategic, or legal reason to 'adjust [the strategy of war] to include' the rescue of Jews who were not its citizens. What Helen Fein called 'the organizational incapacity and unreadiness among nation-states to protect members of other nation-states' made rescue from beyond the Nazi realm a most improbable expectation (Fein, 1979: 166).

8

Humanity, modernity, and the Holocaust

The Allies claimed that they could contribute best to rescuing Jews by winning the war as quickly as possible. Indeed, in the end only the Allied victory put an end to the murder campaign. The gas chambers at Birkenau functioned until November 1944, when, in anticipation of imminent conquest by Soviet forces, the last remaining Jewish and non-Jewish prisoners from Auschwitz and other concentration and labour camps in Poland were evacuated and forcibly marched to Germany proper. Some 250,000 Jews and non-Jews died in these so-called **death marches**. Those who survived spent the final weeks of the war in Dachau, Buchenwald, and other German camps, where they were liberated by British and US forces in April–May 1945. Photographs of these prisoners have become standard images of the Holocaust. At the time they were first published they were greeted with shock and disbelief. They have continued to arouse horror and fascination ever since.

This book began by suggesting that a dispassionate look at the basic facts of the encounter between the Third Reich and the Jews and their placement in a historical context might dispel the sense of mystery and bewilderment that encountering the Holocaust often sparks and render comprehensible events that could not be imagined at the time they occurred. Now, after having laid out the basic features of such a historical approach, it seems appropriate to ask to what extent that proposition has been proved.

Saul Friedländer, who has spent most of his adult life applying the tools of the professional historian in an effort to understand the Holocaust, has written of 'the unease in historical interpretation' of such a seemingly unimaginable set of events. In his words, 'for some historians . . . an opaqueness remains at the very core of the historical understanding and interpretation of what happened' (Friedländer, 1992: 103). Although the accumulation of factual knowledge in the nearly seven decades since the end of the Second World War is impressive, he has argued, 'there is no clearer perspective today, no deeper comprehension than immediately after the war' (Friedländer, 1981: 1).

Death marches: Forced marches of prisoners over long distances, accompanied by brutal treatment. The term is most commonly applied to the march from Budapest to Vienna in November 1944 and to the westward march of prisoners from labour and concentration camps east of Berlin during the first four months of 1945, in flight from the advancing Soviet army.

But if so much factual knowledge has been amassed over the past half century, what exactly remains opaque? Murder investigations generally concentrate upon three questions – motive, means, and opportunity. The story of how the Third Reich, together with some of its allies, acquired the opportunity to cause the deaths of some 5.8 million Jews seems fairly straightforward: the sources of the Nazi party's accession to power in Germany, its diplomatic and military triumphs that brought almost 9 million Jews within its reach between 1933 and 1945, and the frequent (if not unlimited) ability of German agencies to do with those Jews as they wished may still be the subject of debates over details, but in no interpretation do they appear so mysterious as to defy understanding. The same is true regarding the means of murder: no great flights of imagination are necessary to comprehend how a decision to commence mass killing, once taken, could be executed. The unease in interpretation thus would seem to be concentrated about the issue of motive. Indeed, the question of why a decision to commence systematic mass killing of Jews was taken in the first place (together with the corollary questions of when the decision was taken and by whom) has demanded by far the most strenuous efforts at solution.

Not that historical research has not made headway. On the contrary, it has revealed quite clearly the precarious logic by which, at the beginning of the twentieth century, a person prepared to question the data of his senses could infer from certain widely accepted contemporary principles of biology and anthropology that Jews were literally non-human parasites threatening all humanity and needing to be killed for the sake of human survival. It has explicated the social, psychological, and organizational dynamics and the particular historical circumstances that could turn 'ordinary men' into mass killers when prodded by a critical mass of true believers who accepted such a picture of Jews. And it has raised plausible suggestions about how, in the aftermath of the First World War, such a critical mass was generated precisely within *German* society. New facts and insights continue to be adduced constantly and to refine analysis of these matters. Historians disagree strongly, to be sure, about the relative importance of each of these factors in precipitating the decision to kill, but that such factors could, in whatever combination, have generated a Holocaust does not seem unfathomable.

Nonetheless, certain features of the encounter between the Third Reich and the Jews continue to remain a mystery for many historians. Though there are some dissenting voices, most scholars today believe that Nazi leaders viewed the systematic murder of Jews not as a means to any rationally understandable goal but as an *end in itself*, whose success was its own justification. They consider that such murder was intended to be *total*, to lead to the death of every single Jewish man, woman, and child within the Third Reich's reach; no Jew was ultimately to be allowed to escape. They note, too, that the decision to murder had *nothing to do with Jewish behaviour*, even in the word's broadest possible sense. The murderers were unconcerned with where particular Jews lived, what languages they spoke, how they dressed, what they believed about God, or even whether they regarded themselves as Jews or not; anyone whom German law (or the laws of Germany's allies) identified as a Jew was automatically sentenced to death by virtue of that fact alone. Finally, most historians recognize that the ultimate justification for total murder lay in the conviction that Jews were not human beings, that their very existence endangered not only Germany but humanity as a whole, and that therefore the killing of each and every one of them was imperative. Historians have debated whether this conviction had *necessarily* to lead to total murder, but the large majority agree that total murder could not have been pursued in its absence; killing operations would not have reached the dimensions that they did without such ideological justification affirmed at the very highest levels of the Nazi hierarchy.

What continues to baffle many historians about these realizations is their implication that the Third Reich operated within a *totally foreign universe of discourse*, according to rules for perceiving and conceiving reality entirely beyond the experience of any contemporary society. Saul Friedländer called attention to a speech by Himmler to senior SS officers in Poznań in October 1943 to illustrate this absolute foreignness [*Doc. 33*]. He reasoned that Himmler must have grasped that no one but Nazi initiates would ever understand how the slaughter of each and every Jew within the Reich's reach could be considered a 'page of glory' in German history; otherwise he would not have acknowledged that the glorious page could never be written. Present-day readers of the speech must thus, according to Friedländer, ultimately face it with incredulity. Although, in his words, 'on the basis of the assumption of sharing a common humanity and even a common historical experience, and thus basically common perceptions of human existence in society, we try to overcome the feeling of strangeness and horror and try to find the point of psychological identity', all such efforts are doomed to failure, for there is nothing in the experience of non-Nazis that can enable them to penetrate the Nazi conceptual domain (Friedländer, 1992: 108). That conceptual domain, Friedländer has argued, will always remain opaque.

But does that conclusion negate the historical approach altogether? Evidently those historians who share Friedländer's position are prepared to wrestle continuously with the 'non-congruence between intellectual probing and the blocking of intuitive comprehension' (Friedländer, 1992: 111); they continue to find value in historical research, if not as a means to ultimate understanding then at least as a tool for describing the course of the Holocaust accurately. Yet not all share it. For intellectual historian Amos Funkenstein, 'the crime committed by the Nazis was of immense proportions; the horror and the suffering transgress our capacity of imagination, but it is possible to understand them rationally. Even if the perpetrators of the crime were madmen who lost all touch with reality, a reconstruction of their mentality and patterns of action would be possible'. In the end, according to Funkenstein, the Holocaust was perpetrated by flesh and blood human beings subject to the same biological and social constraints as all other humans; indeed, 'it pointed at a possibility . . . of human existence, a possibility as human as the best instances of creativity and compassion'. Thus 'historians, psychologists, sociologists, and philosophers ought to . . . be guided by the reasonable expectation that they can comprehend it' (Funkenstein, 1989: 302–03).

Acknowledging the particular possibility of human existence represented by the Holocaust and facing its implications, however, can be frightening. Perhaps speaking of the Holocaust as mysterious, opaque, or inconceivable is at bottom a way of coping with the fright. Yehiel De-Nur, a Holocaust survivor and prominent fiction writer whose metaphor of Auschwitz as 'another planet' evoked the idea of opaqueness more concisely and memorably than any historian's lament about inability to comprehend, appears himself to have reached this conclusion following an especially upsetting course of introspection. In 1976, at a psychiatric clinic in Leiden in the Netherlands, he underwent therapy to uncover 'the secret of the nightmares that had visited me night after night these last thirty years'. The treatment involved injections of the hallucinogenic drug LSD, which induced a series of terrifying visions. In one episode he saw himself as a corpse on a truck headed to a crematorium; the truck was guarded by a 'yawning German'. 'All I know about this German', De-Nur explained, 'is that on a cold morning like this he'd certainly prefer snuggling under the covers of his warm bed without having to get up this early because of some load that has to leave for the crematorium'. This glimpse of the executioner feeling a human sensation, even one so emotionally detached from the situation, generated

all at once an additional horror . . . . : if this is so, then he could have been standing here in my place, a naked skeleton in this truck, while I, I could have been standing there instead of him, on just such a cold morning doing my job delivering him and millions like him to the crematorium – and like him I, too, would yawn, because like him I'd certainly prefer snuggling under the covers of my warm bed on a cold morning like this.
(Ka-Tzetnik, 1989: x, 10)

As a result of his visions – which also included one in which the smoke rising from the chimney of the Birkenau crematorium turned first into the face of Satan, then into his own face, while Satan's servants proclaimed the young victim sovereign of the universe and named him Nucleus – De-Nur repudiated the 'other planet' image, concluding that 'wherever there is humankind, there is Auschwitz; it wasn't Satan who created . . . Nucleus, but you and I' (Ka-Tzetnik, 1989: 107). It was this realization that freed him from what had until then been his inability to speak of the Holocaust except through the medium of third-person fiction. The Holocaust, he seemed to suggest, is indeed imaginable and expressible, but only to those prepared radically to adjust their thinking about the fundamental nature of human beings.

Unfortunately, he did not indicate what specific adjustment is required. Indeed, beyond some rather commonplace statements about how the Holocaust demonstrates that the capacity of human beings to do evil to one another is far greater than anyone had imagined earlier, the fundamental rethinking that the Holocaust demands does not seem to have proceeded very far. Actually, the most serious attempts at rethinking have focused not upon humanity in general but upon *modern* humanity. Zygmunt Bauman has argued implicitly that not any human society, but only one valuing 'the social norms and institutions of modernity' – rationality and science, planning and efficiency, objectivity and uniformity – is capable of conceiving and per-petrating systematic mass murder of the Nazi variety (Bauman, 1989: 87). What impressed him most about the Holocaust (as it had Hilberg and many others) was the role of the German bureaucracy in laying the groundwork for killing – defining Jews, keeping files on them, segregating and isolating them, and finally arranging the logistics of despatching them to the killing centres. Had there not been a bureaucracy willing and able to take on these tasks, Bauman claimed, the Holocaust could not have happened. But in his opinion, the availability of such a bureaucracy could be taken for granted, for all modern states depend for their very existence upon a large bureaucratic administration, organized and trained to control populations impersonally and impartially, according to whatever rules their state sets for them, without reflecting on the ethical implications of the rules or their administration. Thus, he suggested, any state with a modern 'bureaucracy is intrinsically *capable* of genocidal action', provided it is governed by an 'ideologically obsessed power elite' determined to enforce 'a grand vision of a better, and radically different, society' by any means necessary (Bauman, 1989: 91, 94, 106). Such, for Bauman, was the Nazi leadership, but under certain condi-tions any leadership passionately committed to a utopian vision of a perfect society can, with bureaucratic assistance, destroy all who do not fit its scheme. Hence the Holocaust must precipitate thoroughgoing criticism of modern Western civilization.

Bauman's analysis has many supporters; it has many detractors as well. Some argue that although the Nazis may have employed modern means to perpetrate murder on such a mass scale, their motives were not modern at all: Jews were killed precisely because, having benefited most conspicuously from capitalism, rationalism, and political centralization and the concomitant ideas of individual freedom and equality, they symbolized some of the most notable features of modernity – features the Nazis vigorously denounced. This argument implies that commitment to those modern values, not criticism of them, stands as a safeguard against possible repetition of a Nazi-style total murder programme. Others deny that Jews were killed because they interfered with any particular utopian vision: what prompted the Third Reich to pursue them so relentlessly and systematically was ultimately Hitler's world view, which represented them as a mortal danger to human survival in any form, utopian or not. Still others contend that even modern means, including bureaucracy, were not intrinsic to the Holocaust. They point out that the *Einsatzgruppen* murders in the Soviet Union and killings by shooting squads elsewhere were accomplished without benefit of any bureaucratic preliminaries of identification, segregation, and removal, and that the abandonment of the shooting method was prompted by considerations of convenience, not necessity; thus, they claim, the Germans, had they wished, could have pursued their murder programme without bureaucratic assistance at all.

Who is right? The test of any of the propositions advanced for or against the modernity thesis lies in the documentary record that historians of the Holocaust have been seeking, uncovering, and analysing for nearly seventy years. Since the early twenty-first century, new discoveries in and understandings of that record have pointed to additional reasons for questioning just how essentially 'modern' a phenomenon the Holocaust was. In particular, research into the participation of local populations in the killing of Jews, especially on the eastern front following Germany's invasion of the Soviet Union in mid-1941, together with a number of studies about the manner in which Jews and non-Jews in several east European towns interacted daily with one another in the years before the German conquest, has suggested to some historians that, in some places at least, the mass murder of Jews, far from being the handiwork of a ramified bureaucracy or sophisticated technologies, actually sprang directly from within the fabric of the intimate communal existence that modernity is supposed to have destroyed. In Jedwabne and several dozen other nearby locations studied mainly by Polish scholars since 2000 (where Jews were sometimes burned or clubbed to death – means of murder that had been available long before the advent of modernity) killings were generally not depersonalized acts marked by division of labour, fragmentation of the moral burden, and absence of true community. Quite the contrary, not only did victims and killers see each other face to face at the moment of murder, they actually knew one another; they had lived side-by-side with one another for decades, gone to school together, bought and sold from one another, attended the same entertainments, participated in the same civic ceremonies, even played football with one another. Indeed, Holocaust survivors from Jedwabne recalled that they had been intimately imbricated in the pre-war life of their town; they made up half of its inhabitants and carried on a reasonably calm, if not completely tension-free, day-to-day interaction with their Polish neighbours, to whom they related on a first-name basis. Such was the pattern of existence in thousands of small towns across the east-central European Jewish heartland, where, as the title of a recent book by Shimon Redlich on the east Galician town of Brzeżany (today the west Ukrainian town of Berezhany) suggests, Jews and non-Jews lived simultaneously 'together and apart', their lives intertwined in complex webs of relationships marked by multiple valences and levels of intimacy that fluctuated largely according to the immediate circumstances of interaction (Redlich, 2002). Sometimes those webs provided Jews with connections for escaping the sentence of death that was placed upon them, as they did in the case of Redlich's own family, which was saved thanks to the combined, cooperative efforts of a Pole and a Ukrainian on its behalf. More often, though, they functioned as instruments of entrapment; far from insulating against genocide born of modern depersonalization and alienation, social proximity and familiarity could actually breed genocidal impulses once the restraints of the modern impersonal rule of law were cast off.

In other words, recent research has suggested a new set of images for epitomizing the Holocaust – images that do not supplant entirely the icons of bureaucrat, boxcar, and barbed wire central to most popular representations of the Holocaust but that must now supplement them. These new images – the shooting pit, the burning barn, the murderous neighbour poised to strike his fellow townsman, the look in the face of the fellow townsman upon realizing that his erstwhile schoolmate, customer, supplier, or football opponent was about to take his life – while not undermining entirely the notion that modernity offers no foolproof safeguards against genocide, will not easily support Bauman's contention that 'without modern civilization and its most essential achievements, there would be no Holocaust' (Bauman, 1989: 87) or the suggestion that the smaller-scale, more intimate preindustrial world we have supposedly lost is inherently more secure and beneficent than the impersonal existence of the industrial era.

But neither can the modern features of the Holocaust be easily dismissed. Few scholars will dispute the proposition that the Holocaust would likely not have attained the dimensions it ultimately did without the bureaucratic organization and technological implementation that characterized its central and western European manifestations more than its east European ones. Some historians have also suggested that other features of late nineteenth- and early twentieth-century European history that Bauman did not see implicated directly in the Holocaust – the universalization of the market economy, for example, or the subordination of citizenship to ethnicity by the nation-state, or the incorporation of the countryside into the arena of mass politics – created ultimately catastrophic runs in the fabric of communities like Jedwabne in ways that have yet to be fully fathomed.

These suggestions, in turn, have prompted the question of whether the Holocaust's modern and pre-modern aspects can be understood together within a single conceptual framework. Since the 1960s, most historians have separated out the encounter between the Third Reich and the Jews from all of the other horrors perpetrated by the Third Reich against a wide range of victims and assigned it a name of its own. That assignment has helped them identify some of the peculiar features of that encounter that challenge most powerfully our self-understanding as human beings. But at the same time it turns out to have obscured somewhat the wide variety of experiences that have been subsumed collectively under the single designation, 'the Holocaust'. That variety has suggested to some scholars that perhaps the encounter between the Third Reich and the Jews is best conceived not as one indivisible whole but rather as a composite, as a set of events consisting not of one but of several smaller, local 'holocausts', some complete, others aborted, each having its own particular history. Those particular histories clearly bear important similarities to the histories of the encounter between the Third Reich and the Jews in other places, but they surely display notable differences as well. One of the potential benefits of disaggregating the concept of 'the Holocaust' in this way is that it allows both the modern and the pre-modern features of the encounter their appropriate place in the historical narrative. The degree to which those features figured in the encounter's outcome can be said to have varied significantly from place to place.

Like any other thesis about the Holocaust and its implications for human self-understanding, this thesis too will always be subject to validation by the documentary record. The broad contours of that record have been outlined in the preceding pages, as have some of the difficulties the record presents. The work of discovery and analysis is still far from complete, as is the confrontation with its fundamental import. Whether these efforts will ever reach the point where the feeling of mystery and the sense of 'opaqueness at the core' will be banished altogether is doubtful. But the historical approach to the Holocaust has brought and continues to bring to light a significant body of knowledge that can, when perceptively and judiciously interpreted, help make the core clearer, at least for some.

Part 2

DOCUMENTS

Document 1   THE DEFINITION OF 'GENOCIDE', BY THE WORD'S INVENTOR

Raphael Lemkin had arrived in the United States as a refugee only three years before the Carnegie Endowment for International Peace published his analysis of the legal systems in countries under the influence of the Third Reich. In it he introduced a new concept, 'genocide', defined below.

By 'genocide' we mean the destruction of a nation or of an ethnic group. This new word . . . is made from the ancient Greek word *genos* (race, tribe) and the Latin *cide* (killing), thus corresponding . . . to such words as tyrannicide, homocide [*sic*], infanticide, etc. Generally speaking, genocide does not necessarily mean the immediate destruction of a nation, except when accomplished by mass killings of all members of a nation. It is intended rather to signify a coordinated plan of different actions aiming at the destruction of essential foundations of the life of national groups, with the aim of annihilating the groups themselves. The objectives of such a plan would be disintegration of the political and social institutions, of culture, language, national feelings, religion, and the economic existence of national groups, and the destruction of the personal security, liberty, health, dignity, and even the lives of the individuals belonging to such groups. Genocide is directed against the national group as an entity, and the actions involved are directed against individuals, not in their individual capacity, but as members of the national group. . . .

Genocide has two phases: one, destruction of the national pattern of the oppressed group; the other, the imposition of the national pattern of the oppressor. This imposition, in turn, may be made upon the oppressed population which is allowed to remain, or upon the territory alone, after removal of the population and the colonization of the area by the oppressor's own nationals. Denationalization was the word used in the past to describe the destruction of a national pattern. The author believes, however, that this word is inadequate because: (1) it does not connote the destruction of the biological structure; (2) in connoting the destruction of one national pattern, it does not connote the imposition of the national pattern of the oppressor; and (3) denationalization is used by some authors to mean only deprivation of citizenship. . . .

Genocide is effected through a synchronized attack on different aspects of life of the captive peoples: in the political field (by destroying institutions of self-government and imposing a German pattern of administration, and through colonization by Germans); in the social field (by disrupting the social cohesion of the nation involved and killing or removing elements such as the intelligentsia, which provide spiritual leadership . . .); in the cultural field (by prohibiting or destroying cultural institutions and cultural activities; by substituting vocational education for education in the liberal arts, in order to prevent humanistic thinking, which the occupant considers dangerous because it promotes national thinking); in the economic field (by shifting the wealth to Germans and by prohibiting the exercise of trades and occupations by people who do not promote Germanism 'without reservations'); in the biological field (by a policy of depopulation and by promoting procreation by Germans in the occupied countries); in the field of physical existence (by introducing a starvation rationing system for non-Germans and by mass killings, mainly of Jews, Poles, Slovenes, and Russians); in the religious field (by interfering with the activities of the Church, which in many countries provides not only spiritual but also national leadership); in the field of morality (by attempts to create an atmosphere of moral debasement through promoting pornographic publications and motion pictures, and the excessive consumption of alcohol).

Source: Lemkin, Raphael (1944), *Axis Rule in Occupied Europe: Laws of Occupation, Analysis of Government Proposals for Redress*, Washington: Carnegie Endowment for International Peace, pp. 79–80, xi–xii.

FROM AN EARLY SPEECH BY HITLER ABOUT THE JEWS   Document 2

Hitler gave this speech at a public meeting of the National Socialist German Workers Party in Munich on 13 August 1920.

The Jew, in his role as parasite, is turning and must turn against national purity as a source of a people's strength. The Jew, who is himself more nationally pure than any other people, who has not blended in with any other race for thousands of years but has simply exploited racial interbreeding at propitious moments in order to cause other races to degenerate – this same Jew preaches day by day . . . that all peoples on this earth are equal, that these peoples should be bound together in international solidarity, that no people should lay claim to any special disposition, and above all that no people has any basis to be proud of anything national . . .

First, [the Jew declares,] a race must be denationalized. First it must forget that its strength lies in its blood . . . for what the Jew needs in order to organize, build up, and maintain his definitive mastery over the world is the lowering of the racial level of the remaining peoples, so that he, as racially pure, will be the only one qualified to rule all others. This is the racial deterioration whose effects upon a host of peoples we observe even today . . .

An additional problem is that of the physical incapacitation of all races. This means that the Jew struggles to do away with everything that he finds capable of generating strength or of hardening the muscles. Above all he strives to do away with everything that he finds might make a people healthy enough to decide that it will no longer tolerate the presence of national racial criminals (that is, noxious weeds) in the midst of the racial community but will punish them with death, circumstances permitting. This is the Jew's greatest fear and worry, for even the strongest bolts upon the most secure prison are not so strong, and the prison not so secure, that a few million people cannot open them in the end. There is only one bolt that cannot be opened, and that is death; this he dreads the most, and therefore he yearns for the day when this barbaric punishment will be abolished wherever he continues to live as a race of parasites, although he employs it without mercy wherever he is already in control. (Spirited applause.)

Source: Phelps, R.H. (1968), 'Hitlers "grundlegende" Rede über den Antisemitismus', *Vierteljahrshefte für Zeitgeschichte* 16, pp. 411–12.

Document 3   AN EX-NAZI EVALUATES THE ANTI-JEWISH ASPECT OF NATIONAL SOCIALISM, 1939

The author of the following passage, Hermann Rauschning (1887–1982), joined the Nazi Party in 1932 but resigned in 1934, put off in part by anti-Jewish agitation. He became a refugee in 1937, settling in Great Britain in 1938 before moving to the United States in 1941. His writings after leaving Germany became staples of anti-Nazi propaganda in the West. They helped to popularize the image of Hitler as a man devoid of ideas, interested solely in power for its own sake. That image received its most famous incarnation in Charlie Chaplin's 1940 film, The Great Dictator, *but subsequent scholarship has shown that Hitler had a far more developed and original world view than Rauschning understood.*

[T]he fight against Judaism . . . is now an element in the revolutionary un-settling of the nation, a means of destruction of past categories of thinking and valuation, of destroying the liberalist economic system based on private initiative and enterprise; it is also a sop to the destructive revolutionism of the masses, a first lesson in cynicism . . . It is of functional importance only, a means and nothing more. It is the main element in propaganda. The question to be asked of it is not its meaning but its purpose. It serves mainly for the propagation, in a form assimilable by the masses, of revolutionary aims which can be harbored at first hand only by a small élite. The function of the philosophy is to keep alive the fighting character of the movement . . . Nothing is of more importance to National Socialism than the possession of 'enemies,' objects on which this pugnacity can sharpen its claws. This is the root explanation of such senseless and horrible myths as that of the totally evil character of the Jews. If there is no other enemy available there is always the Jew, whose despised figure can always be made to serve as fuel for the fighting spirit, and at the same time to keep alive the happy feeling of belonging to the company of the elect . . .

All these elements, so primitive and threadbare in their psychology, are nevertheless thoroughly effective in practice. It would be a great mistake to suppose that so cunning an individual as the German Minister of Propaganda [Goebbels] is not perfectly well aware that the atrocity propaganda against the Jews . . . is preposterous nonsense, that he does not see through the racial swindle just as clearly as those compatriots of his whom it has driven out of their country. It would be simply foolish to imagine that any member of the élite truly and sincerely believes in the bases of the 'philosophy.' They have been deliberately concocted for their demagogic effectiveness and for the furtherance of the party's political aims. They have also been chosen with a cunning realization of the needs of the . . . German masses. Other representations of good and evil, of hero and weakling, may 'work' in other countries; the selection for Germany was already indicated by the experience of the pan-Germans and the anti-Semitic 'racial' parties.

Source: Rauschning, Hermann (1939), *The Revolution of Nihilism: Warning to the West*, translated by W.E. Dickes, New York: Longmans, Green & Co, pp. 22, 52–53.

HITLER AND HORTHY DISCUSS THE FATE OF HUNGARIAN JEWRY, APRIL 1943   Document 4

From the minutes of a conversation between Hitler and the regent of Hungary, Miklos Horthy, held at Klessheim Castle near Salzburg, Austria, 17 April 1943.

The Führer [Hitler] . . . described to Horthy the German measures for rationing, which had been implemented in a completely orderly fashion. There is no black market in Germany . . . In this connection Horthy observed . . . that he was not yet able to control the black market. The Führer responded that the Jews were responsible for this . . . When Horthy asked in response what he ought to do with the Jews, since he had already done so much to take away all possibilities for economic survival – after all, he couldn't kill them – the Reich foreign minister [Ribbentrop] explained that the Jews must either be destroyed or placed in concentration camps. There was no other way [to deal with them] . . . [The Führer stated that] the Jews had never had any organizational value. All of the fears that had been repeatedly expressed to him in Germany notwithstanding, everything was proceeding quite well without the Jews. Wherever the Jews were left to themselves – in Poland, for example – the most awful misery and depravity prevailed. They are simply pure parasites. In Poland these conditions have been fundamentally cleared away. Jews who did not want to work there were shot. If they couldn't work, they had to die. They were to be treated like tuberculosis bacteria who might infect a healthy body. This is not cruel if you keep in mind that even innocent creatures of nature, like rabbits and deer, have to be killed so they will do no damage. Why should we treat the animals who thought to bring us Bolshevism any better?

Source: Trials of the Major War Criminals before the International Military Tribunal (1949), 42 vols., Nuremberg: International Military Tribunal, vol. 35, pp. 427–28.

Document 5   *KRISTALLNACHT* IN GERMAN PUBLIC OPINION

This survey, prepared by the Security Service of the Nazi Party (SD) under the direction of Reinhard Heydrich, was one of a series of reports on Jewish affairs written for top echelons of the Third Reich's leadership. The stated purpose of the series was 'to fight the enemy with passion but to be cold as ice and objective in the assessment of the situation and its presentation'.

The atonement operation against the Jews of Germany began uniformly throughout the entire territory of the Reich during the night of 9/10 November [1938]. The activists in the operation were in general the Political Directors, members of the SA, the SS, and in individual instances also members of the Hitler Youth. The civilian population participated only to a very limited extent in the operations . . .

The attitude of the population to the actions, which initially was positive, changed fundamentally when the extent of material damage inflicted became generally known. It was repeatedly emphasized that action against the Jews as atonement for the murder of the legation secretary vom Rath met with approval. However, persons stressed that destruction of firms, offices, and private dwellings was incompatible with the requisite measures called for to implement the Four-Year Plan. In addition, it was noted that this all-too-blatant action against the Jews could lead to new difficulties in foreign policy. There was particular condemnation by members of the armed forces of the methods used against the Jews.

The clear rejection of the entire operation in uniformly Catholic regions proves that the internal political adversaries are exploiting this mood. Commenting that the synagogues were 'the Lord's houses' – which previously were never especially seen as such by the Catholic Church – the attempt was made to upset the population, and fears were articulated that a similar fate now awaited the churches. This action by the Catholic clergy led in some instances to the population in various solely Catholic areas distancing itself from participation in the operation against the Jews, or even demonstratively expressing its sympathies for the Jews . . .

The attitude abroad to the operation was uniformly negative . . . The laws and ordinances from all departments issued against the Jews in Germany in the wake of the operation, as well as those still in preparation, are aimed at achieving the final exclusion of Jewry from all areas of life, with the ultimate goal of their removal from the territory of the Reich, by all means necessary, and in the shortest amount of time. In general, in no case has immigration to a country where immigration by Jews is at all possible been made any easier [by the violence].

Source: Kulka, Otto Dov, and Jäckel, Eberhard (eds) (2010), *The Jews in the Secret Nazi Reports on Popular Opinion in Germany, 1933–1945*, translated by William Templer, New Haven, CT: Yale University Press, pp. 340–42.

GERMANS CONFRONT THE DEPORTATION OF THEIR JEWISH NEIGHBOURS, 1941

Document 6

This Security Service report, dated 6 December 1941, describes the 'attitude of the population to the evacuation of the Jews' from Minden, a town on the Weser River in north-western Germany.

The now factual evacuation of the Jews from this area is viewed by a large segment of the population as a matter of great concern. There are two aspects here of greatest importance for most people. For one, they fear that as a result of this, the many Germans in still neutral foreign countries, especially in America, could suffer anew. People point to 9 November 1938 [*Kristallnacht*] once again, which harmed us more everywhere abroad than it benefited us here at home.

The second point is that it is probably very questionable to ship the people specifically to the East now, during winter with all its dangers. It is quite likely that many Jews will not survive the transport. And people point out that all of the Jews evacuated now are people who have been living for ages in this region. People think that for many Jews, this decision is too harsh. Even if this opinion is not shared by a great many, it can be encountered in a large segment of the population, especially among the financially better-off circles. Here too, older persons are in the overwhelming majority.

But *Volksgenossen* [members of the German *Volk*] who are well informed about the Jewish Question are absolutely in favour and approve of this action . . .

Source: Kulka, Otto Dov, and Jäckel, Eberhard (eds) (2010), *The Jews in the Secret Nazi Reports on Popular Opinion in Germany, 1933–1945*, translated by William Templer, New Haven, CT: Yale University Press, pp. 563–64.

Document 7   THE LUBLIN RESERVATION

The following text is a summary of a report delivered by two Jews, Jonathan Eibeschütz and Jacob Mandelbaum, who had been deported from the town of Bielsko-Biała in south-western Poland to the Lublin reservation, evidently in October 1939. The two escaped and made their way to Wilno, where representatives of the World Jewish Congress recorded their testimony. The document is one of the earliest examples of eyewitness testimony gathered by Jews from other Jews and one of the few extant descriptions of how the Lublin reservation programme actually operated.

When the war between Germany and Poland broke out almost the entire Jewish population of [Bielsko-Biała] ran away . . . A few Jews remained there. When the Germans conquered [the town], on 3 September [1939], they arrested most of the remaining Jews and led them to the yard of the Jewish school. They tortured them there in horrible fashion. They beat them half to death, poured boiling water on them, suspended many of them by the hands, holding them in that position for more than an hour until they fainted . . .

The Germans took all the property of the Jews of Bielsko-Biała for themselves. After torturing them for several weeks in the concentration camp they set up in the schoolyard, they sent all the Jews to the Russian border. The Jews were deported there together with many other Jews from Ostrava-Moravska, Königshütte [Chorzów], and Katowice. The greatest number of deportees came from Katowice – about 1,000 people. All together about 2,000 Jews were expelled from all of these towns and sent to the Russian border.

The way to the Lublin region was paved with suffering and torment. [The deportees] travelled from Bielsko to Nisko in sealed boxcars. For two full days they did not eat. The Germans provided no food. The German sadists would enter the cars and ask if anyone was hungry. If someone said that he was, they would beat him half to death. After the beating they would ask the beaten person if he was satisfied, and he would be forced to respond that he was quite satisfied . . .

Upon reaching Nisko all of the Jews were told to get out of the boxcar, to arrange themselves in groups of four, and to begin marching. The Germans permitted them to place their packs upon peasant wagons that had been rented for this purpose, and all of the Jews marched seven kilometres in the rain and the mud . . . The people who travelled along with the persecuted Jews paid 10 zł. per wagon, but from the Jews they took 4 zł. per person. From this manoeuvre the fellow-travellers filled their pockets with money . . .

The head overseer from the Gestapo took the jewellery of all of the Jews along with whatever money they had left, threatening to shoot them [if they refused].

After having left the persecuted Jews devoid of any possessions, the head overseer announced that by 6 pm they must cover a distance of another 25 kilometres or they would be shot . . .

The poor Jews pushed and shoved one another in order to grab their packs quickly, and they began to run as fast as their strength would allow. The Gestapo men shot in the air in order to frighten them as they ran and to make them go even faster.

The persecuted Jews ran all night until they reached . . . Biłgoraj. From Biłgoraj they were expelled further, all the way to . . . the Russian border.

Before the expulsion from Bielsko the Germans gave the Jews to understand that they were being sent to the reservation in Lublin in order to 'build a Jewish state' there. But [when they arrived] it became clear that they were being driven out of the entire area of German occupation and being pushed to the Russian border.

At the Russian border the . . . Germans made another search of the Jews, taking what little money a few had managed to hide in their belongings.

People who had once been well off came to the Russian border as shadows of their former selves, destitute and afflicted, beaten down by endless sorrow and horrible desperation.

Source: Engel, David (2000), 'Divu'ah miMakor yehudi al gerush yehudei Bielsko-Biała el "haShemurah haYehudit" beEzor Lublin, mars 1940' (A Report on the Jewish Reservation in Lublin, March 1940), *Gal-Ed* 17, pp. CXXXV–CXXXVII.

A GERMAN JEWISH EDITOR ASSESSES THE IMPACT OF THE NUREMBERG LAWS   Document 8

Der Morgen was a bi-monthly Jewish intellectual journal. Founded in 1925 by the philosopher Julius Goldstein, it featured articles by leading Jewish scholars, thinkers, and public figures representing a range of religious and political attitudes. Following Goldstein's death in 1929, editorship passed to Hans Bach, who held a position in the German interior ministry until he was dismissed following the Nazi takeover. Bach wrote the following commentary as a preface to the first issue of Der Morgen *to appear following promulgation of the Nuremberg Laws in September 1935. The journal continued to appear regularly until 1938.*

The new laws promulgated at the Nuremberg party conference set the entire life of the Jews living in Germany not only before new tasks but also on a new plane altogether. If [in promulgating these laws] the German government was acting according to the intention of the *Führer* and Chancellor '... to create a plane ... upon which the German people could find a tolerable relationship with the Jewish people', these laws govern mainly the areas in which the German people does *not* wish to maintain relations. The fundamental positive constitutional idea [embodied in the laws] is to be found not in the legislation itself but in a commentary [on them] by the editor of the German News Agency. [It is] defined by the concept 'minority' ...

[T]he national majority, which holds state power, cannot permanently remain unconcerned with whether the minority is respected or defamed from without or whether it is unified or splintered from within. In an authoritarian state the minority is also not able to allow the will of the individual free play. Thus the *Reichsvertretung* ... has properly placed the demand for state recognition of an autonomous Jewish leadership ... at the top of a grand programme for Jewish self-determination, along with the hope for the possibility of [continued] moral and economic existence.

Source: Der Morgen 11:8 (November 1935), pp. 329–30.

Document 9   A GERMAN JEWISH WOMAN DESCRIBES HER EXPERIENCE IN THE EARLY NAZI YEARS

The author of the following memoir, Marta Appel, was the wife of Rabbi Ernst Appel from Dortmund, an industrial town in north-western Germany, whose 1933 population of 500,000 included some 4,000 Jews. The two left Germany in 1937. She wrote her memoirs in 1940, after arriving in the United States as a refugee.

Our gentile friends and neighbors, even people whom we had scarcely known before, came to assure us of their friendship and to tell us that these horrors could not last very long. But after some months of a regime of terror, fidelity and friendship had lost their meaning and fear and treachery had replaced them. For the sake of our gentile friends, we turned our heads so as not to greet them in the streets, for we did not want to bring upon them the danger of imprisonment for being considered a friend of Jews.

With each day of the Nazi regime, the abyss between us and our fellow citizens grew larger. Friends whom we had loved for years did not know us anymore . . . [W]e were hunted like deer. Through the prominent position of my husband [a rabbi] we were in constant danger. Often we were warned to stay away from home. We were no longer safe, wherever we went.

How much our life changed in those days! Often it seemed to me I could not bear it any longer, but thinking of my children, I knew we had to be strong to make it easier for them. From then on I hated to go out, since on every corner I saw signs that the Jews were the misfortune of the people . . . Never did anything unpleasant happen to me on the street, but I was expecting it at every moment, and it was always bothering me . . .

Almost every lesson began to be a torture for Jewish children. There was not one subject anymore which was not used to bring up the Jewish question. And in the presence of Jewish children the teachers denounced all the Jews, without exception, as scoundrels and as the most destructive force in every country where they were living . . .

The only hope we had was that this terror would not last very long. The day could not be far off when this nightmare would cease to hound the German people. How could anybody be happy in a land where 'freedom' was an extinct word, where nobody knew that the next day he would not be taken to jail, possibly tortured to death . . .

[In 1935 a Jewish doctor fled the country, leaving all that he owned behind.] A few days after the doctor had left with his family, we were invited to a friend's house. Of course the main subject of the evening was the doctor's flight. The discussion became heated. 'He was wrong', most of the men were arguing. 'It indicates a lack of courage to leave the country just now when we should stay together, firm against all hatred'. 'It takes more courage to leave', the ladies protested vigorously. 'What good is it to stay and to wait for the slowly coming ruin? Is it not far better to go and to build up a new existence somewhere else in the world, before our strength is crippled by the everlasting strain on our nerves, on our souls? Is not the children's future more important than a fruitless holding out against Nazi cruelties and prejudices?' . . .

On our way home I still argued with my husband. He, like all the other men, could not imagine how it was possible to leave our beloved homeland, to leave all the duties which constitute a man's life. 'Could you really leave all this behind you to enter nothingness?' . . . 'I could', I said again, 'since I would go into a new life'. And I really meant it.

Source: Richarz, Monika (ed.) (1991), *Jewish Life in Germany: Memoirs from Three Centuries*, Bloomington: Indiana University Press, pp. 352–54, 356.

Document 10   A JEWISH MAN COMMITS SUICIDE IN PROTEST OVER EXCLUSION FROM
                     THE GERMAN NATION

*Fritz Rosenfelder was a businessman from Stuttgart, a manufacturing city in
south-western Germany with a 1933 population of about 450,000, of whom
about 4,500 were Jews. An avid gymnast, Rosenfelder learned that because
he was a Jew he would be expelled from his sports club. In response he
shot himself to death, leaving the following note. He was 31 years old. Some
5,000 German Jews are estimated to have committed suicide between 1933
and 1945.*

[5 April 1933]
Dear Friends,

Here is my final farewell! A *German* Jew cannot bear to live knowing that
the movement to which nationalist Germany looks for salvation regards him
as a traitor to the Fatherland! I leave without hatred or resentment . . . But
because I do not see any way for me to take what I regard as suitable action,
I shall try, by ending my life voluntarily, to shake up my Christian friends.
You will be able to see by this step I am taking how things look to us *German*
Jews. How much more would I have preferred to give my life for my
Fatherland!

Do not be sad, but try to enlighten and help the truth to victory.

Source: Zalzer, Maria (ed.) (1964), *Weg und Schicksal der Stuttgarter Juden*, Stuttgart:
Eernst Klett Verlag, p. 160.

Document 11   A GERMAN JEWISH LEADER DESCRIBES THE 'RETURN TO JUDAISM'

*Eva Reichmann (1897–1998) was a director of the largest German Jewish
organization, the Central Association of German Citizens of the Jewish Faith
(commonly known as the Centralverein or CV). The organization was
founded in 1893 in order to promote the full integration of Jews into German
civic, social, and cultural life. In 1939 she fled to Great Britain, where she
became a leader of the German Jewish refugee community. Following the
Second World War she worked for German–Jewish reconciliation. She wrote
the following observations in 1934.*

People are exploring the boundaries of their existence as Germans and Jews,
and many of them . . . are feeling something like this:

'The era of emancipation is at an end. Our emotional security has been
shattered. Perhaps [our sense of security] actually made us insensate, too
self-confident and satisfied. True, hostility to Jews was never absent, but

we hardly allowed it to affect us. We saw historical developments from too one-sided a perspective to believe in any really earth-shaking convulsions. It is hard to imagine . . . that equality for German Jews could ever be reinstated as it was before. But if it does not return, then we shall be forever excluded from the nation that we made our own with indescribable devotion and about which we feel, painfully, the same way today. In this state of inner uprootedness . . . one inner foothold remains for us – our Jewishness. As we were rising in the surrounding society, we neglected our Jewishness all too much. Who among us continued to be familiar with our holy books? Who knew Jewish history? Who continued to keep our beautiful, gracious, ancient customs? Who bore his Jewishness, even when he knew about it, as anything more than an irrevocable, tired fate? Who experienced it any more as . . . a creative force?'

[T]his path to inner contemplation and collectedness, this path of return to Jewishness, [is one] that we affirm and in which we see one of the great blessings of our time.

Source: Reichmann, Eva G., (1974) *Größe und Verhängnis deutsch-jüdischer Existenz: Zeugnisse einer tragischen Begegnung*, Heidelberg: Lambert Schneider, p. 50.

A ZIONIST EXPLAINS HOW HIS MOVEMENT CAN HELP GERMAN JEWS   Document 12

Chaim Arlosoroff wrote this article for Germany's leading Zionist newspaper, Jüdische Rundschau, *in support of the negotiations that eventually led to the* Haavara *agreement.*

I shall not join the theoretical argument over whether Palestine is *the* solution to the situation of German Jews. . . . But we must not ignore the fact that, unlike other programmes, Palestine is not a temporary solution or an asylum for the night. What we are doing in Palestine carries the stamp of per-manence, and it is being carried out in an atmosphere of self-help and self-determination, which no other country in the world can give us. Thus our accomplishments depend largely upon planning and organization. In my opinion, such planning needs to be spread over several years, let's say a programme of three or four years . . .

The central problem facing German Jewry . . . is that of converting the emigrants' assets into cash. As long as we avoid this problem we are leaving many people, whose assets exceed [in value] the amount that can be removed from Germany according to present currency laws, without a chance to escape. According to a cautious estimate, during recent months 40,000 individuals and families have applied to the Palestine Office in Berlin. Even if only a portion of them end up emigrating to Palestine, the number shows clearly how acute the issue of emigration is. It is folly not to see the problem or to think that it can be solved without agreement with the German government . . . Germany will not strain its foreign currency situation in order to make things easier for the Jews . . . [But] it appears that there is a possibility of reaching an agreement involving exchanging the emigrants' property for German exports in Palestine . . . [This would be] a solution that would satisfy the interests of all participants; it would represent real progress on the road to dealing constructively with the problem of the Jews in Germany.

Source: Jüdische Rundschau, 23 May 1933.

Document 13   A POLISH REPORT DESCRIBES CONDITIONS FOR JEWS AFTER
THE GERMAN CONQUEST

Beginning in 1940, the Interior Ministry of the Polish government-in-exile in London prepared digests of hundreds of reports sent to it clandestinely from occupied Poland describing, among other things, the policies and practices of the German occupation regime. Most of the digests included a section on the persecution of Jews.

From the first days of September [1939] to the present moment the fate of Jews in the occupied territories has been . . . suffering, degradation, persecution, and expropriation. Both the system of exceptional laws introduced by the authorities and the unchecked actions in which the army, Gestapo, administration, and German population engage with impunity contribute to this situation. Officially Jews are the objects of discriminatory laws; in fact they are [treated as] outlaws . . .

A ghetto was established in Warsaw in October 1940, long before then in [other towns] . . . [Establishing] the Warsaw ghetto created the problem of resettling 110,000 Jews and 70–80,000 Poles. It was similar in Łódź. The population density in the ghettos exceeds that of Chinese cities: 5–8 people occupy each room . . . Usually the ghettos are [located in] already overcrowded and filthy areas, without parks, often without sewage disposal systems, but with many buildings that are old or were ruined in the war. Communication with the ghettos is forbidden in principle . . . A high death rate is prevalent (up to 50 per day in Łódź) . . . [Closing the ghettos] separates Jews from the possibility of making a living and existing materially.

There is glaring discrimination against Jews with regard to food supply. They are treated even worse than the Poles. Their bread ration is half that of Poles, their sugar ration one-third. They have no ration cards for meat at all.

They are supposed to receive potatoes, salt, and coal in the same amounts as Poles. Jewish restaurants do not receive any allocations . . .

The free professions have been destroyed. Jewish lawyers have been completely eliminated; Jewish doctors have no right to treat Christians . . . Jews may not own pharmacies. The overwhelming majority of Jewish engineers is unemployed; the same for musicians, journalists, writers . . .

An order by Governor Frank of 26 October 1939 imposes compulsory labour service on all male Jews between ages 14 and 60, with boys over 12 forced to register . . . [The labourers] are treated extremely poorly: they lack food and have wretched living conditions (in barns, cellars, etc.) . . .

The Jews are the object of indescribable mental torture. Face slapping; kicking; insulting address; ridicule; stealing furniture, furs, food reserves – these are daily occurrences . . .

Source: 'Działalność Władz Okupacyjnych na Ter. RP, 1.IX.39–1.XI.40 (Activity of the Occupation Authorities on Polish Territory, 1 September 1939–1 November 1940)', Hoover Institution Archives: Poland, Ministerstwo Spraw Wewnętrznych, Box 4.

GOERING INSTRUCTS HEYDRICH TO PREPARE A 'TOTAL SOLUTION' OF   Document 14
THE JEWISH QUESTION

This document illustrates some of the difficulties in pinpointing when, how, and by whom a decision to begin systematic mass killing of Jews was reached.

Berlin: 31 July 1941

The Reich Marshal of the Greater German Reich
Plenipotentiary for the Four-Year Plan
Chairman of the Ministerial Council for the Defence of the Reich

To: the Chief of the Security Police and the SD,
SS Major General Heydrich, Berlin:

As supplement to the task which was entrusted to you in the decree dated 24 January 1939, namely to solve the Jewish question by emigration and evacuation in a way which is the most favourable in connection with the conditions prevailing at this time, I herewith commission you to carry out all preparations with regard to organizational, factual, and financial viewpoints for a total solution of the Jewish question in those territories in Europe under German influence.

If the competency of other central organizations is touched in this connection, these organizations are to participate.

I further commission you to submit to me as soon as possible a draft showing the organizational, factual, and financial measures already taken for the execution of the intended final solution of the Jewish question.

[Signed] Goering

Source: Trials of War Criminals before the Nuremberg Military Tribunals (1952), 18 vols., Washington: US Government Printing Office, vol. 13, pp. 169–70.

Document 15   NOTES BY GOEBBELS ON A MEETING WITH HITLER CONCERNING THE IMPLICATIONS OF GERMANY'S DECLARATION OF WAR AGAINST THE UNITED STATES

Josef Goebbels, Germany's minister of propaganda, was present at a meeting of top Nazi Party leaders with Hitler, held on 12 December 1941, the day after Germany declared war against the United States. Hitler discussed the significance of the new war situation for a range of policy areas, including treatment of the Jews. The following passage from Goebbels's account of that meeting, written the following day, has figured in the discussion of when the policy of systematic mass murder of Jews throughout Europe began.

Regarding the Jewish question, the Führer is determined to clear the table. He warned the Jews that if they were to cause another world war, it would lead to their own destruction. Those were not empty words. Now the world war has come. The destruction of the Jews must be its necessary consequence. We cannot be sentimental about it. It is not for us to feel sympathy for the Jews. We should have sympathy rather with our own German people. If the German people have to sacrifice 160,000 victims in yet another campaign in the east, then those responsible for this bloody conflict will have to pay for it with their lives.

Source: Gerlach, Christian (1998), 'The Wannsee Conference, the Fate of German Jews, and Hitler's Decision in Principle to Exterminate All European Jews', *Journal of Modern History* 70, p. 785.

Document 16   INVITATION TO THE WANNSEE CONFERENCE

This document announced a conference of administrators held to consider how the murder of European Jewry could be most effectively carried out on a continent-wide scale. The meeting was postponed from 9 December 1941 to

20 January 1942, probably due to the urgent situation created by Japan's attack on Pearl Harbor on 7 December and Germany's subsequent decision to declare war against the United States.

Berlin SW 11 29 Nov 1941
Prinz Albrecht Str. 8
Telephone: Local 120040
Long Distance 126421
Personal

Chief of the Security Police and the Security Service (SD)
IVB 4-3076/41 Secret (1180)

. . .

(Confidential)

To SS Gruppenführer Hofmann
Race and Settlement Main Office
Berlin

Dear Hofmann:

On the 31 July 1941 the Reich Marshal of the Greater German Reich commissioned me to make all necessary preparations in organizational, factual, and material respect for the total solution of the Jewish question in Europe with the participation of all interested central agencies and to present to him a master plan as soon as possible. A photostatic copy of this commission is included in this letter. Considering the extraordinary importance which has to be conceded to these questions and in the interest of the achievement of the same viewpoint by the central agencies concerned with the remaining work connected with this final solution, I suggest to make these problems the subject of a combined conversation, especially since Jews are being evacuated in continuous transports from the Reich territory, including the Protectorate Bohemia and Moravia, to the East ever since 15 October 1941.

I therefore invite you to such a conference, followed by luncheon, on 9 December 1941, 1200 hours, at the office of the International Criminal Police commission, Berlin, Am Grossen Wannsee No. 56/58. . . .

Heil Hitler!
Yours,
[Signed] Heydrich

Source: Trials of War Criminals before the Nuremberg Military Tribunals (1952), 18 vols., Washington: US Government Printing Office, vol. 13, pp. 192–93.

Document 17   AN EYEWITNESS DESCRIBES A MASS SHOOTING IN THE SOVIET UNION

This testimony was offered by Rivka Yoselewska at the trial of Adolf Eichmann, in May 1961. It provided one of the most graphic and memorable depictions of the Holocaust presented by any of the trial's 102 witnesses.

One Saturday evening [8 August 1941] gentiles from nearby villages came to our town and said . . . that the Germans were killing Jews – we'd better flee, disperse and hide . . . We asked grandfather: What shall we do, run away? He consulted with some of his acquaintances, the rabbi, the ritual slaughterer, and other important people, and then said not to run away, to remain where we are, nothing will happen. Perhaps young people will be taken to work, but killing – it can't be . . .

Next morning, at dawn, the town was in an uproar. A Jew came running from the nearby village of Borki . . . He shouted: 'Jews, run away, the Germans are coming to kill us' . . . That very moment we saw the Germans driving into town; they snatched that Jew at once. He barely got into town and was shot on the spot. All the Jews who had heard it began to run away and tried to hide. Grandfather said: 'You children get away . . . nothing will happen to me' . . . That day we made our escape, those who could manage, because the Germans had seized the town. We found refuge in a small forest, where we could hear shooting . . . The next day at daybreak we heard a lot of shooting . . .

When the shooting stopped, we began to make our way back. The gentiles we met told us that we could go ahead; the Germans had left. They killed everyone they found. Nobody was left . . .

[On 22 August 1941] we saw a lot of German policemen surrounding the ghetto . . . We realized that this time it wasn't a matter of counting us . . . A lot of Germans were there. Four or five Germans for every one of our people. This was not in order to count us . . . Then we were told: 'Death is threatening you. You will be shot; whoever wants to buy his way out should bring in whatever he owns in money or jewels that he has hidden'. They tormented us right till the end of the day . . . [But] we did not have anything . . . We had handed over everything before . . .

Then the gate of the ghetto opened and a truck moved in. Those who were strong enough climbed up by themselves, but the weak ones were thrown in. They were piled into the truck like cattle . . . The rest they made run after the truck . . .

We arrived at the place. Those who had been on the truck had already got down, undressed and stood in a row . . . It was about three kilometres away from our town. There was a hill and a little below it they had dug something like a ditch. They made us walk up to the hill, in rows of four, and . . . shot each one of us separately . . . They were SS men. They carried several guns with plenty of ammunition pouches . . .

Some of the younger ones tried to run away. They hardly managed a few steps, they were caught and shot. Then came our turn . . .

[My six-year-old daughter and I] stood facing the ditch. I turned my head. He asked, 'Whom do I shoot first'? I didn't answer. He tore the child away from me. I heard her last cry and he shot her. Then he got ready to kill me . . . He turned me around, loaded his pistol, so that I could see what he was doing. Then he again turned me around and shot me. I fell down . . .

I felt nothing. At that moment I felt that something was weighing me down. I thought that I was dead, but that I could feel something even though I was dead . . . I felt I was suffocating, bodies had fallen on me . . . I pulled myself up with the last bit of strength. When I reached the top I looked around but I couldn't recognize the place. Corpses strewn all over, there was no end to the bodies . . . The Germans were not there. No one was there . . .

When he shot me I was wounded in the head. I still have a big scar on my head, where I was wounded by the Germans. I got to my feet to see that horrible scene . . .

When I saw they were gone I dragged myself over to the grave and wanted to jump in. I thought the grave would open up and let me fall inside alive. I envied everyone for whom it was already over, while I was still alive . . . I . . . tried to dig my way in with my hands . . . The earth didn't open up. I shouted to Mother and Father, why was I left alive? What did I do to deserve this? Where shall I go? To whom can I turn? I have nobody. I saw everything; I saw everybody killed. No one answered.

Source: State of Israel, Ministry of Justice (1993), *The Trial of Adolf Eichmann: Record of Proceedings in the District Court of Jerusalem*, Jerusalem: Yad Vashem, vol. 1, pp. 514–18.

A *SONDERKOMMANDO* MEMBER DESCRIBES THE BEŁŻEC KILLING CENTRE   Document 18

This testimony by Rudolf Reder, one of only a handful of Jews to escape from the Bełżec killing centre, is one of the earliest given by a Jew after the war. It was collected by the Regional Jewish Historical Commission in Kraków in early 1945.

On 16 August 1942 I was taken during an *Aktion* in Lwów to the Janowska camp. The next day I was loaded onto a railroad car . . . The train carried about 5,000 people, [including] women and children . . . [in] closed, sealed freight cars with grates on the windows . . . The journey lasted seven night-marish, desperate, hopeless hours. The train arrived at Bełżec station . . .

The camp was situated in a young coniferous forest, out of which a 3 km square clearing had been cut . . . From a distance it was invisible, because the cut trees had been lashed to the growing ones to create a thicket that blocked the light, hiding the barracks and death chambers that were located there . . .

After unloading, all were ordered to disrobe, men and women together. We were told that we were going to the baths and then to work. For a while the people were glad to hear talk about work. Dozens of Jews from the *Sonderkommando* rummaged through the clothing, removed gold and money. The clothing was taken to the warehouse; valuables were sorted and brought to the camp office.

The building in which the gas chambers were located was a single-storey bungalow painted white. A corridor ran down the middle; there were three chambers to the left, three more to the right. The building was made of concrete. There were no windows. The roof, 3.5 metres high, was covered with roofing paper.

Jewish barbers shaved the women's heads in the yard outside. The women sat naked on stools and were shorn one by one. While waiting they were beaten on the head and face with whips. The people were shoved into the 'baths' *en masse*, with no order, without counting, like cattle to be slaughtered. In the corridor people understood that they were going to die. Whoever balked was prodded with a bayonet by Ukrainian guards . . .

The gassing took twenty minutes. The gas was produced by a gasoline engine worked by two Ukrainian machinists. It was located in a room at the end of the corridor. The gas ran through pipes into the chambers . . .

The corpses were dragged by leather straps to graves 200–300 paces distant. On the way from the building to the graves, ten dentists, selected from among the prisoners, opened the corpses' mouths and extracted the teeth; later they melted the gold into ingots, which went to the camp commandant's office . . .

Immediately upon arrival skilled workers were selected – carpenters, metalworkers, cobblers, tailors. I said I was a machine fitter. I was assigned to the machine that dug sand out of the grave pits . . .

There were 500 people in the *Sonderkommando*. Every day the ranks were thinned by 30–40. The Germans culled the workers who were weak, called out their names at noon, made them run to the grave, and shot them. They brought the number back to 500 out of the new transports . . .

Source: Borwicz, Michał M., Rost, Nella, Wulf, Józef (eds) (1945), *Dokumenty zbrodni i męczeństwa*, Kraków: Wojewódzka Żydowska Komisja Historyczna, pp. 56–58.

THE POLISH UNDERGROUND REPORTS THE LIQUIDATION OF THE
WARSAW GHETTO

Document 19

*The following account of the beginning of mass deportations of Jews from the
Warsaw ghetto was prepared by the Polish underground and sent to the Polish
government-in-exile in London during the last week of July 1942. The process
described is typical of* Aktionen *in many ghettos.*

In the past few days the liquidation of the Warsaw ghetto has begun . . . On
22 July [1942], notices were posted on the walls of the ghetto, according to
which 6,000 Jews from Warsaw were to be resettled daily in the east. This
undoubtedly signifies shipment to a place of execution. The 'resettlees' have
the right to take with them 15 kg of baggage and any jewellery. The resettlement does not include employees of the community or hospitals, doctors,
order police, holders of work cards, and persons certified by the medical
commission as fit for work (no such commission was established). After the
resettlement has been carried out, those Jews remaining in the ghetto will
be quartered in barracks and put to work. That same day machine guns
were stationed at the ghetto gates, and in the streets 'thugs' – Lithuanians,
Latvians, Ukrainians – appeared. Shooting began at passers-by. The deportation action is carried out in the following manner: A closed apartment
building is picked at random, and the Jewish police pull everyone out of it,
without regard to age or state of health. After the elimination of those not
subject to deportation, the remaining are transported by lorry or tram to a
waiting train. Several trains (of open cars enclosed with barbed wire) have
already left. Blocking off of apartment buildings is going on at several points
in the city. Independently of this, acts of hooliganism – so far sporadic – have
begun. The thugs force their way into apartments and shoot all present . . .
The victims of the first day of the 'resettlement' action were mainly old and
sick people, invalids, children, infants, women, and a large percentage of
foreign Jews. The young people attempted to hide. The terrified population
runs into the streets or wanders from apartment to apartment. Complete
depression. Many suicides . . .

Source: 'Pro memoria o sytuacji w Kraju w okresie 1–25 lipca 1942 r.' (Memorandum
on the situation in Poland, 1–25 July 1942), Polish Underground Study Trust,
London, 56/113.

Document 20   AN EARLY ASSESSMENT OF GERMAN POLICY TOWARDS JEWS IN
               OCCUPIED POLAND

Jan Karski, a courier for the Polish underground, presented a detailed report on the situation of Jews in Poland under German and Soviet occupation as part of his secret mission to the Polish government-in-exile in February 1940. The document, from which an extract is presented here, contains one of the earliest eyewitness accounts of German treatment of Polish Jews delivered to the West.

The Germans are attempting at all costs to win over the Polish masses . . . They are attempting [to persuade the masses that] 'the Germans, and the Germans alone, will help the Poles to settle accounts with the Jews'.

Thus the relation of the Germans to the Jews clearly exceeds the strictures of their official ideology and is *one of the elements of their internal policy.*

They are attempting:

1. to extract as much as they can from the Jews (money, stocks, means of production, workshops);
2. to cleanse the lands seized by them of Jews, at the price of Judaizing the Generalgouvernement;
3. to use the Jews as bait to win the sympathy, recognition, and respect of broad strata among the Poles.

'At last the Germans are solving the Jewish question in the General-gouvernement, not so much for themselves as in consideration of the interest of the Polish nation' – this is how, according to the German design, the [Polish] populace ought to understand their behaviour.

Much indicates that it is indeed this that they desire.

They do not particularly care *in principle* about the oppression of Polish Jews in the Generalgouvernement:

A Jew can still buy himself out of wearing an armband or patch if he has a lot of money; he can still go over to the Bolsheviks if he pays; often he can even still get a passport if he gives a bribe. The Germans are not resettling Jews from Zakopane as they had announced, since the Jewish community paid them ransom; they still are not arresting important rabbis or other Jewish personalities when they pay for their freedom; etc., etc. . . . .

Plunder, 'the psychological outlet of the Master Race', and the duping of the Polish populace – these are their real goals.

Source: Engel, David (1983), 'An Early Account of Polish Jewry under Nazi and Soviet Occupation Presented to the Polish Government-in-Exile, February 1940' *Jewish Social Studies* 45, pp. 11–12.

THE STORY OF A MASS SHOOTING IS MET WITH DISBELIEF   Document 21

This testimony by a Jewish physician from Wilno, Mark Dworzecki, was given at the trial of Adolf Eichmann in May 1961. Dworzecki later became a noted early scholar of the Holocaust.

The Germans occupied Wilno on 24 June 1941. They entered the ghetto on 6 September. During these two and a half months, about 40,000 Jews disappeared from Jewish Wilno . . . The Germans said they were taking the Jews to the labour camp of Ponary. But the Poles were saying that they heard shots at Ponary. Ponary is a beautiful forest beyond Wilno . . .

I was at the time a doctor in Wilno . . . One morning I saw in the street a woman with dishevelled hair, barefoot, walking with flowers in her hands and giving the impression of a woman who had gone out of her mind. The woman came into my room and said to me: 'I have come from Ponary'. I asked: 'Have you come from the labour camp at Ponary?' She said: 'No, it is not a labour camp. They are killing the Jews there'. She described how, on the night of 31 August 1941, she was brought there together with . . . about ten thousand Jews . . . She heard the sound of shots. [Wounded,] she fell into the pit . . . She remained amongst the dead bodies until sunset. And that night . . . she got out from amongst the bodies. She crossed the barbed wire fence, escaped, ran through the forest until she came to a little valley, and there she found a simple Polish peasant woman. The peasant woman made a bandage for her from a towel, gave her flowers in her hand and said to her: 'Run away from here, but go with the flowers as if you are a plain peasant woman, so that they should not realize that you are a Jewess'. And then she came up to me and opened the towel-bandage and I saw the wound, the bullet hole, and ants were crawling in the hole – ants of the forest.

Then I realized the truth about Ponary. I went out into a street . . . I turned to the Jews and said: 'Jews, Ponary is not a labour camp – in Ponary they are killing Jews'. And they said to me: 'Doctor, you too are creating a panic? Instead of consoling us, instead of encouraging us, instead of giving us hope, you tell us horror tales – that there are killings in Ponary? How could it be that they should simply take Jews and kill them?'

Source: State of Israel, Ministry of Justice (1993), *The Trial of Adolf Eichmann: Record of Proceedings in the District Court of Jerusalem*, Jerusalem: Yad Vashem, vol. 1, pp. 447–48.

Document 22   THE FIRST JEWISH INTUITION OF A NAZI MURDER PROGRAMME

This record of the origins of the United Partisan Organization in the Wilno ghetto (the earliest known Jewish armed resistance group) comes from the memoirs of Ruzhka Korczak, a local leader of the Zionist youth movement Hashomer Hatsair. It describes a secret meeting of the Wilno Hashomer Hatsair leadership in December 1941, presided over by Abba Kovner.

Abba: Since our last meeting . . . our nearest and dearest have been torn from us and led to death with masses of other Jews . . . With the uprooting of our comrades the naked truth stands before us. That truth says that we must not believe that those who have been taken from us are still alive, that they have merely been deported. Everything that has befallen us to this point means . . . death. Yet even this fact is not the whole truth . . . The destruction of thousands is only a harbinger of the annihilation of millions. Their death is our total ruin.

It is still difficult for me to explain why Wilno is bleeding while Białystok is peaceful and calm . . . But one thing is clear to me: Wilno is not just Wilno. [The shootings at] Ponary are not just an episode. The yellow patch is not the invention of the local SS commander. This is a total system. We are facing a well-planned system that is hidden from us at the moment.

Is there any escape from it? No. If we are dealing with a consistent system, fleeing from one place to another is nothing but an illusion . . . Is there a chance that we might be rescued? Cruel as the answer may be, we must reply: no, there is no rescue! . . . Maybe for dozens or hundreds; but for the . . . millions of Jews under the yoke of German occupation there is no rescue.

Is there a way out? Yes. There is a way out: rebellion and armed resistance . . .

Adam: How can we, in our present state, think of . . . armed resistance when we know that this might precipitate the great, final catastrophe. After all, we have no assurance that we are facing the immediate absolute liquidation of the ghetto, its total annihilation. Once we begin our action will we not be endangering the entire ghetto? . . . Do we have the right to assume responsibility for all Jews, to endanger their lives and to hasten their destruction if we fail? None of the ghetto Jews will stand with us; no one will understand us. They may even curse us and turn against us, for they will think that we are the source of the disaster that is befalling them . . . Collective responsibility hangs over our head like a sword of Damocles . . .

Abba: The unresolved point in the discussion is: How can we be certain that we are facing complete physical extermination? To me the matter is clear enough, but I shall not be able to convince the others. Only the last one of us who remains alive can be completely certain. But anyone who observes what is happening around us with a clear mind, and open heart, and mainly with a healthy instinct, cannot help but be convinced: we are headed for absolute, total annihilation. The day will come when that recognition will be common to all, but what is important is that it not come too late . . . Thus we must choose to act as if we were certain, despite the doubts.

Source: Korczak, Ruzhka (1965), *Lehavot be-efer* (*Flames in the Ash*), Tel Aviv: Sifriat Poalim, pp. 49–51.

A YOUTH MOVEMENT MEMBER BECOMES AN UNDERGROUND COURIER   Document 23

Bronia Klibański, who recorded the oral histories from which this text is composed, was a member of the Zionist youth movement Dror. Once she joined the Jewish underground in her home town of Grodno, she obtained a false identity card as a Pole named Jadwiga Szkibel. Under this assumed identity she was able to carry news between ghettos. The text is a composite of two testimonies given during the 1990s.

In January 1942, Mordechai Tenenbaum came to Grodno from Wilno, where he had experienced the mass killing of Jews. He was one of the most important organizers of the Jewish underground and Jewish fighters in the ghettos in Poland. At that time life in the Grodno ghetto was very difficult, but there was no killing. Mordechai told us what had happened in Wilno. I think he was one of the first and the very few who understood that the mass killing of Jews from Wilno was not just a caprice of the Germans but part of a general German policy to kill Jews . . .

After a month, another girl from our movement came to me in the ghetto in Grodno and informed me that I had to go to Białystok to attend a gathering of the members of our organization . . . My problem was how to leave the Grodno ghetto and how to come back in, since I had no papers. But I was lucky to have a very not-Jewish face. I went out of the ghetto by some hole in the wall and I went to the train station. Of course it was dangerous because there were many non-Jewish people who knew me. But even Polish people had to have permission to buy a train ticket. Of course I had no permission. And I didn't know exactly how to buy a ticket without permission. Then I saw a German at the station. I went to him and I smiled nicely and I asked him if he could buy me a ticket to Białystok.

He said, 'All right'. So I gave him the money and he bought me the ticket . . .

After the meeting I returned to Grodno. Later I was asked to go to Białystok and stay there. When I left I didn't know I was leaving my family forever. I didn't tell them where I was going because it was a secret . . .

This time I went with a boy, a member of our organization. We travelled on foot and sometime by horse cart. On the way from Grodno to Białystok we passed different villages where there were ghettos. One was even a labour camp. We visited them to meet members of our organization. But it was more to support our members and tell them . . . they must not be passive. They had to do something. Maybe they had to fight . . .

One day Mordechai Tenenbaum suggested that I cross to the Aryan side to serve as a liaison officer for the movement. In late 1942 only one liaison officer, Tema Shneiderman, remained alive. Other experienced officers had been caught by the Germans, and I was to replace them. At that time, the Polish population of Białystok was ordered to apply for German identity cards. I did so, too, using a forged birth certificate as proof that I was a Christian. I had to leave the ghetto frequently to carry out each stage of these arrangements . . .

It was dangerous to cross to the Aryan side. I was to leave the ghetto early in the morning with a group of Jewish labourers. Then I would swiftly take off my yellow stars and would leave the group at a suitable moment . . . Each step had risks: I could be caught leaving the ghetto; the Germans might discover that I was Jewish or that my birth certificate was forged. But luck was with me . . . On the Aryan side, Tema Schneiderman helped me find a room and a job as a maid in the apartment of three German railroad operators. I later used their help when I rode the trains to purchase arms and deliver them to Białystok . . . This, my main task, was the most dangerous of all . . .

On my very first day on the Aryan side, the fact that I was living alone, which was not customary for a young woman of my age at that time, naturally provoked my neighbours' suspicions that I was Jewish . . . [T]o this day I am puzzled about how I managed . . . to avoid arrest . . . Because of my reserved, polite, and detached demeanour, the Poles perceived me as a girl of fine upbringing who did not fear to speak her mind. This image, my non-Jewish appearance, and my knowledge of Polish permitted me to survive and act as I did . . .

We lost several brave women; one tragedy occurred when several veteran couriers and liaisons were stopped at the checkpoint between Białystok and Warsaw and were caught with money that had been given them for delivery to the underground . . . Others, such as Tema Shneiderman, were killed in resistance operations in the ghetto.

Sources: Mais, Yitzchak (ed.) (2007), *Daring to Resist: Jewish Defiance in the Holocaust*, New York: Museum of Jewish Heritage, pp. 74–76; Ofer, Dalia, and Weitzman, Lenore J. (eds) (1998), *Women in the Holocaust*, New Haven, CT: Yale University Press, pp. 180–82.

A JEWISH UNDERGROUND PARTY INFORMS THE POLISH GOVERNMENT-IN-EXILE OF A PLAN TO MURDER ALL POLISH JEWS

Document 24

This document was composed in mid-May 1942. On 21 May it was transferred by a Swedish citizen living in Warsaw, Sven Normann, who departed for neutral Stockholm the next day. From there he forwarded the letter to the Polish government-in-exile in London. It reached London on 31 May 1942.

From the day the Russo-German war broke out, the Germans embarked upon the physical extirpation of the Jewish population on Polish soil, using Ukrainians and Lithuanians for that purpose. This began in the summer months of 1941, first in eastern Galicia . . . In Lwów 30,000 Jews were murdered, in Stanisławów 15,000, in Tarnopol 5,000, in Złoczów 2,000, in Brzeżany 4,000 . . .

In October–November the same thing began to happen in Wilno and environs and in the Kaunas area in Lithuania. During November 50,000 Jews were murdered in Wilno. At present there are 12,000 Jews there. According to various estimates, the overall number of Jews in the Wilno and Kaunas regions who have been bestially murdered reaches 300,000 . . .

In November–December the murder of Jews in Polish territories annexed to the Reich (the so-called Warthegau) began. Murder was carried out here by means of gassing, which was done in the village of Chełmno . . . A special motor vehicle (gas chamber), into which ninety people were loaded at a time, was used for gassing. The victims were buried in special dumping pits in the Lubardzki forest . . . Between November 1941 and March 1942, the Jews of Koło, Dąbie, Bugaj, and Izbica Kujawska (altogether 5,000 people), plus 35,000 Jews from the Łódź ghetto and a certain number of Gypsies, were gassed at Chełmno.

In February 1942 the extirpation of the Jews began in the so-called Generalgouvernement. It started in Tarnów and Radom, where Gestapo and SS men began visiting the Jewish quarters daily, systematically killing Jews in streets, courtyards, and apartments. In March the massive expulsion of Jews from Lublin began, during whose course children and old people in the orphanages and old-age homes, as well as patients in the general and communicable disease hospitals, were brutally murdered . . . About 25,000 Jews were transported from Lublin in sealed railroad cars 'in an unknown direction'; all trace of them has been lost. About 3,000 Jews were housed in barracks in Majdanek Tartarowy, a Lublin suburb. In Lublin there is no longer a single Jew . . .

Since 18 April [Gestapo officers] have been killing a number of Jews [in Warsaw] daily in broad daylight, at home or outside. This action is conducted according to prepared lists and encompasses all places where Jews move about in the Warsaw ghetto. There is talk of more bloody nights.

According to an estimate, to date the Germans have murdered 700,000 Polish Jews.

These facts demonstrate irrefutably that the criminal German regime has begun to realize Hitler's prediction that five minutes before the end of the war, no matter how it ends, he will murder all the Jews of Europe . . . Immediate annihilation threatens millions of Polish citizens of Jewish nationality.

Therefore we ask the Polish Republic, as the protector and representative of all people living on Polish territory, immediately to take the necessary steps to prevent the annihilation of Polish Jewry. To this end the Polish Republic must exert its influence upon the Allied governments and the responsible agents in those countries immediately to apply a policy of reprisal against German citizens . . . [The German government] must know that Germans in the United States and other countries will have to answer *now* for the bestial extirpation of the Jewish population.

We understand that we are demanding extraordinary steps from the Polish Republic. This is the only way to save millions of Jews from certain annihilation.

Source: 'Raport Bundu w sprawie prześladowań Żydów (Bund report on the persecutions of Jews)', Hoover Institution Archives: Stanisław Mikołajczyk, Box 12.

Document 25   THE WARSAW *JUDENRAT* OFFERS TO REGULATE JEWISH FORCED LABOUR

The following description was written by Szmul Zygielbojm, a member of the Warsaw Judenrat, following his escape from Poland in December 1939. Zygielbojm spent two years in the United States before moving to London to serve as a representative of the Bund in the exiled Polish National Council. On 12 May 1943 he committed suicide in protest over the evident unwillingness of Western governments to come to the aid of Jews threatened with death.

One of the most awful torments picking away at Jewish life in Poland under the Nazis is kidnapping for labour service. The Germans are seizing old and young in the streets and carrying them away to perform the hardest labour . . . When this happens Jews are brutally beaten with regularity and often murdered . . .

[The day after the Germans entered Warsaw] lorries parked near the places where Jews were standing in long rows to obtain a piece of bread. Nazis in blue uniforms, holding rifles, revolvers, and whips, undertook to cleanse the queues of Jews. Jewish women, young and old, were beaten out of the queues with fists, pulled out by the hair, knocked out with kicks to the stomach. Jewish men were grabbed by the collar, dragged out of the queues and thrown onto the dark, sealed lorries . . .

That was the beginning. Where the people were being taken, what would happen to them – no one knew . . .

[Since then] groups of Germans stand on street corners, looking at the faces of passers-by. Whoever is a Jew is ordered, 'Jew, come here!' When that happens he is already lost, a captive. Often young Polish antisemites stand with the Germans and help the Nazis recognize who is a Jew. The honest Poles are angry about this . . .

I will never forget the faces of some Jews who came to the *Judenrat* offices to tell about the horrors . . . One . . . was one of the best-known and finest Yiddish actors. His clothes were torn and smeared with mud and blood. His hands were cut and torn from the hard labour he was forced to perform . . . [Another] banged his fist against his own face and wailed . . . 'Look! I'm being forced to soak myself in blood . . . I won't survive this! Help, do something, help save me from this, because I'm liable to commit some horrible deed' . . .

We [in the *Judenrat*] could not bear the humiliating kidnapping of Jews from the streets the way dogcatchers catch dogs. We tried to figure out how to counteract this. The Warsaw *Judenrat* approached the Gestapo with a proposal: if the German occupation authorities need people for labour, they should obtain them in an organized fashion; but the kidnapping of people in the streets must stop. Let the daily quota of Jews required by the Germans be determined, and the community will provide people.

The Gestapo accepted the proposal on the surface. From that time (November 1939) the Warsaw *Judenrat* did indeed provide two thousand Jews a day for labour service. But the kidnapping of Jews from the streets did not stop.

When the community protested, the Gestapo replied . . . that the military authorities were the ones doing the kidnapping, and the Gestapo had no control over them. Nonetheless, the obligation that the *Judenrat* had undertaken remained in force: it had to continue providing two thousand workers every day, even though kidnappings from the street went on anyway.

Source: Hertz, J.S. (ed.) (1947), *Zygielbojm-Bukh*, New York: Unzer Tsayt, pp. 142–50.

THE LEADER OF THE BIAŁYSTOK *JUDENRAT* PREACHES 'SALVATION Document 26
THROUGH WORK'

This document is taken from the minutes of a meeting of the Białystok Judenrat on 16 August 1942. Few sets of Judenrat minutes have been preserved. The speaker is the head of the Judenrat, Efraim Barash.

Today's meeting is being held under the severe impression of the events of the last weeks [the mass deportations from Warsaw and Slonim]. We must not shut our eyes to our own fate; we must face the truth squarely.

Białystok has been living a more or less peaceful life during the past year . . . Our task is to maintain that situation and to extend it to the end, which has to come someday.

But by what available means . . . can we do this? . . . We cannot simply come and say, 'We want to live, we have wives and children'! There is no pity. There is only one recourse: deeds! [We must] turn the ghetto into an element that is too valuable, too useful to destroy.

And we are doing this.

You yourselves have seen how in recent weeks . . . delegations have come here. Some have included the highest ranks in the regime. They are coming . . . to resolve the question of whether the ghetto should exist. These are the days when our fate will be determined . . . We have now put 40 per cent of the Jewish population – almost all who are physically able – to work. This makes a powerful impression and to a certain extent blunts the hostile actions of our enemies . . .

Source: Blumenthal, Nachman (ed.) (1962), *Darko shel Judenrat: Te'udot miGeto Białystok*, Jerusalem: Yad Vashem, p. 236.

Document 27   THE HEAD OF THE ŁÓDŹ GHETTO ANNOUNCES THE DEPORTATION OF CHILDREN

Mordechai Haim Rumkowski, head of the Łódź ghetto (the second largest in Nazi-occupied Poland), made this public speech on 4 September 1942.

The ghetto has been hit with a painful blow. They are demanding from us our most precious fortune – children and the elderly. I was not privileged to have a child of my own, so I gave the best years of my life to children . . . In my old age I must stretch out my hands and beg: 'Brothers and sisters, turn them over to me! Fathers and mothers, give me your children' . . .

Yesterday I was commanded to expel twenty-odd thousand Jews from the ghetto, and if not – 'We will do it!' And the question presented itself: 'Should we take over and do it ourselves or leave it for others to carry it out?' Thinking not about how many will perish but about how many might be saved, we . . . came to the conclusion that, no matter how hard it is for us, we should take it upon ourselves to execute the evil decree.

I must perform this difficult and bloody operation. I must amputate limbs in order to save the body! I must take children because, if not, others could be taken as well, heaven forbid . . .

In the ghetto we have many tuberculosis patients whose life expectancy is numbered in days, or maybe in weeks. I don't know – maybe this is a devilish plan, maybe not – but I can't hold it back: 'Give me those sick people, and in their place we can save healthy ones' . . . Each evil decree forces us to weigh and measure: who should, can and may be saved? And common sense dictates that the ones to be saved must be those . . . who have a chance of being rescued, not those who cannot be saved in any case.

Remember that we live in the ghetto. Remember that our life is so constricted that we do not have enough even for the healthy, let alone for the sick. Every one of us feeds the sick at the expense of our own health: we give up our bread to the sick . . . And the result of all this is not only that the sick don't get better but that we become sick ourselves . . .

Standing before you is a broken Jew. Don't be jealous of me. This is the worst decree I have ever had to carry out. I stretch out my broken, trembling hands to you and beg: Place the victims in my hands so that they can help us avoid having further victims and protect a community of a hundred thousand. So I have been promised: if we deliver our victims by ourselves, we shall have quiet . . .

What do you want, for 80–90,000 Jews to survive or for everyone to perish, heaven forbid? . . . Judge me as you will; my obligation is to protect the remaining Jews.

Source: Trunk, Isaiah (ed.) (1962), *Lodzher geto*, New York: Marston Press, pp. 311–14.

A WARSAW GHETTO RESIDENT COMMENTS ON CZERNIAKÓW'S SUICIDE   Document 28

Henryk Makower, a Polish physician of Jewish origin who, despite having been baptized, was forced to reside in the Warsaw ghetto, composed a memoir of his twenty-eight months in the ghetto shortly after escaping in January 1943.

The chairman of the *Judenrat*, engineer Adam Czerniaków . . . refused to sign the [deportation] order. After a conference with the authorities on the second day of the action, 23 July, the bold and resourceful Adam Czerniaków committed suicide . . . He was found dead in the *Judenrat* office. Clearly he had not wanted to put his own name to the deportation (it is rumoured that the Germans announced publicly that they had begun deporting Jews from Warsaw at the *Judenrat*'s behest!). Czerniaków had not wanted to be a witness to this tragedy, whose extent he certainly foresaw. He did a bad thing, for following his departure almost 400,000 people were left without leadership. In my opinion he should have foreseen this and demonstrated even greater courage by staying alive. Perhaps he no longer had the strength . . .

At the time we were stupid. The shock of Czerniaków's death made us think not that he had been brave but that he had had a nervous breakdown, and we dismissed any thought of extermination as unreal and impossible.

Source: Makower, Henryk (1987), *Pamiętnik z getta warszawskiego*, Wrocław: Ossolineum, p. 56.

Document 29   SELF-HELP AND ALTERNATIVE LEADERSHIP IN WARSAW

The author of this text is unknown. It is taken from a manuscript recovered after the war and deposited at the Jewish Historical Institute in Warsaw.

In the building where I lived there were 30 needy families . . . They occupied a boarded-up office at the rear of the building, where there was no electricity, gas, or water . . . They stubbornly battled the harsh conditions of life as best they could. [But] prices soared, and their strength and reserves became exhausted . . . A house committee organized to get food for the children, distributed holiday gift packages, bought medicines, summoned doctors, set up a club in a heated room where they could sit by day, tried to find clothing, sought employment for those able to work, and gave grants or loans whenever possible. Several dozen house committees organized a people's kitchen . . . that distributed several hundred portions of soup daily to the neediest.

The house committees . . . often played an important role . . . in building people's political awareness. The *Judenrat* opposed the house committees, because it could not control the activities of so many such bodies. It wanted to transform them into organs of administrative pressure.

Source: Grynberg, Michał (ed.) (1993), *Pamiętniki z getta warszawskiego*, Warsaw: PWN, pp. 41–42.

Document 30   HIDING IN A BUNKER

This testimony, by Wiktor Littner, is one of the earliest postwar accounts of survival in hiding. It was given to the Regional Jewish Historical Commission in Kraków in 1945.

We thought about arranging a hiding place; but building a bunker was not easy, for our hut was not detached and had no basement. There was a tiny table next to the kitchen stove. The floorboard that ran between the legs of the table could be removed easily. Underneath the board we gouged out a hole and covered it so that those who didn't know about it couldn't notice anything. But we had to do everything in such a way that the floorboards would have dirt underneath them, so that they wouldn't make a hollow sound, different from the rest of the floor. We managed with great difficulty to remove many buckets of dirt. Finally the bunker was ready. There was enough room in the cave under the floor for four people to squeeze in tolerably. On one side we dug out a recess, where we put the floorboard and some water, and even a small thermos. Thus we passed many nights and days in terror.

Source: Borwicz, Michał M., Rost, Nella, Wulf, Józef (eds) (1945), *Dokumenty zbrodni i męczeństwa*, Kraków: Wojewódzka Żydowska Komisja Historyczna, pp. 155–56.

ŻEGOTA APPEALS FOR FUNDS TO RESCUE POLISH JEWS   Document 31

This letter, composed on 12 May 1943, reflects the difficulties faced by the underground Council for Aid to Jews in Warsaw in procuring the necessary funds for its activities. It is taken from the Council's voluminous secret archive, which survived the war.

To the [Polish] Minister of Social Welfare, London:

The occupier's murder of the country's Jewish population, which is increasing daily and now reaching culmination, imposes ever greater and more difficult obligations . . . for rescuing the remaining . . . Jews and supporting active resistance units. In the fourth year of the war the Polish people have become so impoverished that, although we can demand that they give their lives to aid and hide hunted Jews . . . it is impossible to demand . . . material contributions . . . The Council for Aid to Jews . . . possesses so relatively few material resources received from the [underground authorities] that they represent only symbolic assistance in the face of the enormity of the demands and needs that mount each day. The Council . . . has already requested the Polish government-in-exile . . . to send it 6–8 million zł per month if assistance is to be real and not a fiction. Unfortunately, so far the Council has received neither assistance nor a response.

The prime minister's words . . . about extending aid to the ill-fated Jewish population found a lively response here . . . but in order for documents to remain of large-scale humanitarian activity by the Polish population . . . great amounts of funds are needed for establishing aid centres, for continuous and not merely haphazard assistance to the victims, for the inclusion of as many victims as possible, and for reaching wherever aid is needed, wherever it is still possible to release a person from the hands of the criminals.

Thus the Council for Aid to Jews . . . conscious of its obligations and responsibilities . . . asks you to intervene in this matter, to allocate the needed funds for this purpose, and to send the Council a response as quickly as possible. The Council's future plans depend on this.

Warsaw, 12 May 1943

Source: Yad Vashem Archives, O6/48.10a.

Document 32   A PLEA TO COMBAT BLACKMAIL OF JEWS IN HIDING

This document from the Żegota archive, dated March 1943, was addressed to the leadership of the Polish underground.

The plague of blackmail carried out by criminal elements of society against Jews . . . is already a mass phenomenon . . .

A determined struggle against this hideous practice of extorting and denouncing the victims of German terror is becoming the burning problem of the moment, and the condemnation of this disgraceful plague is a matter of our community's honour and self-respect.

The Aid Council *Żegota*, at its meeting on 25 [March 1943], decided to request of the government delegate:

1. Publication and posting of death sentences against blackmailers that have already been carried out. Only street placards including the grounds for the sentences and a categorical admonition against other [such deeds] will create the necessary effect and bring real results. Only in this way will the broad mass of the populace realize that the government delegate regards blackmail as a capital crime . . .

2. Stepping up the active struggle against blackmailers by . . . regularly assigning . . . the death penalty. Such a decisive stand by state officials will undoubtedly bring the expected result and radically change the demoralizing state of affairs.

Source: Prekerowa, Teresa (1982), *Konspiracyjna Rada Pomocy Żydom w Warszawie 1942–1945*, Warsaw: Państwowy Instytut Wydawniczy, pp. 370–71.

HIMMLER COMMENTS ON MASS MURDER   Document 33

An extract from a speech to senior SS officers given by Himmler at Poznań, 4 October 1943.

I . . . want to speak to you . . . of a really grave chapter. Amongst ourselves . . . it shall be said quite openly, but all the same we will never speak about it in public . . .

I am referring . . . to the extermination of the Jewish people . . . Most of you men know what it is like to see 100 corpses side by side, or 500, or 1,000. To have stood fast through this and . . . to have stayed decent – that has made us hard. This is an unwritten and never-to-be-written page of glory in our history. . . . All in all . . . we can say that we have carried out this most difficult of tasks in a spirit of love for our people. And we have suffered no harm to our inner being, our soul, our character.

Source: Arad, Yitzhak, Gutman, Israel, and Margaliot, Abraham (eds) (1999), *Documents on the Holocaust: Selected Sources on the Destruction of the Jews of Germany and Austria, Poland, and the Soviet Union*, Eighth edition, Lincoln, NE: University of Nebraska Press, pp. 344–45.

Guide to further reading

The Holocaust has inspired a vast and rapidly growing scholarly literature in most major European languages and in Hebrew. This essay lists only books and articles in English. Unfortunately, as of 2011 there is no up-to-date, comprehensive, multilingual bibliography of the subject.

The standard anthology of primary documents related to the encounter between the Third Reich and the Jews is *Documents on the Holocaust*, edited by Yitzhak Arad, Israel Gutman, and Abraham Margaliot (Lincoln: University of Nebraska Press, 1999). The documents reflect the evolution of Nazi policy towards Jews in Germany and Austria, Poland, and the Soviet Union, as well as the responses of Jews in those countries to Nazi actions. An older collection, *Documents of Destruction*, edited by Raul Hilberg (Chicago: Quadrangle Books, 1971), highlights Nazi policy, while *A Holocaust Reader*, edited by Lucy S. Dawidowicz (New York: Behrman House, 1976) focuses on Jewish behaviour under Nazi impact. Beginning in 2010 the United States Holocaust Memorial Museum has begun to publish a series of documentary anthologies, based mainly on its own archival holdings, entitled *Jewish Responses to Persecution*. Volume 1, edited by Jürgen Matthäus and Mark Roseman, encompasses the years 1933–38; volume 2, edited by Alexandra Garbarini, extends coverage to 1940. Both volumes contain bibliographies. Specific themes in Holocaust history are highlighted in the series *The Holocaust: Selected Documents in Eighteen Volumes*, edited by John Mendelsohn (Clark, NJ: Lawbook Exchange, 2010). The volumes reproduce facsimiles of original documents held at the United States National Archives.

There are several comprehensive scholarly overviews of the Holocaust. Foremost among them is Saul Friedländer's magisterial two-volume history, *Nazi Germany and the Jews* (New York: Harper Collins, 1997–2007). The first volume, entitled *The Years of Persecution*, describes the interval from the Nazi accession to power until the beginning of the Second World War; the second, entitled *The Years of Extermination*, treats the war years. An outstanding feature of these books is their integration of German and Jewish perspectives, along with those of so-called bystanders: witnesses to the encounter between the two groups who belonged to neither. A one-volume work that offers a similar integration is Leni Yahil, *The Holocaust: The Fate of European Jewry, 1932–1945* (Oxford: Oxford University Press, 1990). A classic study of the evolution of Nazi Jewish policy and its execution is Raul Hilberg, *The Destruction of the European Jews*. Originally published in 1961, it was released in an expanded, three-volume edition in 1985 and in a third edition in 2003 (New Haven, CT: Yale University Press). Similarly German-centred is Peter Longerich, *Holocaust: The Nazi Persecution and Murder of the Jews* (Oxford: Oxford University Press, 2010).

An indispensable reference work for students and scholars is *Encyclopaedia of the Holocaust*, edited by Israel Gutman (New York: Macmillan, 1990). A more compact reference is *The Holocaust Encyclopaedia*, edited by Walter Laqueur (New Haven, CT: Yale University Press, 2001). *The Columbia Guide to the Holocaust*, edited by Donald Niewyk and Francis Nicosia (New York: Columbia University Press, 2000), offers a good overview of the literature of the field, as does Saul Friedländer's article, 'The Holocaust and its Aftermath', in the *Oxford Handbook of Jewish Studies* (Oxford: Oxford University Press, 2002). Still useful for the same purpose is Michael Marrus, *The Holocaust in History* (Lebanon, NH: University Press of New England, 1987). *Atlas of the Holocaust*, by Martin Gilbert (New York: William Morrow, 1993), provides an excellent orientation to the geographical dimensions of the Nazi murder campaign and of Jewish life in Europe under Nazi impact. *Encyclopaedia of Jewish Life Before and During the Holocaust*, edited by Shmuel Spector (New York: New York University Press, 2001), is a condensed version of the Hebrew *Pinkas haKehilot*, an encyclopaedic listing of every individual Jewish community touched by Nazi rule, with histories constructed largely from survivor testimony. Another fundamental reference is *The Yad Vashem Encyclopaedia of the Ghettos during the Holocaust*, edited by Guy Miron (Jerusalem: Yad Vashem, 2009).

Several collections of scholarly articles offer valuable introductions to multiple dimensions of the subject. These include *The Holocaust: Origins, Implementation, Aftermath*, edited by Omer Bartov (London: Routledge, 2000); *The Holocaust and History: The Known, the Unknown, the Disputed, and the Reexamined*, edited by Michael Berenbaum and Abraham J. Peck (Bloomington: Indiana University Press, 1998); *The Final Solution: Origins and Implementation*, edited by David Cesarani (London: Routledge, 1994); *Unanswered Questions: Nazi Germany and the Genocide of the Jews*, edited by François Furet (New York: Schocken Books, 1989); and *The Holocaust as Historical Experience*, edited by Yehuda Bauer and Nathan Rotenstreich (New York: Holmes and Meier, 1981). Detailed historiographical surveys of 24 different aspects of the encounter between the Third Reich and the Jews are offered in *The Historiography of the Holocaust*, edited by Dan Stone (New York: Palgrave Macmillan, 2004).

Two books by Yehuda Bauer, *Rethinking the Holocaust* (New Haven, CT: Yale University Press, 2001) and *The Holocaust in Historical Perspective* (Seattle: University of Washington Press, 1978), offer reflections on employing historical methods to fathom the fate of European Jewry at Nazi hands. *Memory, History, and the Extermination of the Jews of Europe*, by Saul Friedländer (Bloomington: Indiana University Press, 1993), examines difficulties with the historical approach, as does the seminal volume edited by Friedländer, *Probing the Limits of Representation: Nazism and the Final Solution* (Cambridge, MA: Harvard University Press, 1992). Dan Michman, *Holocaust Historiography: A Jewish Perspective* (London: Vallentine Mitchell, 2003) considers the implications of studying Jewish history under Nazi impact using the historian's tools.

Analyses of the Holocaust through the lens of other instances of genocide or ethnic cleansing include Ben Kiernan, *Blood and Soil: Genocide and Extermination in World History from Carthage to Darfur* (New Haven, CT: Yale University Press, 2007); Eric D. Weitz, *A Century of Genocide: Utopias of Race and Nation* (Princeton, NJ: Princeton University Press, 2003); Norman M. Naimark, *Fires of Hatred: Ethnic Cleansing in Twentieth-Century Europe* (Cambridge, MA: Harvard University Press, 2001); and Robert Melson, *Revolution and Genocide: On the Origins of the Armenian Genocide and the Holocaust* (Chicago: University of Chicago Press, 1992). *Bloodlands: Europe between Hitler and Stalin*, by Timothy Snyder (New York: Basic Books, 2010), places the Holocaust in eastern Europe in the context of the murderous policies pursued by the German and Soviet regimes in the border regions between the two countries between the early 1930s and the end of the Second World War. On Nazi persecution of groups other than Jews on racial grounds see, among others, Guenter Lewy, *The Nazi Persecution of the Gypsies* (Oxford: Oxford University Press, 2000); Michael Burleigh and Wolfgang Wippermann, *The Racial State: Germany 1933–1945* (Cambridge: Cambridge University Press, 1991); and Henry Friedlander, *The Origins of Nazi Genocide: From Euthanasia to the Final Solution* (Chapel Hill: University of North Carolina Press, 1995). Daniel Blatman, *The Death Marches: The Final Phase of Nazi Genocide* (Cambridge, MA: Harvard University Press, 2011), ponders the connection between the Holocaust and the killing of other 'enemies of the Aryan race' during the final months of the Second World War.

Readers seeking a basic overview of the history of the Jews should consult John Efron *et al.*, *The Jews: A History* (Upper Saddle River, NJ: Pearson Prentice Hall, 2009). Attitudes towards Jews in antiquity are surveyed by Peter Schäfer, *Judeophobia* (Cambridge, MA: Harvard University Press, 1997). Several important books treat attitudes towards Jews in medieval Christian

Europe, including Robert Chazan, *Medieval Stereotypes and Modern Antisemitism* (Berkeley: University of California Press, 1997) and Jeremy Cohen, *The Friars and the Jews: The Evolution of Medieval Anti-Judaism* (Ithaca, NY: Cornell University Press, 1982). A useful survey of Jewish history since the seventeenth century is Lloyd P. Gartner, *History of the Jews in Modern Times* (Oxford: Oxford University Press, 2001). A comparative look at the process of emancipation in different European countries is offered in *Paths of Emancipation: Jews, States, and Citizenship*, edited by Pierre Birnbaum and Ira Katznelson (Princeton, NJ: Princeton University Press, 1995). The history of the large Jewish communities of eastern Europe is best approached through Israel Bartal, *The Jews of Eastern Europe, 1772–1881* (Philadelphia: University of Pennsylvania Press, 2005), and Ezra Mendelsohn, *The Jews of East Central Europe between the World Wars* (Bloomington: Indiana University Press, 1983). Antony Polonsky's three-volume work, *The Jews in Poland and Russia* (London: Littman Library of Jewish Civilization, 2010–12) presents a more detailed history of the region's Jewish population, including a substantial section on the Holocaust. The multi-authored, four-volume *German-Jewish History in Modern Times*, edited by Michael A. Meyer (New York: Columbia University Press, 1996–98), does the same for the first Jewish community to encounter the Third Reich.

Important general histories of the Third Reich include the trilogy by Richard J. Evans, *The Coming of the Third Reich* (2003), *The Third Reich in Power, 1933–1939* (2006), and *The Third Reich at War* (2009) (all published in New York by Penguin) and Michael Burleigh, *The Third Reich: A New History* (New York: Hill & Wang, 2001). *Hitler's Empire: How the Nazis Ruled Europe*, by Mark Mazower (New York: Penguin, 2008) examines the so-called Nazi New Order, including the murder of Jews, as it was implemented throughout Europe. Ian Kershaw's *The Nazi Dictatorship: Problems and Perspectives of Interpretation* (London: Arnold, 2000) is a lucid guide to the historiographical debates over the character of the Nazi regime. *Hitler*, Kershaw's two-volume life of the Nazi leader (W. W. Norton, New York, 1999–2000), abridged to a single volume in 2008, is now the standard biography. Biographies of other Nazis who played a significant role in the killing of Jews include Richard Breitman, *The Architect of Genocide: Himmler and the Final Solution* (Hanover, NH: Brandeis University Press, 1991); Robert Gerwarth, *Hitler's Hangman: The Life of Heydrich* (New Haven, CT: Yale University Press, 2011); and David Cesarani, *Becoming Eichmann* (Cambridge, MA: Da Capo Press, 2007).

The foundational work for understanding Hitler's world view and the place of the Jews in it is Eberhard Jäckel, *Hitler's World View: A Blueprint for Power* (Cambridge, MA: Harvard University Press, 1981). Insights have been added by Rainer Bucher, *Hitler's Theology: A Study in Political Religion*

(London: Continuum, 2011). An important study of the possible intellectual origins of Hitler's world view is Nicholas Goodrick-Clarke, *The Occult Roots of Nazism* (New York: New York University Press, 1992).

There are many works on German popular attitudes towards Jews during the Nazi era, including David Bankier, *The Germans and the Final Solution: Public Opinion under Nazism* (Oxford: Blackwell, 1992); Sarah Gordon, *Hitler, Germans, and the 'Jewish Question'* (Princeton, NJ: Princeton University Press, 1984); and Otto Dov Kulka, 'Public Opinion in Nazi Germany and the "Jewish Question"', *Jerusalem Quarterly* 25 (1982): 121–44. Important essays by Ian Kershaw on the subject have been collected in *Hitler, the Germans, and the Final Solution* (New Haven, CT: Yale University Press, 2008). Otto Dov Kulka and Eberhard Jäckel have published an extensive, thoroughly annotated selection of surveillance reports on German public opinion concerning Jews commissioned by the Nazi regime under the title, *The Jews in the Secret Nazi Reports on Popular Opinion in Germany, 1933–1945* (New Haven, CT: Yale University Press, 2010). The volume includes a CD with original copies of nearly 4,000 documents on the subject.

The evolution of Nazi Jewish policy leading up to mass killing, the factors that triggered the transition, and the dating of the implementation of the murder policy remain subjects of intense examination and debate. Of works focusing on the period before the invasion of Poland, Karl A. Schleunes, *The Twisted Road to Auschwitz* (Urbana: University of Illinois Press, 1970) remains of seminal importance. Besides the more general works by Friedländer, Hilberg, and Longerich listed above, essential literature includes Götz Aly and Susanne Heim, *Architects of Annihilation: Auschwitz and the Logic of Destruction* (Princeton, NJ: Princeton University Press, 1991); Christopher R. Browning, *The Origins of the Final Solution* (Lincoln: University of Nebraska Press, 2004); Philippe Burrin, *Hitler and the Jews: The Genesis of the Holocaust* (London: Edward Arnold, 1994); Peter Longerich, *The Unwritten Order: Hitler's Role in the Final Solution* (Stroud: Tempus, 2001); and Mark Roseman, *The Wannsee Conference and the Final Solution: A Reconsideration* (New York: Henry Holt, 2002). Adam Tooze, *The Wages of Destruction: The Making and Breaking of the Nazi Economy* (New York: Viking, 2006), links the decision for mass killing to economic factors. *National Socialist Extermination Policies: Contemporary German Perspectives and Controversies*, edited by Ulrich Herbert (New York: Berghahn Books, 2000) is a collection of local and regional studies of killing operations in which the role of lower-level Nazi commanders and officials in deciding upon and implementing mass murder is highlighted.

Local dimensions of the encounter between the Third Reich and the Jews are examined in the collection *The Holocaust and Local History*, edited by Thomas Kühne and Tom Lawson (London: Valentine Mitchell, 2011). Another valuable collection in this category is *Collaboration and Resistance during the Holocaust: Belarus, Estonia, Latvia, Lithuania*, edited by David Gaunt, Paul A. Levine and Laura Palosuo (Bern: Peter Lang, 2004). Studies of the Holocaust in individual countries include Dan Michman, (ed.) *Belgium and the Holocaust: Jews, Belgians, Germans* (Jerusalem: Yad Vashem, 1998); Frederick Chary, *The Bulgarian Jews and the Final Solution, 1940–1944* (Pittsburgh: University of Pittsburgh Press, 1972); Livia Rothkirchen, *The Jews of Bohemia and Moravia: Facing the Holocaust* (Lincoln: University of Nebraska Press, 2005); Leni Yahil, *The Rescue of Danish Jewry: Test of a Democracy* (Philadelphia: Jewish Publication Society, 1969); Anton Weiss-Wendt, *Murder Without Hatred: Estonians and the Holocaust* (Syracuse, NY: Syracuse University Press, 2009); Michael R. Marrus and Robert O. Paxton, *Vichy France and the Jews* (New York: Basic Books, 1981); Renée Poznanski, *Jews in France during World War II* (Hanover, NH: Brandeis University Press, 2001); Avraham Barkai, *From Boycott to Annihilation: The Economic Struggle of German Jews 1933–1943* (Hanover, NH: Brandeis University Press, 1989); Marion A. Kaplan, *Between Dignity and Despair: Jewish Life in Nazi Germany* (Oxford: Oxford University Press, 1998); Steven B. Bowman, *The Agony of Greek Jews, 1940–1945* (Stanford, CA: Stanford University Press, 2009); Randolph L. Braham, *The Politics of Genocide: The Holocaust in Hungary* (Detroit: Wayne State University Press, 2000); Joshua D. Zimmerman (ed.) *Jews in Italy under Fascist and Nazi Rule 1922–1945* (Cambridge: Cambridge University Press, 2005); Andrew Ezergalis, *The Holocaust in Latvia, 1941–1944* (United States Holocaust Memorial Museum, 1996); Bob Moore, *Victims and Survivors: The Nazi Persecution of the Jews in the Netherlands 1940–1945* (London: Arnold, 1997); Samuel Abrahamsen, *Norway's Response to the Holocaust* (New York: Holocaust Library, 1991); Radu Ioanid, *The Holocaust in Romania* (Chicago: Ivan R. Dee, 2000); and Yitzhak Arad, *The Holocaust in the Soviet Union* (Lincoln: University of Nebraska Press, 2009).

Perhaps surprisingly, no comprehensive history of the Holocaust in Poland exists in English. Nevertheless, more has been written about that country than about any other. Studies of individual Polish Jewish communities include Israel Gutman, *The Jews of Warsaw, 1939–1943: Ghetto, Underground, Revolt* (Bloomington: Indiana University Press, 1982); Barbara Engelking and Jacek Leociak, *The Warsaw Ghetto: A Guide to the Perished City* (New Haven, CT: Yale University Press, 2009); Gordon J. Horowitz, *Ghettostadt: Lodz and the Making of a German City* (Cambridge, MA: Harvard University Press, 2008); Isaiah Trunk, *Łódź Ghetto: A History* (Bloomington: Indiana University Press, 2006); Yitzhak Arad, *Ghetto in Flames: The Struggle and Destruction of the Jews in Vilna in the Holocaust* (Jerusalem: Yad Vashem, 1980); and Sara Bender, *The Jews of Białystok during World War II and the Holocaust* (Hanover, NH: Brandeis University Press, 2008). Yehuda Bauer, *The Death of the Shtetl* (New Haven, CT: Yale University Press, 2009), analyzes

Jewish responses to Soviet and Nazi occupation in eleven small towns in Ukraine and Belarus, examining factors that might account for divergent behaviour patterns identified in them. *Neighbors: The Destruction of the Jewish Community in Jedwabne, Poland*, by Jan T. Gross (Princeton, NJ: Princeton University Press, 2000), is one of the few works in English about the Holocaust in the Polish countryside. It set off a storm for its depiction of the role played by Polish residents of a small town in the murder of their Jewish neighbours.

An overview of Polish-Jewish relations under Nazi impact is Yisrael Gutman and Shmuel Krakowski, *Unequal Victims: Poles and Jews During World War II* (New York: Holocaust Library, 1986). The articles in *Contested Memories: Poles and Jews during the Holocaust and its Aftermath*, edited by Joshua D. Zimmerman (Chapel Hill, NC: Rutgers University Press, 2003), are also valuable. Polish-Jewish political relations have been the subject of two books by David Engel: *In the Shadow of Auschwitz: The Polish Government-in-Exile and the Jews, 1939–1942* (Chapel Hill: University of North Carolina Press, 1987) and *Facing a Holocaust: The Polish Government-in-Exile and the Jews, 1942–1945* (Chapel Hill: University of North Carolina Press, 1993). The experience of Jews trying to survive by hiding on the so-called 'Aryan side' of Warsaw is examined in Gunnar S. Paulsson, *Secret City: The Hidden Jews of Warsaw, 1940–1945* (New Haven, CT: Yale University Press, 2002). Another sort of experience in hiding is the subject of Ewa Kurek, *Your Life is Worth Mine: How Polish Nuns Saved Hundreds of Jewish Children in German-Occupied Poland, 1939–1945* (New York: Hippocrene Books, 1997). The motives of Poles who risked their lives to assist Jews is explored in Nechama Tec, *When Light Pierced the Darkness: Christian Rescuers of Jews in Nazi-Occupied Poland* (Oxford: Oxford University Press, 1986).

There are several important studies of perpetrators of mass murder and of the sites where mass killings took place. Yitzhak Arad, *Belzec, Sobibor, Treblinka: The Operation Reinhard Death Camps* (Bloomington: Indiana University Press, 1999) is a detailed study of three major killing centres. A number of books treat Auschwitz-Birkenau: Sybille Steinbacher, *Auschwitz: A History* (London: Penguin, 2005); Yisrael Gutman and Michael Berenbaum (eds), *Anatomy of the Auschwitz Death Camp* (Bloomington: Indiana University Press, 1994); and Debórah Dwork and Robert Jan van Pelt, *Auschwitz, 1270 to the Present* (New York: Norton, 1996). Christopher Browning's *Ordinary Men: Reserve Police Battalion 101 and the Final Solution in Poland* (New York: Harper Collins, 1992) delves into the actions and motives of Germans involved in shooting Jews *en masse*. Browning later turned his attention to a labour camp where many perished but many also survived: *Remembering Survival: Inside a Nazi Slave-Labor Camp* (New York: W. W. Norton, 2010). His collection of essays, *Nazi Policy, Jewish Workers, German Killers*

(Cambridge: Cambridge University Press, 2000), explores interactions between perpetrators and victims. Another sort of interaction and experience is represented in Gideon Greif, *We Wept Without Tears: Testimonies of the Jewish Sonderkommando from Auschwitz* (New Haven, CT: Yale University Press, 2005).

The subject of Jewish responses to the Nazi regime has called forth a large literature. Books of particular note are Isaiah Trunk, *Judenrat: The Jewish Councils in Eastern Europe under Nazi Occupation* (New York: Macmillan, 1972); Shmuel Krakowski, *The War of the Doomed: Jewish Armed Resistance in Poland, 1942–1944* (New York: Holmes & Meier, 1984); and Daniel Blatman, *For Our Freedom and Yours: The Jewish Labour Bund in Poland 1939–1949* (London: Vallentine Mitchell, 2003). Bob Moore, *Survivors: Jewish Self-Help and Rescue in Nazi-Occupied Western Europe* (Oxford: Oxford University Press, 2010), offers the first comparative study of Jewish behaviour in the face of Nazi rule in Belgium, France, Germany, and the Netherlands. Isaiah Trunk, *Jewish Responses to Nazi Persecution* (New York: Stein & Day, 1979), offers 62 eyewitness testimonies illustrating a broad range of experiences. *Women in the Holocaust*, edited by Dalia Ofer and Lenore J. Weitzman (New Haven, CT: Yale University Press, 1998), and *Resistance and Courage: Women, Men, and the Holocaust*, by Nechama Tec (New Haven, CT: Yale University Press, 2003), consider the gendered aspects of Jewish behaviour under Nazi impact.

Personal narratives offer a special window onto the Holocaust. Hundreds of diaries kept during the Nazi period and even more memoirs composed after the fact have been published. An excellent introduction to this literature is Alexandra Garbarini, *Numbered Days: Diaries and the Holocaust* (New Haven, CT: Yale University Press, 2006). *Holocaust Chronicles: Individualizing the Holocaust through Diaries and other Contemporaneous Personal Accounts*, edited by Robert Moses Shapiro (New York: KTAV, 1999), contains nineteen articles on various wartime diaries from Warsaw, Łódź, and Wilno and on methodological problems associated with using diaries as a historical source. *Words to Outlive Us: Eyewitness Accounts from the Warsaw Ghetto*, edited by Michał Grynberg (New York: Henry Holt, 1993), offers selections from survivor testimonies housed at the Jewish Historical Institute in Warsaw. A volume edited by Jack Kugelmass and Jonathan Boyarin, *From a Ruined Garden: The Memorial Books of Polish Jewry* (Bloomington: Indiana University Press, 1998), offers selections from essays and memoirs written after the war by Jews whose communities had been destroyed.

Only a handful of scholarly biographies of Jews who figured prominently in the history of the Holocaust have appeared. Among them are Samuel D. Kassow, *Who Will Write Our History? Emmanuel Ringelblum, the Warsaw Ghetto, and the* Oyneg Shabes *Archive* (Bloomington: Indiana University

Press, 2007); Dina Porat, *The Fall of a Sparrow: The Life and Times of Abba Kovner* (Stanford, CA: Stanford University Press, 2010); Nechama Tec, *In the Lion's Den: The Life of Oswald Rufeisen* (Oxford: Oxford University Press, 1990); Tom Segev, *Simon Wiesenthal: The Life and Legends* (New York: Doubleday, 2010); and Yechiam Weitz, *The Man Who Was Murdered Twice: The Life, Trial, and Death of Israel Kasztner* (Jerusalem: Yad Vashem, 2011). A more journalistic approach is taken by Carol Ann Lee in her biography of the father of Anne Frank, *The Hidden Life of Otto Frank* (New York: William Morrow, 2002). There are also several biographies of non-Jews other than Nazi leaders; most of them involve people generally classified as 'rescuers'. They include Saul Friedländer, *Kurt Gerstein: The Ambiguity of Good* (New York: A. E. Knopf, 1969); Thomas E. Wood and Stanisław M. Jankowski, *Karski: How One Man Tried to Stop the Holocaust* (New York: John Wiley, 1994); Harvey Rosenberg, *Raoul Wallenberg* (New York: Holmes & Meier, 1995); and David M. Crowe, *Oskar Schindler: An Untold Account of his Life, Wartime Activities, and the True Story Behind* The List (Cambridge, MA: Westview Press, 2004).

There is a large literature on the responses of Allied and neutral governments to the Holocaust. Many of the works about the Western Allies (mainly Great Britain and the United States) that remain foundational were composed during the 1970s and 1980s; they are discussed in David Engel, 'The Western Allies and the Holocaust: A Bibliographical Essay', *Polin* 1 (1986): 300–315. Some notable subsequent additions to the works discussed in that essay are Richard Breitman and Alan M. Kraut, *American Refugee Policy and European Jewry, 1933–1945* (Bloomington: Indiana University Press, 1987); Tony Kushner, *The Holocaust and the Liberal Imagination: A Social and Cultural History* (Oxford: Basil Blackwell, 1994); Richard Breitman, *Official Secret: What the Nazis Planned, What the British and Americans Knew* (New York: Hill & Wang, 1998); David Bankier (ed.) *Secret Intelligence and the Holocaust* (New York: Enigma Books, 2006); and Marion A. Kaplan, *Dominican Haven: The Jewish Refugee Settlement in Sosúa, 1940–1945* (New York: Museum of Jewish Heritage, 2008). On neutral governments see Haim Avni, *Spain, the Jews, and Franco* (Philadelphia: Jewish Publication Society, 1982); Stanford J. Shaw, *Turkey and the Holocaust* (New York: New York University Press, 1993); and Paul A. Levine, *From Indifference to Activism: Swedish Diplomacy and the Holocaust, 1938–1944* (Uppsala: Almqvist & Wiksell, 1996). Two important nongovernmental agencies that figured in the history of the Holocaust are explored in Michael Phayer, *The Catholic Church and the Holocaust, 1930–1965* (Bloomington: Indiana University Press, 2000), and Jean-Claude Favez, *The Red Cross and the Holocaust* (Camridge: Cambridge University Press, 1999).

The activities of Jews beyond the Nazi orbit in response to persecution and murder have similarly been extensively studied. Some of the many important works on the subject are Yehuda Bauer, *American Jewry and the Holocaust: The American Jewish Joint Distribution Committee, 1939–1945* (Detroit: Wayne State University Press, 1981); Dina Porat, *The Blue and the Yellow Stars of David: The Zionist Leadership in Palestine and the Holocaust, 1939–1945* (Cambridge, MA: Harvard University Press, 1990); Gulie Ne'eman Arad, *America, its Jews, and the Rise of Nazism* (Bloomington: Indiana University Press, 2000); Richard Bolchover, *British Jewry and the Holocaust* (Oxford: Littman Library of Jewish Civilization, 2003); and Yosef Gorny, *The Jewish Press and the Holocaust 1939–1945: Palestine, Britain, the United States, and the Soviet Union* (Cambridge: Cambridge University Press, 2012).

Books on the significance of the Holocaust are legion. Some works that will help readers begin to think about the complex issues involved are James E. Young, *Writing and Rewriting the Holocaust: Narrative and the Consequences of Interpretation* (Bloomington: Indiana University Press, 1990); Alvin H. Rosenfeld (ed.) *Thinking about the Holocaust after Half a Century* (Bloomington: Indiana University Press, 1997); Inga Clendinnen, *Reading the Holocaust* (Cambridge: Cambridge University Press, 1999); Michael A. Signer (ed.) *Humanity at the Limit: The Impact of the Holocaust Experience on Jews and Christians* (Bloomington: Indiana University Press, 2000); and Moishe Postone and Eric Santner (eds) *Catastrophe and Meaning: The Holocaust and the Twentieth Century* (Chicago: University of Chicago Press, 2003).

References

Adam, Uwe Dietrich (1976), 'An Overall Plan for Anti-Jewish Legislation in the Third Reich?', *Yad Vashem Studies* 11, 33–55.

Allen, William Sheridan (1966), *The Nazi Seizure of Power: The Experience of a Single German Town 1930–1935*, London: Eyre & Spottiswoode.

Arad, Yitzhak, Gutman, Israel, and Margaliot, Abraham (eds) (1999), *Documents on the Holocaust: Selected Sources on the Destruction of the Jews of Germany and Austria, Poland, and the Soviet Union*, Eighth edition, Lincoln, NE: University of Nebraska Press.

Aschheim, Steven E. (1994), 'Small Forays, Grand Theories and Deep Origins: Current Trends in the Historiography of the Holocaust', *Studies in Contemporary Jewry* 10, 139–63.

Bauer, Yehuda (1978), *The Holocaust in Historical Perspective*, Seattle: University of Washington Press.

Bauer, Yehuda (1980), 'Genocide: Was it the Nazis' Original Plan?' *Annals of the American Academy of Political and Social Science* 450, 35–45.

Bauman, Zygmunt (1989), *Modernity and the Holocaust*, Ithaca, NY: Cornell University Press.

Blumenthal, Nachman (ed.) (1962), *Darko shel Judenrat: Te'udot miGeto Białystok*, Jerusalem: Yad Vashem.

Borwicz, Michał M., Rost, Nella, Wulf, Józef (eds) (1945), *Dokumenty zbrodni i męczeństwa*, Kraków: Wojewódzka Żydowska Komisja Historyczna.

Breitman, Richard D. (1991), *The Architect of Genocide: Himmler and the Final Solution*, Hanover, NH: Brandeis University Press.

Broszat, Martin (1979), 'Hitler and the Genesis of the "Final Solution": An Assessment of David Irving's Theses', *Yad Vashem Studies* 13, 73–125.

Browning, Christopher R. (1992), *Ordinary Men: Reserve Police Battalion 101 and the Final Solution in Poland*, New York: HarperCollins.

Browning, Christopher R. (1996), 'Daniel Goldhagen's Willing Executioners', *History and Memory* 8, 88–108.

Browning, Christopher R. (2004), *Thee Origins of the Final Solution: The Evolution of Nazi Jewish Policy, September 1939–March 1942*, with contributions by Jürgen Matthäus, Lincoln, NE: University of Nebraska Press.

Bucher, Rainer (2011), *Hitler's Theology: A Study in Political Religion*, London: Continuum.

Burdick, Charles, and Jacobsen, Hans-Adolf (eds) (1988), *The Halder War Diary 1939–1942*, Novato, CA: Presidio Press.

Dawidowicz, Lucy S. (1975), *The War Against the Jews 1933–1945*, New York: Holt, Rinehart & Winston.

Dawidowicz, Lucy S. (ed.) (1976), *A Holocaust Reader*, New York: Behrman House.

Engel, David (1983), 'An Early Account of Polish Jewry under Nazi and Soviet Occupation Presented to the Polish Government-in-Exile, February 1940' *Jewish Social Studies* 45, 1–16.

Engel, David (1987), *In the Shadow of Auschwitz: The Polish Government-in-Exile and the Jews, 1939–1942*, Chapel Hill: University of North Carolina Press.

Engel, David (1991), 'Moshe Kleinbaum's Report on Issues in the Former Eastern Polish Territories, 12 March 1940', in Norman Davies and Antony Polonsky (eds), *Jews in Eastern Poland and the USSR, 1939–1946*, London: Macmillan, pp. 275–300.

Engel, David (2000), 'Divu'ah miMakor yehudi al gerush yehudei Bielsko-Biała el "haShemurah haYehudit" beEzor Lublin, mars 1940' (A Report on the Jewish Reservation in Lublin, March 1940), *Gal-Ed* 17, CXXXI–CXXXIX.

Esh, Shaul (1979), *Iyunim beHeker haSho'ah veYahadut Zemanenu* (Studies in the Holocaust and Contemporary Jewry), Jerusalem: Institute of Contemporary Jewry.

Fein, Helen (1979), *Accounting for Genocide: National Responses and Jewish Victimization during the Holocaust*, Chicago: University of Chicago Press.

Fleming, Gerald (1984), *Hitler and the Final Solution*, Berkeley: University of California Press.

Friedlander, Henry (1995), *The Origins of Nazi Genocide: From Euthanasia to the Final Solution*, Chapel Hill: University of North Carolina Press.

Friedländer, Saul (1971), *L'antisemitisme nazi: histoire d'une psychose collective*, Paris: Éditions de Seuil.

Friedländer, Saul (1981), 'On the Possibility of the Holocaust: An Approach to a Historical Synthesis', in Yehuda Bauer and Nathan Rotenstreich (eds), *The Holocaust as Historical Experience*, New York: Holmes & Meier, pp. 1–21.

Friedländer, Saul (1992), *Memory, History, and the Extermination of the Jews of Europe*, Bloomington: Indiana University Press.

Friedländer, Saul (1997), *Nazi Germany and the Jews*, vol. 1, *The Years of Persecution*, New York: HarperCollins.

Friedländer, Saul (2007), *Nazi Germany and the Jews*, vol. 2, *The Years of Destruction*, New York: Harper Collins.

Funkenstein, Amos (1989), 'Theological Interpretations of the Holocaust: A Balance', in François Furet (ed.), *Unanswered Questions: Nazi Germany and the Genocide of the Jews*, New York: Schocken Books, pp. 275–303.

Gerlach, Christian (1998), 'The Wannsee Conference, the Fate of German Jews, and Hitler's Decision in Principle to Exterminate All European Jews', *Journal of Modern History* 70, 759–812.

Goldhagen, Daniel Jonah (1996), *Hitler's Willing Executioners: Ordinary Germans and the Holocaust*, New York: Alfred E. Knopf.

Graetz, Heinrich (1866), *Geschichte der Juden*, vol. 4, Leipzig: Verlag von Oskar Leiner.

Grynberg, Michał (ed.) (1993), *Pamiętniki z getta warszawskiego*, Warsaw: PWN.

Gutman, Israel (2008), *Sugiyot beHeker haSho'ah: Bikoret uTerumah* (Issues in Holocaust Scholarship: Research and Reassessment), Jerusalem: Zalman Shazar Center.

Heiber, Helmut (1958), 'Der Generalplan Ost', *Vierteljahrshefte für Zeitgeschichte* 6, 281–325.

Hertz, J.S. (ed.) (1947), *Zygielbojm-Bukh*, New York: Unzer Tsayt.

Hilberg, Raul (1985), *The Destruction of the European Jews*, Second edition, New York: Holmes & Meier.

Hilberg, Raul, Staron, Stanisław, Kermisz, Josef (eds) (1979), *The Warsaw Diary of Adam Czerniaków: Prelude to Doom*, New York: Stein & Day.

Hitler, Adolf (1943), *Mein Kampf*, translated by Ralph Mannheim, Boston: Houghton Mifflin.

Hitler, Adolf (1961), *Hitler's Secret Book*, translated by Salvator Attanasio, New York: Grove Press.

Jäckel, Eberhard (1981), *Hitler's World View: A Blueprint for Power*, translated by Herbert Arnold, Cambridge, MA: Harvard University Press.

Jäckel, Eberhard (1984), *Hitler in History*, Hanover, NH: Brandeis University Press.

Karski, Jan (1944), *Story of a Secret State*, Boston: Houghton Mifflin.

Katz, Jacob (1975), 'Was the Holocaust Predictable?' *Commentary* 59, 41–48.

Katz, Steven T. (1994), *The Holocaust in Historical Context*, vol. 1, *The Holocaust and Mass Death Before the Modern Age*, New York: Oxford University Press.

Ka-Tzetnik 135633 (Yehiel De-Nur) (1989), *Shivitti: A Vision*, San Francisco: Harper & Row.

Kellermann, Heinz (1933), 'Ende der Emanzipation?' *Der Morgen* 9, 173–77.

Kershaw, Ian (1981), 'The Persecution of the Jews and German Popular Opinion in the Third Reich', *Leo Baeck Institute Year Book* 26, 261–89.

References

Kershaw, Ian (2008), *Hitler, the Germans, and the Final Solution*, New Haven, CT: Yale University Press.

Korczak, Ruzhka (1965), *Lehavot ba-efer (Flames in the Ash)*, Tel Aviv: Sifriat Poalim.

Kulka, Otto Dov, and Jäckel, Eberhard (eds) (2010), *The Jews in the Secret Nazi Reports on Popular Opinion in Germany, 1933–1945*, translated by William Templer, New Haven, CT: Yale University Press.

Lamberti, Marjorie (1997), 'The Jewish Defence in Germany after the National-Socialist Seizure of Power', *Leo Baeck Institute Year Book* 42, 135–47.

Lemkin, Raphael (1944), *Axis Rule in Occupied Europe: Laws of Occupation, Analysis of Government Proposals for Redress*, Washington: Carnegie Endowment for International Peace.

Lemkin, Raphael (1952), 'My Battle with Half the World', *Chicago Jewish Forum*, Winter.

Lipstadt, Deborah E. (1986), *Beyond Belief: The American Press and the Coming of the Holocaust 1933–1945*, New York: Free Press.

Lukas, Richard C. (1986), *The Forgotten Holocaust: The Poles under German Occupation 1939–1944*, Lexington: University Press of Kentucky.

Mais, Yitzchak (ed.) (2007), *Daring to Resist: Jewish Defiance in the Holocaust*, New York: Museum of Jewish Heritage.

Makower, Henryk (1987), *Pamiętnik z getta warszawskiego*, Wrocław: Ossolineum.

Margaliot, Abraham (1971), 'The Struggle for Survival of the Jewish Community in Germany in the Face of Oppression', in *Jewish Resistance during the Holocaust*, Jerusalem: Yad Vashem, pp. 100–11.

Mendelsohn, Ezra (1983), *The Jews of East Central Europe between the World Wars*, Bloomington: Indiana University Press.

Michman, Dan (2011), *The Emergence of Jewish Ghettos during the Holocaust*, Cambridge: Cambridge University Press.

Morgenthau, Hans (1961), *The Tragedy of German-Jewish Liberalism* (Leo Baeck Memorial Lecture 4), New York: Leo Baeck Institute.

Neumann, Franz (1944), *Behemoth: The Structure and Practice of National Socialism 1933–1944*, New York: Oxford University Press.

Ofer, Dalia, and Weitzman, Lenore J. (eds) (1998), *Women in the Holocaust*, New Haven, CT: Yale University Press.

Peled (Margolin), Yael (1993), *Krakov haYehudit 1939–1943* (Jewish Kraków 1939–1943), Tel Aviv: Hakibbutz Hameuchad.

Phelps, R.H. (1968), 'Hitlers "grundlegende" Rede über den Antisemitismus', *Vierteljahrshefte für Zeitgeschichte* 16, 390–420.

Poliakov, Léon (1954), *Harvest of Hate: The Nazi Program for the Destruction of the Jews of Europe*, Philadelphia: Jewish Publication Society of America.

Prekerowa, Teresa (1982), *Konspiracyjna Rada Pomocy Żydom w Warszawie 1942–1945*, Warsaw: Państwowy Instytut Wydawniczy.

Pridham, Geoffrey (1973), *Hitler's Rise to Power: The Nazi Movement in Bavaria, 1923–1933*, New York: Harper & Row.

Rauschning, Hermann (1939), *The Revolution of Nihilism: Warning to the West*, translated by W.E. Dickes, New York: Longmans, Green & Co.

Redlich, Shimon (2002), *Together and Apart in Brzezany: Poles, Jews, and Ukrainians, 1919–1945*, Bloomington, Indiana University Press.

Reichmann, Eva G. (1974), *Größe und Verhängnis deutsch-jüdischer Existenz: Zeugnisse einer tragischen Begegnung*, Heidelberg: Lambert Schneider.

Richarz, Monika (ed.) (1991), *Jewish Life in Germany: Memoirs from Three Centuries*, Bloomington: Indiana University Press.

Roseman, Mark (2002), *The Wannsee Conference and the Final Solution: A Reconsideration*, New York: Henry Holt & Co.

Rosenbaum, Alan S. (ed.) (1996), *Is the Holocaust Unique? Perspectives on Comparative Genocide*, Boulder, CO: Westview Press.

Rubinstein, William D. (1997), *The Myth of Rescue: Why the Democracies could not have Saved more Jews from the Nazis*, London: Routledge.

Schleunes, Karl A. (1970), *The Twisted Road to Auschwitz: Nazi Policy toward German Jews 1933–1939*, Urbana: University of Illinois Press.

Schleunes, Karl A. (1989), 'Retracing the Twisted Road: Nazi Policies toward German Jews, 1933–1939', in François Furet (ed.), *Unanswered Questions: Nazi Germany and the Genocide of the Jews*, New York: Schocken Books, pp. 54–70.

Shirer, William L. (1941), *Berlin Diary*, New York: Pocket Books.

State of Israel, Ministry of Justice (1993), *The Trial of Adolf Eichmann: Record of Proceedings in the District Court of Jerusalem*, Jerusalem: Yad Vashem.

Tal, Uriel (1979), 'On the Study of the Holocaust and Genocide', *Yad Vashem Studies* 13, 7–52.

Tooze, Adam (2006), *The Wages of Destruction: The Making and Breaking of the Nazi Economy*, New York: Viking.

Trials of the Major War Criminals before the International Military Tribunal (1949), 42 vols., Nuremberg: International Military Tribunal.

Trials of War Criminals before the Nuremberg Military Tribunals (1952), 18 vols., Washington: US Government Printing Office.

Trunk, Isaiah (ed.) (1962), *Lodzher geto*, New York: Marston Press.

Wasserstein, Bernard M.J. (1979), *Britain and the Jews of Europe 1939–1945*, Oxford: Oxford University Press.

Wood, E. Thomas and Jankowski, Stanisław (1994), *Karski: How One Man Tried to Stop the Holocaust*, New York: John Wiley.

Zalzer, Maria (ed.) (1964), *Weg und Schicksal der Stuttgarter Juden*, Stuttgart: Eernst Klett Verlag.

Index

Aid and Rescue Committee 81
Aktion xviii, 69, 119
Albania 3, 17
Algeria 3
Allen, W. S. 26
Allies xiii, xiv, 87–89, 90. *See also* Great Britain,
    Soviet Union, United States
Ältestenrat 75
Aly, Götz 62
Amidah 78–79
Amsterdam 17
'Antisemites' 16
Antonescu, Ion xv, xix, xxiii, 64, 83
Appel, Marta and Rabbi Ernst 108
Arab revolt 54
Arlosoroff, Chaim xv, 51–52, 111–12
Armed resistance 79–80
Armenians 7
Arrow Cross xviii, 84
Arrow Cross xviii
'Asocials' xviii, xx, 6, 62, 67
Association des Juifs en Belgique 75
Auschwitz-Birkenau xiii, xviii, xix–xxi, xxvi, 6, 9,
    66, 84, 87, 88; asphyxiation by Zyklon B at 67;
    evacuated xiv, 90; medical experiments at 67
Austria xx, xxi, 3, 5, 15, 37, 41, 48, 56, 68; annexed
    by Germany xi; Jewish emigration from 54;
    percentage of Jews in 17
Axis 61
Axis Rule in Occupied Europe 6

Bach, Hans 107–108
Bach-Zelewski, Erich von dem 63
Baltic States 41, 68, 80, 84. *See also* Estonia, Latvia,
    Lithuania
Barash, Efraim xv, 78, 127

Bauer, Yehuda 37, 71
Bauman, Zygmunt 8, 94, 96
Bavaria 25
Becker, Rudolf 35
Będzin xvi
Belarus, Belorussians 63
Belgium xii, 3, 41, 68, 82; Jews deported from xiii;
    Judenrat in 75; percentage of Jews in 17; takes in
    St. Louis refugees 55
Bełżec xiii, xviii, xxi, xxiii, 6, 66, 68, 117;
    asphyxiation by diesel exhaust at 67; news about
    reaches Jews in Warsaw 74
Benelux 78. *See also* Belgium, Luxembourg,
    Netherlands
Bergen-Belsen 5
Berlin xx, xxv, 17, 59, 73; Jews deported from xvi,
    60
Bermuda conference xix, 87
Bessarabia xv, xix, xxiii, xxv, 64, 65, 82, 83
Białystok xv, xvii, xxi, xxv, 66, 69; armed resistance
    in 80; *Judenrat* in 78, 127
Bielsko-Biała 106
Birkenau. *See* Auschwitz-Birkenau
Blackmail 86
Bolshevik revolution 17
Bolshevism: *See* Communism
Boycott: anti-Jewish 39, 50, 53; anti-Nazi 52–53
Bratislava 81
Breitman, Richard 61
Broszat, Martin 31, 33, 59, 60
Browning, Christopher 28, 29, 30, 58–59, 62; on
    origins of 'final solution' 61
Brzeżany 96
Buber, Martin 50
Buchenwald 5, 67, 90
Budapest xiv, xvii, xx, 81, 84, 88, 90

Bug River xxv, 64, 65, 83

Bukovina xv, xxiii, xxv, 64, 65, 82, 83

Bulgaria 3, 41, 82, 85; as German ally 68; deports Jews from Thrace and Macedonia xiii; percentage of Jews in 17

Bund xiii, xix, 74, 75, 87, 125, 126

Burleigh, Michael 62

Burrin, Phillipe 61

Bystanders 70. *See also* Allies, Local populations

Capitalism 14

Carnegie Endowment for International Peace 100

Carpathian Mountains xix, 64

Central Association of German Citizens of the Jewish Faith (*Centralverein*) 110

Central Committee for Aid and Reconstruction 49, 50

Central Office for Adult Jewish Education 50–51

Central Office for Jewish Emigration xi, xv, xix, 41. *See also* Jewish Emigration Office

Chaplin, Charlie 102

Chełmno xiii, xx, xxi, 6, 66; gas vans used at 67; news about reaches Jews in Warsaw 74

China 4

Christianity 12

Communism (Bolshevism), Communists 5, 27, 40, 45, 58, 59, 68, 83; Jews and 16–17

Concentration camps xx, 5, 6, 45, 90; distinguished from killing centres 67

Concentration of Jews 39

Council for Aid to Jews: *See* Żegota

Croatia, Croats xxv, 41, 63, 82, 86; as German ally 68

Cromwell, Oliver 14

Crusades 13

Cuba 55

Czech lands: *See* Czechoslovakia; Protectorate of Bohemia and Moravia

Czechoslovakia xii, xvii, xxiii, 3, 37, 41, 83; Jewish emigration from 54; percentage of Jews in 17. *See also* Protectorate of Bohemia and Moravia

Czerniaków, Adam xv, 76–77, 78, 129

Częstochowa 69

Dachau 5, 67, 90

Danzig 23

Dawidowicz, Lucy 19, 37

De-Nur, Yechiel 9, 93–94

Death marches xiv, xx, 90

Definition of Jews: historical 11–12; Nazi 38

Denmark xii, 3, 68, 81; Jews rescued in xiii; percentage of Jews in 17

'Destruction process' 38–40

Diaspora 11

Diels, Rudolf 35

Dniester River xix, xxv, 64, 65, 83

Dortmund 108

Dror 123

Dworzecki, Mark 121

East Africa 56

Edict of Toleration (1782) 15

Edward I (King of England) 14

Eibeschütz, Jonathan 107

Eichmann, Adolf xiii, xv, 23, 57, 68; trial of 116, 121

Einsatzgruppen xvi, xx, 57, 59, 66, 83, 84, 95

Eisner, Kurt 27

El-Alamein xiii

Elbe River 15

Elbogen, Ismar 49

Emancipation 15

Emigration: as aim of Nazi policy 35–37, 41–42, 60–61; from Germany 48, 50, 108–109; Jewish communal debates over 50; obstacles to 47–48, 53–55

England 14, 16. *See also* Great Britain

Estonia, Estonians 3, 63; local militia shoots Jews in 64, 66; percentage of Jews in 17. *See also* Baltic states

Evian conference xi, xix, xx, xxi, 54–55, 87

Expropriation of Jews 38–39

Fein, Helen 85, 89

Feuchtwanger, Lion 46–47

'Final solution' xiii as designation for mass murder 65; debate over origins of 32–34, 57–63; German deception tactics in 69; local German commanders and 63; missing order for 60; role of local populations in 63–65

Finland 3, 82; as German ally 68; percentage of Jews in 17

First World War xxvi, 16, 76, 91; and Nazi 'true believers' 27

'Flight tax' 48

Four-Year Plan xvi, xx, 42

France xii, 3, 16, 41, 42, 56, 57, 68, 75, 78, 82, 85; grants Jews equality 15; Jews deported from xiii, 68; *Judenrat* in 75; medieval Jews expelled from 14; percentage of Jews in 17; takes in *St. Louis* refugees 55; Vichy government xii, 41

Frank, Anne 86

Frank, Hans xv, 23; opposes Nisko reservation 72; view of Jews 25; view of Slavs 24

Frankfurter, Felix 71–72
Friedlander, Henry 62
Friedländer, Saul 22, 26, 30, 31, 90, 92; on origins of 'final solution' 61
Führer xx, 33
Funkenstein, Amos 92–93

Galicia xx, 24, 64, 72, 96
Gas chambers 67
Generalgouvernement xii, xv, xx, xxii, xxiii, xxv, 24, 66, 68–69, 72, 74, 79. *See also* Poland
Genocide xvi, xxi, 6, 24, 100–101
Gens, Jakob xv, 78, 79
Gerlach, Christian 61–62
German Enamel Works 72
German foreign ministry xxii, 35–37
German Jewish Cultural Association xi
German Ministry of Economic Affairs 52
Germany xx, xxi, 3, 5, 56, 75, 82, 85; and Hungary 83–84; annexes Austria xi, 41; economic conditions in 52; expulsions of Jews from 57; invades Poland xii, 36, 55; invades Soviet union xiii, xix, 41, 95; Jews deported from xiii, 59–60, 105–106; Jews escape from 81; conditions for Jews in before Nazis 17–18; Jews settle in 12–13, 16; occupies Czechoslovakia xii; offers to exchange Jews for trucks 88; percentage of Jews in 17; plans invasion of Soviet Union 58; population policies of 62; prohibits Jewish emigration 57; surrenders xiv
Gestapo xxiii, 35, 68
Gewecke, Hans 63
Ghettos xii, xxi, 39, 62, 72, 75; conditions in 58; in middle ages 14; role of in Nazi policy 58–59
Globocnik, Odilo xv, 68
Goebbels, Josef xv, 62, 114
Goering, Hermann xiii, xvi, xx, 23, 42, 52; commissions 'total solution of the Jewish question' 60, 113
Goldhagen, Daniel 19, 29–30
Goldstein, Julius 107
Great Britain 42, 56, 61; and Palestine xii, 54, 88; informed about murder of Jews xvi; Jewish leaders in 52; takes in *St. Louis* refugees 55. *See also* England
Great Depression 25
Great Dictator, The 102
Greece 3, 41, 75, 78, 82; Jews deported from xiii; percentage of Jews in 17; under Italian occupation 68

Grodno 123
Grynszpan, Herszel xii
Gypsies xxv, 6. *See also* Sinti and Roma

Haavara agreement xi, xv, xxi, 52–53, 55
Habsburg Empire xix, 64
Hamburg 60
Hannover 26
Hashomer Hatsair 122
Havana 55
Hebrew 14
Heim, Susanne 62
Heydrich, Reinhard xii, xiii, xvi, xxiii, xxiv, 37, 59, 60, 68, 104, 113; 'express letter' of 36; and Wannsee conference 65
Hilberg, Raul 28, 38, 39, 40
Himmler, Heinrich xvi, xxiv, 23, 63, 68; favours Jewish reservation 37; Poznań speech of 92, 133
Hindenburg, Paul von xi
'Historicization of National Socialism' 31
Hitler, Adolf xi, xvi, xx, xxii, xxiv, xxv, 19, 23, 31, 41, 42, 57, 73, 103, 114; and 'Jewish bolshevism' 27–28; and order for 'final solution' 60; appointed German chancellor 45; as author of Nazi Party programme 34; confrontation with Horthy 24; early statements about Jews 47, 101–102; Jews in world view of 20–22, 58, 63; speaks to Reichstag about Jews 36, 42; statements of about fate of Jews 35
Hitler Youth xxi, 30
Holland: *See* Netherlands
Holocaust: and modernity 8, 94–97; and other Nazi persecutions 6–7, 62–63; as composite concept 97; as product of Nazi indoctrination 30; as product of ordinary human psychology 29; debate over 'uniqueness of' 6–7; etymology of word 65; historical study of 10, 91–93; usage of term 4–9
Homosexuals 5, 6
Homosexuals 6
Horthy, Miklos xvi, xviii, 83–84, 88; confrontation with Hitler 24, 103
Hungary xii, xvi, xviii, 3, 16, 24, 41, 75, 78, 86, 88; as German ally 68; changing Jewish policies of 83–84; Jews deported from xiv; percentage of Jews in 17. *See also* Budapest
Hydrogen cyanide 67

Iaşi xiii, 17, 64, 83
IG-Farben xviii
'Indirect extermination' 58

Intergovernmental Committee on Refugees xix, xx, xxi, 55, 87
International Settlements (Shanghai) 57
Israel xxv
Italy xxi, 3, 14, 41, 78, 82; as German ally 68; Jews escape through 57; percentage of Jews in 17

Jäckel, Eberhard 42
Jacob 11
Janowska 67
Japan 57
Jedwabne 64–65, 95–96
Jehovah's Witnesses 5, 6
Jerusalem 11
Jewish Agency for Palestine xv, xxi, 51
Jewish Cultural Association 49
Jewish Emigration Office xii. *See also* Central Office for Jewish Emigration
Jewish Fighting Organization xiii, xxi, 80, 85
Jewish police 69, 84
'Jewish reservation' 36–37, 56, 62, 106–107
Jewish Winter Aid 49
Jews: and communism 16–17, and nationalism 15–16; as forced labourers 83; Ashkenazic 12–14; become enemy aliens 56; businesses of boycotted 39; Catholic church and 13–14; concentration measures for 39; distinguishing characteristics of 14; early Nazi proposals concerning 34–35; economic conditions for under Nazi rule 45; economic profile of 13; emancipation of 15; escape routes for 57; expropriation of 38–39; first mass killings of 57; flee Nazi occupation 81; in eastern Europe 16–17; in free professions 17; in German public opinion 25–26, 104–106; in Hellenistic times 11–12; in hiding 80–81, 130; in Hitler's world view 20–22, 58, 63; in middle ages 12–14; in modern times 14–18; in Nazi Party programme 34; in Poland 45–46; in Romania 46; in tsarist Russia 15–16; modern migrations of 16; Nazi definition of 38; origin of name 11; percentage of in European countries 17; perceptions of Nazi intentions by 46–47, 74–75; population growth of 15; Reform 15; relations with Germans 45, 46; religious characteristics of 12; Nazi-era schools for 49; Sefardic 12; self-help 49, 78–79, 130; settlement in Europe 12–13; subjected to street violence 39; synagogues destroyed 39–40
Joodse Rad xiii, 75

Jordan River 11
Joseph II (Emperor of Austria) 15
Judah, Judea 11, 12
Judenrat xv, xvi, xxi, 35, 79; responses of to mass killing 77–78, 128, 129; responses of to Nazi rule 75–77, 126, 127
Jüdische Rundschau 111–12

Ka-Tzetnik: *See* De-Nur, Yechiel
Kaplan, Marion 48
Karski, Jan xvi, 71, 87, 120
Katz, Jacob 47
Kaunas 17
Kaunas 60; ghetto liquidated in xiv; *Judenrat* in 78, 79
Keitel, Wilhelm 58
Kiev xiii, 66
Killing centres xxi, xxiii, xxv, 6, 57, 66; advantages of 66–67
Kleinbaum, Moshe 73
Klibański, Bronia 123
Korczak, Ruzhka 122
Kovner, Abba xvi, 73–74, 79, 122
Kraków xvii, xviii, xx, xxi, 9, 24, 69, 72, 130; armed resistance in 80
Kripo xxiii, 68
Kristallnacht xii, xvi, xxi, 40, 54; and German public opinion 26, 104–105; impact of on emigration 48

Labour camps xx, xxii, 67, 90
Laqueur, Walter 88
Latin America 55
Latvia 3
Latvia 17, 66. *See also* Baltic states
Law for the Protection of German Blood and Honor xxii, 26, 38, 39
Law for the Restoration of the Professional Civil Service xi, xxii, 38
Law on Reich Citizenship xxiii, 26, 38
League of German Girls xxi, 30
Leiden 94
Lemkin, Raphael xvi, xxi, 6, 24, 100
Libya 3
Liebeskind, Dolek 80
Lisbon 57. *See also* Portugal
Lithuania, Lithuanians 3, 16, 63, 79; Jews escape through 57; mass shootings of Jews in 66; percentage of Jews in 17. *See also* Baltic states
Littner, Wiktor 130
'Living space' 40

Local populations 81–86

Łódź xii, xvi, 59, 66; ghetto liquidated in xiv; *Judenrat* in 78, 128

London 87

Lublin xiii, xv, xviii, xx, xxii, 24, 37, 56, 66, 68, 69, 74, 106; *Judenrat* in 78

Luxembourg 3, 41, 68, 72; percentage of Jews in 17. *See also* Benelux

Luxemburg, Rosa 27

Lwów xviii, 66, 69, 72

Macedonia 82

Madagascar xxi, xxii, 36, 37, 56

Majdanek xx, xxi, xxii, 6, 66; asphyxiation by diesel exhaust at 67; Soviet army liberates xiv

Makower, Henryk 129

Mandelbaum, Jacob 106

Mauthausen 67

Medical experiments 67

Mein Kampf xxii, 20, 27, 34, 47, 73

Mentally ill 6

Merin, Moshe xvi, 78

Michman, Dan 58–59

Minden 105

Minsk 60; *Judenrat* in 78, 79

Mischling xxii, xxiii, 38

Moldavia xxiii, 64, 83

Monowitz xviii, 9. *See also* Auschwitz-Birkenau

Moravia xvii

Morgen, Der 107–108

Morocco 3

Munich 39

Napoleon 15

Nazi Party xv, xx, xxi, xxii, xxiv, 5, 15, 19, 26, 114; election campaigns of 25, 28; programme of 34–35

Nazism 22–23, 25

Netherlands xii, xiii, 3, 41, 68, 75, 86, 94; Jews deported from xiii; *Judenrat* in 75; percentage of Jews in 17; takes in *St. Louis* refugees 55

Neumann, Franz 23, 24

Nisko reservation xii, xxi, xxii, 36, 37, 56, 106–107; opposed by Frank 72

Normann, Sven 125

North Africa 68

North America: indigenous populations of 6, 7

Norway xii, 3, 41, 68, 82, 86; percentage of Jews in 17

Nuremberg 40

Nuremberg Laws xi, xxii–xxiii, 26, 38, 39, 47, 108

Occupied Eastern Territories, Ministry of 24

Odessa 17

Operation Reinhard xv, xxiii, 68–69

Organization of Independent Orthodox Communities 47

Oświęcim xviii, 9. *See also* Auschwitz-Birkenau

Palestine xii, xv, xxi, xxvi, 16, 51–53, 57; Arab revolt in 54; Jewish immigration to 54; British restrictions on immigration to 88

Paris 17

Paris Peace Conference (1919) xix, 64

Partisans 68

Pavelić, Ante xxv, 64, 82

Physically disabled 5, 62

Piotrków Trybunalski xii

Płaszów 67

Poland xii, xv, xviii, xix, xx, xxii, xxvi, 3, 14, 24, 37, 41, 56, 57, 59, 60, 64, 67, 68, 74, 75, 80, 84–85, 90; anti-Jewish violence in 46; government-in-exile xiii, xvi, 74, 85; Jewish population of 16; Jews escape from 81; Jews settle in 13; mass shootings of Jews in 66; percentage of Jews in 17; signs nonaggression pact with Nazi Germany 46; underground in xvi, 84–85

Poles 7, 24, 25, 63, 72, 96; as Nazi victims 6

Poliakov, Léon 33

Polish government-in-exile 74, 85, 112, 119, 120, 125

Polish National Council 126

Polish underground 84–85, 119, 120

Political prisoners x, 6, 45, 67

Portugal 72. *See also* Lisbon

Poznań 92, 133

Prague xii, xv, 17, 41, 57

Pridham, Geoffrey 25

Protectorate of Bohemia and Moravia xii, xvi, xx, xxii, xxiii, 56, 59, 68. *See also* Czechoslovakia

Prussic acid 67

Prut River xix, 64

Radom xx, 24

Rath, Ernst vom xii

Rauschning, Hermann 23, 24, 102

Redlich, Shimon 96

Regat xv, xxiii, 83

Reder, Rudolf 117

Reich Citizenship Law. *See* Law on Reich Citizenship

Reich Labour Service xxiii, 30

Reich Labour Service xxiii

Reichman, Eva 110–11

Reichsvereinigung der Juden in Deutschland xii, xxiii, 54, 75
Reichsvertretung der deutschen Juden (*Reichsvertretung der Juden in Deutschland*) xi, xxiii, 49–50, 51, 52, 54
Rescuers of Jews 86, 96
'Resettlement in the East' xxiii, 69, 75
Resistance xiii. *See also* Amidah, Jewish Fighting Organization, 'Spiritual resistance'
Riga 60
Ringelblum, Emmanuel xii, xvi, 74
Roma: *See* Sinti and Roma
Romania xii, xix, xv, xxiii, xxv, 3, 16, 41, 46, 85–86, 88; as German ally 68; changing Jewish policies of 82–83; Jews escape to 81; mass killing of Jews in 64; offers to release Jews from Transnistria 87–88; percentage of Jews in 17
Romanians 63, 65
Roosevelt, Franklin 54–55, 71
Rosenfelder, Fritz 110
Royal Air Force 54
RSHA xiii, xv, xvi, xxiii, xxiv, 36, 68
Rumkowski, M. H. 78, 128–29
Russia xix, 15. *See also* Soviet Union

SA xxiv, 45
Sachsenhausen 67
St. Louis (ship) 55
'Salvation through work' xxiv, 77, 127
San Francisco 4
Schindler, Oskar xvii, 72, 86
Schleunes, Karl 34
SD xxiii, xxiv, 36, 37, 68, 104, 105
Second World War 4, 5, 9, 36, 68, 88–90
'Selection' xxiv, 67
Serbia 41, 68
Shanghai 57
Shirer, William L. 47
Šiauliai 63
Siberia 59, 60
Silesia, Upper: *See* Upper Silesia
Sinti and Roma xix, xxiv, 5, 7, 62, 67. *See also* Gypsies
Slave labourers 5
Slavs 7, 24, 62
Slovakia xii, 41, 78, 81, 82, 85, 86; as German ally 68; Jews deported from xiii, xiv, 68
Sobibór xiii, xxi, xxiii, xiv, 6, 66, 68; asphyxiation by diesel exhaust at 67
Socialists 5
Solmssen, Georg 46

Sonderkommando xxiv, 67
Sonderkommando xxiv, 67, 117
Sosnowiec xvi
South America: indigenous populations of 6, 7
Soviet prisoners of war xix, 5, 67
Soviet Union xii, xiii, xix, xx, xxi, xxii, 3, 6, 14, 16, 40, 41, 42, 57, 59, 60, 61, 62, 68, 75, 79, 80, 82–83, 84, 87, 90, 95; annexes northern Bukovina 64; German invasion of xiii, 63; Jewish population of 17, 58; killing of Jews in 57, 66; liberates Wilno xiv; occupies eastern Poland xii; testimonies from about mass shootings 73; war front in 68
'Spiritual resistance' 51
SS xv, xvi, xx, xxii, xxiii, xxiv, 57, 64; conflicts of with German army 72; oversees 'final solution' 67–68
'Stab-in-the-back' 27
Stalingrad xiii
Star of David 50
Stuttgart 110
Sweden xvii, 81, 82, 88, 125
Szálasi, Ferenc 84

T4 xxv, 62
Tenenbaum, Mordechai xvii
Thessalonike 17
Thrace 82
Tiyyul 81
Tooze, Adam 61
Trans-Siberian railroad 57
Transnistria xiii, xv, xix, xxv, xxiii, 64, 65, 83, 87, 88
Trawniki 67
Treaty of St. Germain xix, 64
Treaty of Versailles 42
Treblinka xiii, xxi, xxiii, xxv, 6, 66, 68, 69; asphyxiation by diesel exhaust at 67
Tunisia 3
Turkey 7
'Twisted road to Auschwitz' 33, 34

Ukraine, Ukrainians xix, 63, 84, 96; and murder of Jews 64, 72
Union Génerale des Israélites de France 75
United Nations Genocide Convention (1948) xxi, 6
United Partisan Organization xvi, 122
United States xvii, xxv; Germany declares war on 61–62; informed about murder of Jews xvi; Jewish leaders in 52; recalls ambassador from Germany 54
United States War Department 6

Upper Silesia xvi; *Judenrat* in 78
USSR: *See* Soviet Union
Ustaše xxv, 82

Vienna xi, xii, xv, xix, xx, 17, 20, 41, 56, 57, 90
Volk xxv, 20
Volkswart 35

Wallachia xxiii, 83
Wallenberg, Raoul xvii, 88
Wannsee conference xiii, xxv, 65, 67, 68, 82, 114
War Refugee Board xvii, xxv, 88
Warsaw xii, xv, xx, xxi, xxv, 24, 59, 66, 72, 74, 85, 126; armed resistance in 80; ghetto conditions in 58, 130; ghetto liquidated in 69; ghetto uprising in xiii; Jews deported from xiii; Jews hiding in 80–81, 129; *Judenrat* in 76–78, 129
Washington, D. C. 87
Wasserstein, Bernard 87
Weimar Republic xxv, 27, 28
Weser River 105

Wetzel, Eberhard 24
Wilno xiii, xv, xvi, 121, 122; ghetto liquidated xiii; *Judenrat* in 78, 79; Soviet army liberates xiv. *See also* United Partisan Organization
Wippermann, Wolfgang 62
Working Group 81

Yad Vashem xxv, 86
Yiddish 14, 16
Yiddish 16
Yoselewska, Rivka 116
Youth movements 74, 122, 123
Yugoslavia 3, 63, 82, 83; percentage of Jews in 17

Zagłębie xvi
Zagreb 64
Zionism, Zionists xv, xxi, xxv–xxvi, 16, 51–53, 71, 73, 81, 111–12, 122, 123
Zygielbojm, Szmul 126
Zyklon B xxvi, 67
Żegota xxvi, 85, 86, 131–32